THE WRITE STUFF: VOICES OF UNITY ON LABOR'S FUTURE

*Edited by Nick Dyrenfurth
and Misha Zelinsky*

Connor Court Publishing

Published in 2020 by Connor Court Publishers Pty Ltd.

Connor Court Publishing Pty Ltd.
PO Box 7257
Redland Bay QLD 4165
sales@connorcourt.com
www.connorcourt.com

ISBN: 9781922449429

Cover Design by Matt Knapp

Printed in Australia.

Acknowledgements

Nick and Misha would like to sincerely thank all of the contributors to *The Write Stuff* for their thoughtful essays and hard work in bringing this ambitious project to fruition. Many generously read various chapters and our introduction. Thanks also to Anthony Cappello and the team at Connor Court, especially Michael Gilchrist, for publishing this edited collection. This book is dedicated to the magnificent working women and men of Australia.

Nick Dyrenfurth and Misha Zelinsky
November 2020

About the Editors

Nick Dyrenfurth is the Executive Director of the John Curtin Research Centre, a leading social democratic thinktank. Nick worked in both the retail industry and academia for over a decade, as a ministerial speechwriter and advisor, was secretary of the Labor Party's National Policy Forum and has been an ALP member for twenty two years, serving as a branch secretary and president, and is a lifelong unionist. He is the author or editor of ten books, including *Getting the Blues: the Future of Australian Labor* (2019), *A Little History of the Australian Labor Party* (2011, with Frank Bongiorno), *Mateship: A Very Australian History* (2015) and *'A powerful influence on Australian affairs': A new history of the AWU* (2017). He writes for *The Age*, *Sydney Morning Herald*, *The Australian*, *Australian Financial Review*, *Herald Sun*, *Guardian*, and *The Monthly*. Nick lives in Melbourne with his three young children.

Misha Zelinsky is the Assistant National Secretary of the Australian Workers' Union, Australia's oldest blue-collar trade union. He is a director of Cbus Super, an industry superannuation pension fund with nearly $60 billion under management. Misha holds a Bachelor of Laws and Bachelor of Commerce (Economics) and recently completed a Master of Public Administration at the London School of Economics. He began his career as a criminal defence lawyer for the Aboriginal Legal Service and was an advisor to the NSW Government. As the Secretary of the ALP's National Policy Forum, Misha has responsibility for the development of the party's 2019 platform. Misha is the host of the foreign policy podcast *'Diplomates – A Geopolitical Chinwag'* and is a regular contributor for the *Sydney Morning Herald and Daily Telegraph*.

CONTENTS

Foreword

Stephen Loosley

It was the Canberra journalist for the *Daily Telegraph*, 'the Red Fox', Alan Reid, who famously defined the ALP Federal Conference as the agent of change in Australian politics. He was perceptive on this, though wrong on many other occasions.

The history of the ALP has been to move Australia in the direction of being a more confident and resilient country; possessed of optimism and a desire to build a more equitable and just society which does not leave some of our citizens behind.

To achieve this noble goal, it remains essential to generate informed discussion within our ranks and to offer fresh ideas and original solutions to the Australian electorate. This is needed in 2020, perhaps more than at any time in our recent history. Nick Dyrenfurth and Misha Zelinsky have rendered the Labor movement an extraordinary service in having *The Write Stuff* published. It encourages a contest of ideas, but perhaps more importantly provides a signpost which begins the journey back to government in Canberra.

It was Gough Whitlam who made the undeniable point that in politics, only the impotent are pure. Gough was federal Labor leader for part of our long period in the wilderness between 1949 and 1972. He made the observation at a Victorian ALP conference in 1967. Consistently, the Victorian ALP, under the narrow and rigid dictates of an obtuse machine had underperformed electorally and been dead weight in the ALP saddlebags.

Whitlam sought to change our party before he could change Australia for the better. It was utterly necessary, for federal Labor had lost elections in 1954 and in 1961 which should have seen us form government. As everyone reading this knows, it wasn't until 2 December 1972 that federal Labor won a majority of seats in the

House of Representatives and was called back to the government benches.

The essential point about Whitlam's success, as it has been of every success of state and federal Labor administrations, stemmed from dominance of the centre ground of Australian politics. The leaders of the time, from Chris Watson and Andrew Fisher to Bob Hawke and Paul Keating, understood this reality very clearly. The ALP, under their leadership, not only shaped platform and policy which was appealing in content and effective in execution but enabled the leader to cut right through to the electorate. The best example of this is Andrew Fisher's bold statement on the eve of the Great War: 'We are in this war to the last man and the last shilling'. This was Fisher the empire loyalist, a working-class Scotsman who had served Queensland Labor well but who had opposed Australian involvement in the Boer War. Fisher understood the surge in Australian patriotic opinion for Britain at the time and sought to lead and to shape it.

This is definitely true of Whitlam, whose reforming legislation from Medibank to social securities through Indigenous policy to the cities; from ending conscription to the recognition of the People's Republic of China, modernised Australia dramatically, courtesy of his two governments over a short three-year span. Indeed, Gough dragged Australia into the 1960s, as one wag put it best, after a long period of somnolent Tory rule. Remarkably, given the disposition on the High Court at the time, all of the Whitlam Government's pioneering legislation, when challenged, was upheld constitutionally. It was an extraordinary record of achievement.

The Whitlam Government should be regarded accurately and fairly by Labor reformers of this generation as a reconnaissance in force. The Hawke and Keating Governments built upon this success but also of Labor governments in the states which had tacked to the centre and observed Neville Wran's famous dictum: 'The first decision of any Labor government is to stay there'.

Thirteen years of federal Labor government, buttressed by policy achievement and electoral endorsement was a consequence of learning the lessons of the 1970s. Now, along come Misha Zelinsky and Nick Dyrenfurth with an impressive series of essays charting the future course for Labor.

The editors understand something of critical significance about Australian politics which is often overlooked, especially by self-referential inner-city elites.

Australian political parties, like their American counterparts, must be successful geographical, as well as philosophical constructs. To fail to recognise the significance of regional and rural Australia, especially in the outlying states of Queensland, Tasmania and Western Australia is to languish in opposition in perpetuity.

What is more, the issues which galvanise the kitchen tables in the regions – job security; economic opportunity; kids' education; affordable healthcare; accessible transport; cost of living and a welcoming environment – are also those issues which are discussed in the kitchens of great suburban seats of our cities. Gough understood this and made these outer metropolitan electorates our own. It's a lesson we should not have to relearn.

This book is both creative and constructive; aspirational and astute in its philosophical commitment and practical application. If the Chinese proverb 'every journey of a thousand miles begins with a single step' is true, and it is, then *The Write Stuff* offers both clear direction and certainty of destination.

Stephen Loosley AM FRSN
November 2020

Introduction:
Power with Purpose

Nick Dyrenfurth and Misha Zelinsky

Running the Place

"Labor has a most sacred mission and should rise above all petty things. It seeks to secure justice for all who dwell in the land. It seeks to govern and has for the first time brought into politics aims and aspirations which are worth fighting for." So wrote the great William Spence in his weekly *The Worker* newspaper editorial in 1896.

These words were true then and for Labor to win national government they must become true once again. Labor seeks power, unashamedly so, for a purpose – to better the lives of working people. Not just to prevent the unacceptable, or to make things 'less bad' but to create an Australian society worth living in and dying for.

Millions of Australians need Labor to represent their values – family, work, and love of country – and to deliver their aspirations of the Good Life. We are a party of government, formed by working people to exercise power in their interests.

This is an urgent task and a sacred mission. Politics is not a parlour game for protestors. Nor is it a cyclical game of pass the electoral parcel where suited-up technocrats each get a turn. Public life is for the exercise of executive power in the service of a major project – as Paul Keating would say 'running the place'.

Losing our way

Political history is brutal and defined by winners. For a party whose story is very much *the story* of Australia, of its achievements and sometimes its failings, we are fast losing our ability to write the history of our nation. We are losing this right because we are losing too many elections. In national elections, we have forgotten how to win and win often. In 2020, Labor finds itself with only one in three Australians prepared to give it their vote nationally. We have arrived at a historic tipping point; a three decades-in-the-making existential crisis that potentially spells the end for one of the world's oldest and most successful social democratic parties. If not for compulsory, preferential voting, Labor would be in the position of its European comrades, polling under 30 per cent – the threshold of irrelevance for a party of government. Yet, as the recent Queensland state election shows, Labor can compete in the regions when it gets it right – but we aren't translating this into success at a national level.

Since 1993, the ALP has won just one federal election outright (2007), with one draw (2010), after which it formed an ill-fated, one term minority government (2010-13). At the past three elections, Labor's primary vote has slumped to between 33 and 34 per cent. By comparison during the 1950s and 1960s – an era considered one of Labor's worst – the ALP's House of Representatives primary vote averaged 45 per cent over nine elections. If Scott Morrison's government wins the next election and serves out a full term, the Coalition will potentially have held office for 23 of the last 29 years.

Federal Labor finds itself caught between its more conservative working and middle-class base in Australia's suburbs and regions and its inner-city progressive activists, and we appear unable to bridge that growing chasm, and unable to build winning national coalitions. To restore the party to its rightful place, we must change.

The Right Way

It is the eternal task of the Labor Right – variously known as Labor Unity, Centre Unity or National Unity – to remind the party of this founding mission in politics, and of the pathway to, and purpose of, political power. For more than a century the Right lived this creed. This meant that Labor was first party of its type – labour or social democratic – in the world to form government at a state level in

1899, as well as nationally as a minority government (1904) and then in its own right (1910).

Ideas matter. Leaders come and go, but ideas prevail and cannot be left to wither and die. Hence Labor Unity must be in the contest of ideas and be in it to win. There exists a clear correlation with the decline of the Unity's once vibrant culture of ideas, a stultifying ideological conformity, its ability to produce significant, transformation leaders, and federal Labor's decline. That this group produced prime ministers such as Chris Watson, Andrew Fisher, Billy Hughes (originally!), Jim Scullin, Ben Chifley, Gough Whitlam, Bob Hawke, Paul Keating and Kevin Rudd should be a badge of pride. Labor's most revered state premiers have mostly been Unity figures.

Labor governments make the world

Long before the terms 'Labor Right' and 'Labor Unity' entered party lexicon, William Spence – the founder of the Australian Workers' Union and Member of State and Federal Parliament – embodied its intellectual tradition, tempering idealism with pragmatism. He knew there was something urgent about the task of Labor:

> Patience with enthusiasm is required. We cannot change in a day the mental habits of a million years, but we can quickly pull down those political and social barriers which coerce man to do what he for ages has not desired to do ... Our hope is in the masses, in government by self, and by [all] self consciously taking an active part in the ruling of the collective life ... The desire has ever been present in all ages, but the time had not come. It is with us now. Let us not miss the opportunity. The work lies in our hands. Let us Agitate, Educate, Organize. We have the power if we have the will. Let each remember that man has failed before because each carelessly left to some other the work of the Common Good ... Each must take his or her share ...The best start we can give to our children is the certainty of better conditions; the sweetest memory of us to them the fact that we did so.

Over a century later those Biblically-inspired, beautiful words still capture the magnificent purpose of Australian Labor, and must be our New Jerusalem.

We are prone to forget how successful the party of Spence was in international terms. Henry Boote, the famous editor of the *Australian Worker* newspaper, published on a weekly basis by Spence's union, counselled party supporters against disappointment when Labor narrowly lost the 1913 federal election: "We have reached a stage of progress which has no parallel elsewhere on earth. A Labor government here is no longer a wild improbability, but the probable outcome of every appeal." Whereas the British Labour Party was little more than a parliamentary rump, barely distinguishable from the Liberals, and the mass member socialist parties in France and Germany remained remote from power, in Australia the planks of Labor's platform were being made into law by Labor governments. Minority Federal Labor governments were in office in 1904, 1908-09 and then Labor won an election in 1910 to govern in its own right. No comparable Labor party existed whatsoever in the United States.

Australian Labor's successes should not merely be measured in votes. Whether by forming governments or exerting pressure from opposition, over the course of the twentieth century state and federal Labor did much to civilise capitalism in the interests of working people. The role of Labor's Right was critical, whom some commentators erroneously dismiss as mere 'moderates' or, worse, 'centrists' – as if those terms describe timid, shy reformers. Historically, the Right has provided the ballast – the essential ingredient of a Labor leader who is typically more centrist and more popular than the party they lead – to elect nation-building Labor governments.

Two Labor Parties

Somewhat curiously this remains a uniquely 'national' problem for Labor. At a state and territory level, Labor holds government in five of Australia's eight states and territories (Victoria, Queensland, and Western Australia, along with the Northern Territory and ACT, where it was recently re-elected, along with Queensland). Labor has governed in states and territories for 66 per cent of the time since 1996. Yet, even then, Labor has performed poorly in its one-time stronghold of NSW: once the natural party of government. NSW Labor has not won an election in thirteen years.

For two decades, effectively two Labor parties have been in existence: state and federal. COVID-19 has acted to highlight the ALP's state-based strengths and further expose its frailties federally. In the short-term, state Labor's domination bears out a national and global trend of COVID-19 benefitting incumbent governments, but over the long-term reflects the ALP's strengths in state government service delivery: health, education, essential services, and infrastructure delivery. At a federal level, issues of economic management and national security tend to dominate, and since 1996 federal Labor has repeatedly been subjected to effective scare campaigns on these grounds. This need not be the case. Labor is more than capable prosecuting these policy areas – but only if it takes them on and defines them in a patriotically Labor image.

What's the problem?

The *Write Stuff* starts from the position that, despite sensationalist media coverage, organised factions are not the ALP's major weakness. The decline of ideas and values is the true problem. This is because of the erosion of a distinctive, guiding philosophy and set of core beliefs binding what is known as the Labor Right.

A loss of purpose and a confusion of ends with means has left the broader party listless. A group that once believed in the ruthless pursuit and use of power for a clear and practical purpose has given way to a shell that seeks power as an end of itself. Without a return to this clear-eyed focus and belief in the value and execution of ideas, Labor and its supporters will remain powerless, and this matters for working people. Without its Unity engine, Labor cannot operate at full capacity.

As editors we do not assert the right to speak for every contributor, nor ague that there is one 'true' interpretation of the traditions of Labor Unity or to dogmatically insist that the Left or the unaligned are not an important and valued part of the Labor family. Nonetheless, in our view Unity has been the life force behind Labor's historic achievements and the incubator of its best and most electorally successful ideas and leaders. "Where goes the Labor Right, so goes federal Labor", Paul Keating might say. Unless the Right can get its act together, reform, lead a renewal of the ALP's culture of ideas, modernise its governing philosophy, and train the next generation of Labor leaders, there is little hope of halting Labor's slow but reversible decline.

Winning starts at home

We must get back to a culture of winning – because nothing else matters. And to do so we must relentlessly focus on the things that matter to working people. Bemoaning the difficult path for Labor oppositions to government – no doubt true – is also no path to salvation. As the party who wants to challenge the status quo, we need a higher degree of confidence to be entrusted with the keys to the Lodge. Labor must change and listen carefully to the Australian people in their full diversity. A contempt for 'backward' voters who are perceived as not 'with' the issues of the day or a belief they have been 'tricked' by the wicked 'Tories' will not do. As the people's party, we must get back to being of the people and work with them, not be for them and do things to them. Blaming the customer is not a useful method in business and blaming the voters will not work as a political strategy. No partnership ever succeeds on the latter terms. Labor needs to be bigger, not smaller: a bigger and more diverse party reflective of modern Australia, and a party of bigger ideas and national ambition.

This edited collection of thirty essays includes contributions by leading party members, MPs, unionists, and activists broadly identified with Labor Unity on the task ahead. With the postponement of Labor's national conference there is a vacuum at the heart of the ALP – a genuine battle of ideas and vigorous policy debate.

The *Write Stuff* provides that contest. As the essays here testify, ideas remain powerful weapons in our debate, and underpin a way of doing Labor politics with purpose in the twenty-first century. We do not intend to be the last ones to turn out the lights on the way out for the ALP. Millions of Australians rely on the nation's oldest political party and now more than ever they need Labor to light the way nationally.

The Australian way is the Labor way. It can remain so if we choose the Right way.

1. The Right Way

Nick Dyrenfurth

The Battle of Ideas

"Strategy matters. Policies matter. But behind them all stands the vision". "Scorn not the vision; scorn not the idea. Power grows out of the barrel of a gun. A gun is certainly powerful, but who controls the man with the gun? A man with an idea." The words belong to Sir Keith Joseph, addressing the 1976 British Conservative Party Conference, even if he was channelling, improbably, a youthful Mao Zedong.

The Tories were then two years into a five-year stint in Opposition. Against the odds, Margaret Thatcher snatched the party leadership from Edward Heath in 1975. Joseph was not yet recognised as Thatcher's philosopher-king, but rather the object of derision, not least by fellow Tories. Yet he and his ilk enjoyed the last laugh. "This Party of ours has been on the defensive for too long", Thatcher told the Tory's youth-wing in 1978. "If we can win the battle of ideas, then the war is already half won".

Thatcherism and, in America what became known as Reaganism, took free-market theories from the eccentric fringes of the academy to mainstream public policy reality. Australia escaped their worst excesses because the Hawke and Keating Labor governments of the 1980s and 1990s pursued policies towards market liberalisation but governed with a big Labor heart. Yet overall, Joseph's vision prevailed, dominating Western democratic politics until the 2008/09 Global Financial Crisis.

Social democratic and labour parties are in prolonged crisis worldwide. The 2019 federal election merely confirmed the Coalition's recent electoral dominance. Federal Labor's precipitous decline and electoral weakness is the direct result of the growing disconnect between its ideas and values and the Australian electorate. Fundamentally federal Labor is no longer seen to represent working-class people's basic concerns and needs. Too often it does not speak for but rather talks at working-class and middle Australia. As Labor continues to deal with the fallout from its 2019 federal election defeat, the primacy of ideas incarnate in Joseph's Thatcherite philippic can be a source of inspiration to True Believers, and motivate the party's Right to right the ship.

Where goes Labor unity so goes the ALP

In the eyes of the public and commentariat, factions have a bad rap in modern Labor. Yet it is not the existence of factions per se which is the problem. Rather, Labor's woes are the result of the decline of cohesive factions as fulcrums of ideas. The balkanisation of the Right (Labor Unity in Victoria, Centre Unity in New South Wales, and similar titles in other states and territories) and the erosion of a distinctive, guiding philosophy binding its parts, is the real source of trouble.

Historically, especially in NSW, Centre Unity was re-nowned for its political realism, adopting a pragmatic, incremental approach to implementing social and economic reform, and ruthless electioneering methods. Nonetheless, it sought to win and subsequently wield political power for a purpose – to advance the interests of working people, their families, and the nation. Over the past few decades, however, Unity's core ideas, backgrounds of affiliated politicians and raison d'etre have increasingly become indistinguishable from its ostensible opponents on the Left.

Connected to the decline of an animating, unifying set of core ideas, the Right has found it increasingly difficult to say 'no' to bad policies or resist Labor's cultural dalliances with politically correct identity 'woke' politics and virtue signalling.

Too often we fall back on nostalgia or past glories. A section of the Right fetishises the Hawke-Keating era. A governing model par excellence and worthy of imitation has become a block to philosophical renewal in the twenty-first century. The faction of earthy realism, in touch with the humble concerns of working-class and middle Australia, is regrettably defensive about its historic and decisive leadership role in Labor. Granted talented women and men fill the Right's parliamentary, union, and organisational ranks. Collectively, however, the Labor Right has lost its mojo.

These are not academic points. "Where goes the Labor Right, so goes federal Labor", to amend a phrase of former prime minister Paul Keating, and co-founder of the Right's Centre Unity faction in NSW. Unity is not producing enough leaders, often ceding state and federal leadership to the Left. Yet to date every federal leader to have taken Labor from opposition into government at an election has been aligned with the party's Right: Andrew Fisher (1910/1914), Jim Scullin (1929), Gough Whitlam (1972), Bob Hawke (1983) and Kevin Rudd (2007). Unity's atrophy matters. During the twentieth century, it set Labor's governing agenda, and agenda of being a party of government rather than impotent opposition – power was accrued for a purpose, rather than an end in of itself. It sanctified the ALP's central organising principle: labourism, the idea that parliamentary politics, in tandem with strong unionism, could civilise capitalism in the interests of working people, through policies such as compulsory arbitration, tariff protection, the now rightly discredited White Australia policy, and evolving welfare initiatives. This is the case even if a tightly formalised Left-Right factional system did not materialise prior to the 1950s Labor Split.

From Labor's beginnings in the 1890s, inchoate factionalism featured in its affairs. Shortly after its founding, NSW Labor split over the question of whether politicians were autonomous agents or servants of affiliated unions and branches and bickered over the party's 'socialism'. A proto-Unity faction of sorts made up of members such as Billy Hughes, William Holman and the William Spence-led Australian Workers' Union eventually took control of the party. Bread and butter politics were the priority they insisted

– wages, working hours and safety – rather than millenarian obsessions. "It's votes that count," NSW MP W.J. Ferguson warned supporters in 1897. "Two-thirds of the Sydney workers are not prepared to go to the lengths of Unionism, and Socialism is a step beyond." The Right's rejection of purist impotency led to the forming of the first Labor or social democratic governments in the world: Queensland (1899), federally as a minority government (1904) and in its own right (1910).

For Labor's first fifty years, factional conflict was fleeting, issue-based and waged between personalities and unions such as the AWU, as per the split over conscription in 1916, the byzantine struggles that bedevilled the NSW branch over the 1920s, or the tripartite schism during the Great Depression. The reformed NSW party which emerged at a 1939 'Unity' Conference would underpin what became known as the McKell model, named after its long-serving premier. The model not only aimed to harmonise relations between the parliamentary and industrial wings – which it did effectively – but was also the making of the NSW Right and its perennial opponent, various nomenclatures of the Left. That division hardened with the 1955 Cold War split over Labor's attitude to communism and the role of the Church in party affairs. With the exception of NSW, where the Cardinal urged his flock to "stay in and fight another day", the party's anti-communist wing defected in Victoria and later, mostly, in Queensland, and in pockets in other states. The Right has thus been a predominantly NSW and Sydney-centric grouping, acquiring a reputation for political pragmatism and relative social conservatism. In Queensland, it became a matter of the leviathan AWU versus the rest; elsewhere Unity was a less cohesive force, depending on a scattering of unions, individual MPs, and brave branch activists.

The early 1980s witnessed a hardening of factional divisions, spurred by the shift to proportional representation in party affairs the previous decade. The system properly emerged in 1983 after the formation of a national 'anti-faction' Centre-Left faction, which in turn encouraged the unity of state-based Left and Rights. Led by Graham Richardson and Robert Ray, the National Right had three aims: to get Bob Hawke elected as Labor leader, to position itself to claim a share of the spoils of office, and ensure that the next government would avoid the schisms of its predecessors and Whitlam's short-lived government. The system worked as intended, managing ideological and internal conflict. The longest-lived Labor administration ensued. Earlier, the Right made possible Whitlam's modernising late 1960s project, taking on the 'aged doctrinaires' of the extreme Left, notably forces aligned with Victoria's Bill Hartley, which led to Whitlam's election and made possible Hawke's triumph.

In the 1980s, the Right buttressed the Hawke government's historic rebalancing of the role of the state and market by virtue of floating the dollar, financial market deregulation, dismantling tariffs, privatising assets and, in 1993, introducing a form of enterprise bargaining that heralded a major shift away from centralised wage fixing. This model bequeathed Australia with three decades of growth, yet, if inadvertently, hollowed out the old Right labourist model and weakened its industrial base. Nonetheless, the stable factional structure of Federal Caucus 1983-96 ironically enhanced the authority of Hawke and Keating. Hawke, in particular, had loyal lieutenants, Cabinet Ministers, in all three factions able and willing to deliver the consensus outcomes he wanted. The ill-fated decision of Caucus in 2007 to surrender the election of ministers to the new exciting Rudd-Gillard leadership team was a fatal flaw that ultimately derailed the high hopes Labor had for that government.

Ironically, the factional system ossified just as rigid ideological divisions were dissolving. The Cold War's end had profound implications for social democratic parties worldwide. In Australia it disorientated the Labor Right more so than the Left – 'stopping' the radical ambitions of the Left carried less and less credence. Yet ideological convergence around social and economic liberalism came at a cost. Creative tension between factions was long a source of policy dynamism and its demise has contributed to the broader labour movement's intellectual inertia.

We should not underestimate the decline of religion as an animating force in the lives of Right figures. The post-1960s decline of a distinctive Australian Catholic identity acted to weaken the solidarity which existed between Right activists. Faith was an important glue which held them together. Today, people of faith are made to feel unwelcome in the ALP or feel compelled to hide or apologise for their beliefs.

But more than numbers, the Right has suffered from a perception of moral decline. In NSW the Richo creed of 'whatever it takes' has seemingly come to mean 'whatever we can take' through the actions of certain individuals. In 2011, in the wake of NSW Labor's implosion over electricity privatisation and subsequent electoral wipeout, Paul Keating eviscerated the direction of the faction he co-founded more than three decades earlier. "I think the problem with Centre Unity in NSW is that it lacks now an ideology ... other than the sheer pursuit of power ... But power for what?"

Today's balkanised factional system is often formed in the toxic world of student politics. It turns more on shifting alliances and personal rivalries than ideas. Too many young Laborites, if they do join the Right, struggle to identify a compelling ideological reason for signing up in the first place. Young people need a reason to join the Right other than career advancement or 'beating' the Left. After all, this cohort will set the agenda in and outside parliament in the decades to come. A reticence to fight the battle of ideas creates a vicious circular effect: the Right attracts fewer – and less capable – members. It loses policy debates and cedes authority. Where go the ideas, so go the numbers. It is difficult to find a once-in-a generation figure prepared to crash through and unite the maddening array of sub-factions, especially in Victoria. NSW Centre Unity has held together but has suffered from civil war and been hollowed out intellectually due to corruption and foreign interference. Echoes of this concern have been heard nation-wide and played a role in the 2019 election.

Getting back in the battle of ideas

The ALP is unlikely to renew its purpose without the Right's imprimatur. It demands fighting the battle of ideas and seeking to wield power for a defined purpose.

Ideas can help parties avoid the tendency to prioritise tactics over strategy, to focus on the ebb and flow of the four-quarter contest rather than, in football speak, a bone-jarring tackle, spectacular mark or – more likely in 2020 – a Twitter burn. The Right's decline has led many to miss the critical distinction between pursuing 'progress' on behalf of working-class and middle Australia and left-liberal social and economic 'progressivism', the cross-faction ideology of choice in modern Labor.

Unity's renewal involves reconceptualising how power works, the means of accruing it, and to what ends it is used. Confusing ends and means leads to an absence of 'why'? Labor represents the labour interest, broadly conceived, the majority of Australians who work for a living and who own little capital. The labour interest winning, and exercising power, is the pathway to them living a good life, a means to self-realisation and human flourishing. Power is the key to people leading good lives. In its absence, working people have less control over their lives, individually and collectively, in workplaces, communities and the nation-at-large. Labor's mission in life – and Unity's central mission – must rest on a conception of what constitutes a good life and a good society where people can lead long, meaningful, productive, and healthy lives.

The good life is not lived on some island. Humans are innately social beings who, for that reason, have obligations and duties towards each other and not simply owed 'rights'. This conception however requires a nuanced view of the State. Labor exists to exercise power to create and redistribute power and wealth to people, rather than expanding the state to redistribute wealth *without* power or to create rights-based legislation. The latter style of transactional, technocratic politics is a dead-end. For a social democratic party, this modus operandi is neither social nor democratic, but paternalistic and statist, doing politics to and for people but never with them.

Some Unity figures are prone to claim that Labor's mission in life is merely to 'civilise capitalism'. Their opponents on the left were equally wrong to claim Labor's mission in life equated to ushering in some abstract socialist society. Unquestionably, most early Laborites believed that their party would create a more civilised society than what had resulted from free markets and *were* influenced by socialism in so far as they opposed, in ethical and often Christian-inspired terms, capitalism's tendency to relentlessly commodify all aspects of life, notably the labour and lives of working people. Labor's early activists also understood the party to be a means by which working men and women could themselves wield power over their lives and the places they worked in, lived, and socialised. They saw their task as protecting hard-fought democratic liberties, freedoms and yes, rights, won in New World Australia.

Labourism, properly understood, is the strategy by which the labour interest seeks to wield power, power not as an end in itself, but the means to subject the economy to democratic forces: parliamentary action, robust unionism and by means of other self-governing civil society associations, including faith groups. Labor's mission in the political life of our nation is the same as it was 129 years ago: winning power so that all Australians are empowered to live long, fulfilling, good lives rich in meaning. This is Labor's true 'social'-ist objective. It's not rocket science. Yet re-engaging with that core purpose means hard thinking about where Labor has been – and is – heading.

Importantly, the early labour movement aimed to *conserve* as much as it hoped to bring about change, namely preserving the so-called 'workingman's paradise' of high wages and social mobility. This much was suggested by the famous report of the Sydney-based Labor Defence Committee issued in the wake of the disastrous 1890 Maritime Strike. Only by forming a Labor Party and securing representation in parliament its authors suggested: "can we ... ensure to every man, by the opportunity of fairly remunerated labour, a share in those things that make life worth living." If you excuse the masculine language, that's Labor's mission spelled out pithily and exquisitely. It is not as famous as Ben Chifley's 'Light on the Hill', but certainly should be. Its beauty lies in the eye of the beholder, however. For some, it entails equality while others might see it as an ode to equality of opportunity, what some call aspiration. Then there is the simple nod to the fundamental desire to lead a good life within the bounds of a common life: the reason Labor was put on this earth.

Even then a closer inspection of Chifley's memorable speech reveals a vision of a party committed to the common good, towards progress not progressivism, and founded on a belief that material well-being is an essential precondition of leading a good life: "I try to think of the Labour movement, not as putting an extra sixpence into somebody's pocket, or making somebody Prime Minister or Premier, but as a movement bringing something better to the people, better standards of living, greater happiness to the mass of the people. We have a great objective – the light on the hill – which we aim to reach by working for the betterment of mankind not only here but anywhere we may give a helping hand." Most Laborites stop there. Yet Chifley went on to express an inherently small 'c' conservative Labor view of life: "If the movement can make someone more comfortable, give to some father or mother a greater feeling of security for their children, a feeling that if a depression comes there will be work, that the government is striving its hardest to do its best, then the Labour movement will be completely justified." Thus Labor exists to conserve – working people's status, dignity and living standards – as much as it seeks to change the world to better their lives. The English writer Jonathan Rutherford has similarly observed of our British comrades: "the Labour Party has embodied the paradox of being both radical and conservative, and so it has played a vital role both in maintaining the traditions of the country and shaping its modernity. These dispositions are not party political. They are qualities of mind and character that are woven into the fabric of our English culture."

This conception was once part of Labor's DNA. Writing in 1909, federal MP and Australian Workers' Union co-founder William Spence wrote that Labor's focus was "the bread and butter question", but maintained his party was "dominated by two moral convictions: the Ethic of Usefulness and the Ethic of Fellowship". With Labor in power, Spence envisaged "an active and enlightened democracy". Shorter working hours, better wages, safer and secure work were not an end in themselves but would allow working people and their families to participate in their communities, voluntary organisations, and political life – to be useful to themselves and others. Spence wanted to create a good life for all Australians based upon an ethical understanding that markets needed regulation but that governments could not solve all ills.

Here is another reminder of what labourism was really about: it was about taking the parliamentary road, and taking office, but was never *limited* to putting bums on seats in parliament, or upholding union rights, improving wages and conditions, or making provision for basic services and welfare. Labourism was a radically new idea of politics – social democracy. It was democratic in seeking to have the voice of working people, the majority of the population, represented in parliament and, in turn, subjecting the market to the force of democratic institutions, including self-governing unions. Needless to say, Labor rejected the revolutionary road and opposed communism. Revolution was seen as both a violation of tradition and a betrayal of the democratic institutions that labour had helped build, to say nothing of the potential for state terror and oppression. It was also an idea of the good society – a 'social-ist' idea with little to do with the means or ownership of production – and more about human freedom and liberty. Labourism held that individuals flourish within strong collectives – family, community, and nation. It insisted working people were fundamentally different from commodities and were not to be bought and sold on the market at a going rate. It is this moral or ethical understanding of material politics, as Spence shows, that underpins the Labor idea of a good life and good society.

Finally, a word on liberalism, which is an important element of the Labor tradition. Indeed, Spence embodied something of the Australian tradition of working-class liberalism, of self-help, self-government and liberty revered by his fellow trade unionists. But liberalism was not and can never be Labor's defining creed. Labourism is not a project of abstract goals such as equality, diversity or inclusivity, in other words a technocratic vision of politics that has little to say about people's need to earn, belong, care for others or speak to their innate human desire for security and stability. Liberalism has much to say about rights, but not enough of responsibility, virtue, and tradition. Its proponents are wedded to delineating some neat and false divide between the individual and the collective. As a result, liberalism is less capable of conceptualising how democratic, self-governing institutions – unions, for instance, but also stakeholder companies, mutuals, cooperatives and faith groups – are in many ways better placed to constrain the power of the market *and* the State.

As I have argued previously, we can derive inspiration from the Blue Labour tendency within British Labour, founded by Maurice Glasman, a Labour life peer in the House of Lords. Here perhaps is Unity's new one big idea – a centre-left proposition that both the market and the State have become too powerful and are in need of reform by way of employee representation on company boards, welfare policy that devolves power to local communities, and a renewed focus on vocational labour market entry. A practising Jew, Glasman's 'Blue Labour' panacea offers up an optional side-serve of Catholic social thought. As Glasman reminded an audience on his 2015 visit to Australia, Aristotle once defined courage as the middle way between recklessness and cowardice. For Labor's sake, members of Unity will need to pluck up a sufficient amount of that cardinal virtue in order to change us and modern Labor.

What comes next?

In the wake of the global financial crisis, cracks first began to appear in the post-late 1970s ascendancy of an elite, cosmopolitan neo-liberalism. First weakened by the 2008-09 global financial crisis, this orthodoxy appears fatally wounded by the COVID-19 pandemic.

Economic insecurity not seen since the 1930s, a power imbalance between labour and capital driven by the emasculation of the union movement, conspired to disrupt liberal democratic politics. Far from aiding parties of the left and centre-left, popular anger over these trends, is *lessening* support for social democrats. It is driving the working-class into the arms of populist, far-right demagogues who seek to divide people on the basis of race and religion. Australian has not been immune to the global, populist trends: Trumpism, the alt-right, Brexit in the United Kingdom (and Corbynisation of the British Labour Party) have been mirrored by One Nation's electoral re-emergence in our polity, and the growth of micro-right parties.

As we negotiate COVID-19 and its aftermath, Labor needs its MPs and activists armed to the teeth with practical, relevant ideas connected to the basic needs and aspirations of Australians, whether they reside in our outer suburbs or inner cities, regions, or remote areas. While the task ahead necessitates encouraging freethinkers and freethinking, the Right requires more ideological coherence, coalescing around a revived common good agenda – modernising but reverent of tradition; pro-worker and pro-business; patriotic and internationalist – the type of agenda capable of building a broad coalition of voters to win national office. By necessity, this coalition includes small 'c' conservative voters and voters of faith and entails a policy agenda grounded in the tangible concerns of Australians: family, work, and love of country.

In 2020, there is a centre-left, social democratic alternative: a post-liberal, communitarian politics of the common good. Taking as its starting point people's grounding in family, community, and nation, this politics rejects market fundamentalism yet is sceptical of centralised statism. It upholds virtue, hard work, decency, responsibility, and patriotism. It seeks not to ape populism but rather broker a popular common good, or settlement, in the national interest. This, after all, was the animating idea of Australian labourism in its most successful electoral phases: the Curtin (1941-45) and Hawke-Keating (1983-1996) governments, and the original

'Australian settlement' of the 1900s, with the living wage at its core, was driven by the Labor oppositions and governments of Chris Watson and Andrew Fisher.

What must hallmark Labor's national reconstruction plan after COVID-19? We are not all Keynesians again, nor should the public's acceptance of an increased role for government during this crisis be mistaken for the return of a pre-1980s statism. Rather, Labor's focus should be strengthening institutions, fixing structural faults in the economy, nation-building social and physical infrastructure, and rebuilding national sovereignty. This entails a thorough revision of enterprise bargaining and reinstating the value of vocational education. COVID-19 has seen business and labour come together to save jobs and people's livelihoods. Labor should institutionalise these arrangements to prepare the economy and its workplaces for future crises. Following the lead of Germany and much of Scandinavia, large companies should be required to have employees represented on their boards – 'codetermination'. Embedding employees in the private sector's corporate governance, as per the case of Industry Super funds, could help recharge Labor's links with business, and remind the ideologues of private enterprise that talking to Labor is a smart thing to do

Conclusion

In 2020, Australia can develop a new policy framework for economic prosperity with fairness, preparing its citizens for the rolling challenges of this crisis and inevitable future shocks. Labor's task is to inspire and convince Australians that it is the only party capable of protecting the economy and jobs, and national security, broadly conceived, that it can be trusted to secure the national recovery and build a stronger, fairer nation. As Australia deals with a once-in-a-century pandemic and plots its recovery, a once-in-a-generation nation-building opportunity is upon Labor.

Yet Labor must change before it can change Australia. It is incumbent on the forces of Unity to lead the party's renewal. Change must come for Australia's sake.

2. Family is Everything

Marielle Smith

Family is everything. That is the sentiment that drives almost every Australian I've come across. And it should be at the heart of all that we do and all that we promise in the Labor Party. Family is a defining common factor for us all. Every Australian was born into one, and most Australians will spend their lives building another. Family is at the heart of many joys in life – it motivates, inspires, drives, and supports. We want to be proud of our family and deliver for them, and we want our family to be proud of us. Family failure is also at the heart of what can go terribly wrong in communities, leaving children vulnerable, women abused, our elderly abandoned – the darkest of ills. To make a compelling case at the next federal election and beyond, Labor must leave no Australian in doubt that we stand with them and the aspirations, hopes and dreams they hold for their family. And for those for whom family has failed them, including the youngest and most vulnerable in our community, we need to make and keep a promise that we will never leave them behind.

Embracing modern families

If Labor is to be the party for families, we first need to refresh our thinking about what the Australian family looks like. In 2009, when the television show *Modern Family* was first broadcast, it defied ratings expectations. Rather than being turned-off by its depiction of non-traditional families, the show's huge following suggests it struck a chord by depicting families *as they are* for an increasing number of Australians. I count my own family here: as a child of a broken and then rebuilt family, I distinctly remember how my step-brothers and I felt to see our family structure portrayed in that show not as a failure or second rate, but as an equally legitimate family unit full of love.

The Australian family unit has changed drastically in just a matter of decades. Men and women are choosing to have fewer children, those children are staying at home for longer, the nuclear family is no longer the established norm and we have seen a rise in 'extended' households (those with three or more generations living under one roof). Single parent families, usually headed by a female, have also become more common, as have 'blended' families and 'step' families. Last census there were almost 47,000 Australians living as same-sex couples, over 6,000 of whom are now married. To most Australians, modern families don't equate to family disfunction and shouldn't be treated as such. Our language, and our policy, must be inclusive of those many Australians living in a modern family unit. We must ensure that those Australians know we speak and stand for their families, as much as we do for those in a more traditional family environment – family must be a broad franchise that connects with the lived experience of Australians, rather than a postcard from the past.

Backing in the aspirations of Australian families

Just as we need to refresh our conception of the Australian family in our political narratives, we also desperately need to revisit the message we deliver to them. To be the party for families, Labor needs to speak to the key objectives and aspirations held by so many families. Our messaging should reflect the premium Australians place on promoting the welfare of their families and those closest to them. We all value the ability to provide our families with security, stability, and greater opportunity generation upon generation. Therefore, the most important message we must take to Australian families, whatever their make-up, is that we back the unique dreams and hopes they hold for themselves and for future generations. If we are to reach more Australians we must offer a more relevant promise: we need to leave Australian families with no doubt that whatever their dreams, goals and aspirations, Labor is the party that will stand with them.

In doing so, it is not for Labor politicians to determine what Australians should aspire to. Our role is to listen, and to use our hard fought for place as one of two parties of government to do everything we can to deliver for families in a meaningful way. Families must know that in their aspirations, we stand behind them and with them. In doing so, Labor politicians must never look down on the vast majority of Australians who identify financial security among their top goals. Financial security for family is a core goal and failing to feel this anxiety and respond to it fulsomely can make Labor seem aloof or not connected with what is occurring on the ground in Australian communities. Priorities that go beyond the financial to those which are grievance based, as often espoused by the Green Left, are frequently a luxury reserved for those in secure and well-paid work. For too many Australians, that is not the case – and we must not devalue their lived experience.

We have seen wages stagnate during the life of this Coalition Government, from an average of 1.8 per cent growth from 2008-2013, to a measly 0.5 per cent in the five years since. This has been coupled with a rise in underemployment and the ongoing casualisation of the workforce. Of those Australians fortunate enough to have a job, over 11 per cent of workers are willing and able to work more hours. One in four are classed as casual – close to double the nearly one in eight in 1982 – and thus enjoy little employment security. The impact of a highly casualised workforce came into stark focus during the pandemic when more than one million casual workers were excluded from the JobKeeper wage subsidy.

This is where our union movement, in partnership with our party, has essential work to do. Historically, the achievements our union movement has delivered vastly improved working conditions and security for Australian workers. Unions were instrumental in delivering paid annual leave, penalty rates, unfair dismissal protections, equal pay for women and compulsory superannuation, to list just a few examples. But despite these successes for families, there is a growing suspicion among too many Australians that our collective efforts to provide greater employment security and higher wages act as impediments to their aspirations.

For example, according to the most recent Australian Election Study, union membership as a percentage of the workforce has declined from 42 per cent in 1987 to 19 per cent in 2019, while the percentage of Australians who favour stricter laws to control unions has remained high, bouncing around the 40–50 per cent range. An Essential poll from 2020 found that while people believe workers would be better off if unions were stronger, 49 per cent still believed unions add an unnecessary layer of bureaucracy for business and 47 per cent believed them to be corrupt. Rather than writing off these fellow Australians sceptical of unions as incompatible with our movement, it is incumbent upon us to convince them of the benefits that a strong union movement, working in partnership with the ALP, can deliver for their families. We should also not be afraid to celebrate the victories our union movement achieves by working in partnership with business, as both Hawke and Keating so powerfully demonstrated. Often our movement's greatest wins have been achieved through collaboration over hostility and that is a history worth celebrating and where possible repeating.

Delivering on aspiration depends on delivering growth

Another way to reassure Australian families that we stand with them in the achievement of their goals and dreams is to reorient our political narrative from one focused on redistribution to one that centres on growth. While a focus on redistribution is understandable given Labor's key mission has always been fairness for working people, it is far too easy for redistribution narratives to be characterised as hostile to aspiration. Of course, focusing on growth as opposed to redistribution does not mean adhering to outdated models of 'trickle down' economics nor does it mean ignoring policy-based questions of redistribution entirely: proactive government intervention in the economy will always be required, and we must always prioritise fairer outcomes from the generation of greater growth and prosperity. Indeed, contemporary economic studies from both the International Monetary Fund and the OECD have shown that inequality itself can act as a handbrake on economic growth, dampening economic demand and preventing disadvantaged Australians from investing in the skills and education required to meet their goals. Tackling inequality is therefore an important part of what should become our economic narrative.

A broad focus on growth clearly says to Australian families of all varieties that there's room for their success and aspirations in our movement, whilst also making plain that we will leave no family behind. And given the challenges ahead for our economy in a post-COVID world, achieving growth through the three Ps of population, productivity and participation will be essential. The increased child care fee support policy launched by Anthony Albanese at the 2020 Budget Reply is a fine example of one that seeks growth above redistribution through the prism of productivity and participation, yet still ensures equitable outcomes for those who need support most. Removing the barriers to workplace participation for thousands of young parents, most of whom are women, grows our economy and does so in a way that supports the dreams and aspirations of young families.

Of course, a focus on growth also requires an acknowledgement of the important role the private sector plays in delivering jobs. Most Australians work in the private sector, and many of them see their opportunities and job security as intrinsically linked to the success of their employer. Whilst we must always hold the private sector to account when businesses fail workers, a general demonisation of business jars with the way many Australians feel about their employers and workplaces.

The role of education and skills in the advancement of Australian families

Australian families don't just dream for themselves in the moment: they hold high dreams for their futures. Modern Australia has been defined by its capacity to deliver better opportunities for the next generation than the ones that came before. In my own family, this story can be mapped simply through education outcomes:

my grandfather concluded his education at primary school level in Australia, yet his children – thanks to a great public education system and Commonwealth university scholarships – had the opportunity to study to post-graduate level. Parents, whatever their background or the makeup of their family, want a better life and greater opportunities for their children than they had themselves. And the best way to achieve this, alongside economic growth, is through a serious and strategic investment in skills and education.

When it comes to school education, our challenge is to ensure that the public education system – the very foundation of a fair and prosperous society – is equitably funded to deliver genuinely fair outcomes for all children. But in doing so, we must also be respectful of those Australian families who aspire not just to a quality education for their children, but choice in who delivers it. Whilst I personally loathe public funding propping up the elite schools in our community already boasting rifle ranges and second swimming pools, there is a space within our education system for private provision, especially when delivered by faith-based institutions. There are valid reasons so many families work countless overtime shifts and make significant financial sacrifices to send their children to low-fee private schools. We can be the party of public education without being a party that scoffs at those who seek something different to the public system and who are prepared to make sacrifices to provide that for their kids.

On higher education and skills, Labor has a proud record but there is room for improvement. We have always fought to ensure that cost isn't a barrier for those Australians for whom university will be key to a brighter future, and that should forever remain our shining star. But university education isn't the be all and end all for every Australian, nor should it be. Rather, fostering a broader diversity of skills, resilient to the expected and unexpected changes in our economy, will be essential for workers across almost all industries. We know that with the rise of artificial intelligence, for instance, it will be crucial for Australians to continually learn and develop new skills throughout their careers, whether that be through traditional educational institutions like universities and TAFEs, or on-the-job training. Our focus on education must include significant support for TAFE and vocational training and also be open to supporting alternative models such as micro-credentialing (short, skill-based accreditations) in high growth sectors, to ensure these industries remain accessible to more Australian workers. In doing so, we can better support a wider cross section of aspiration for even more Australian families.

When family goes wrong: support for failed families

To be the party for families, we need to speak to the aspirations for financial security and greater opportunity that Australian families hold. But we also need to be there for those left most vulnerable when families don't operate in the way this essay assumes – as is too often the case. The devastating reality is that not every parent acts in the best interests of their children, and not every family provides the foundation for a strong community. Estimates vary, but according to the Australian Institute of Health and Welfare, around 1 per cent of Australian children are subject to some form of abuse or neglect each year. These children are most likely to come from the lowest socioeconomic group and are disproportionately Indigenous. The Australian Institute of Family Studies considers substance misuse, mental health problems and domestic violence 'key risk factors' for abuse and neglect. Children exposed to these problems are much more likely to have developmental changes during childhood and psychological challenges well into adulthood.

When combined with the added burden of poverty, family disfunction can severely limit a child's ability to ever catch up with their peers. Just under 18 per cent of Australian children live in poverty, with those in regional areas and single parent households the worse affected. Children from disadvantaged areas, where these issues can compound, are twice as likely to experience developmental vulnerability as their peers in the wealthiest areas. To support these children, we need to make widescale and genuine investments in early childhood education and ensure our social security system is targeted to adequately support and provide protection for children and families in need. Critically, as I have long advocated, and as early childhood development experts widely support, we need a sharper focus within our education and health systems on the first 1000 days of a child's life where the greatest impact can be had.

When children in our community suffer, we are all worse for it – and these problems can impact on the individual and their communities for decades. To meaningfully support all Australian families, that must mean not just supporting the aspirations of the stable ones, but ensuring that all children have the opportunity to dream their own dreams, and not let a start in life that they cannot control or do not deserve stand in the way of a positive future.

Where and how we speak to families matters

Labor is without doubt the party best placed to deliver for Australian families. Our focus on fairness and commitment to meaningful policy reform has demonstrated that decade upon decade. Where we have failed in recent years is to convince enough Australian families this is the case. That's why, beyond our policy offering, we must also be interrogating how we reach Australian families, and the tone with which we engage.

Australians are increasingly going online for their news, with an ever-increasing share relying heavily on social media, particularly via Facebook. Given social media's ability to deliver tailored information that confirms people's biases, we must be thoughtful and creative about penetrating information silos and reaching families where they devote their attention. Whilst it can be daunting to refocus away from our traditional campaigning strengths, a digital-first approach would enable us to connect better to families where they are receptive to our message. Crucially, we must also take care to avoid the condescending tone often adopted on the far left, one that seeks to stifle debate and dismiss those with different views as antiquated oddities. Such a tone is not only morally wrong, but also self-defeating if we want to convince Australian families to trust us with their aspirations.

Concluding thoughts

The road back to government for Federal Labor is not going to be easy. Our fundamentals are good, but to convince Australians to re-turn us to office requires us to speak directly to that which is most important to them: their family. That ultimately requires recognition that the Australian family has changed and a commitment to deliver-ing on the aspirations and dreams each family holds for themselves. This means delivering policy reform that will produce outcomes for Australian families in terms of secure jobs, quality education and care for those families most in need. Given the importance of family to so many Australians, family must be at the heart of how we speak to Australians, and how we design and prioritise the policies we take to each election. We can leave no Australian in doubt that when it comes to their future, Labor stands firmly with and for their family.

* * *

Marielle Smith was elected as a Senator for South Australia in May 2019. Prior to entering Parliament, Marielle was a professional public policy adviser, with diverse experience as an international policy adviser for the Department of the Prime Minster and Cabinet, and as an adviser on early childhood education to former Minister Kate Ellis MP. Marielle also served as senior adviser to former Prime Minister Julia Gillard, Chair of the Global Partnership for Education and Chair of the Global Institute for Women's Leadership at Kings College London, advising on gender and global education policy issues. She has served on private and public sector boards, and as a manager within her family's former business. Marielle holds a Masters of Science with Distinction in Public Policy and Administration from the London School of Economics, and a first class honours degree from the Australian National University. She lives in Adelaide with her husband, two children and, depending on the week, her three step-children.

3. UNIONS MATTER

Gerard Dwyer

In September 2007, former Federal Labor Leader and Deputy Prime Minister Kim Beazley rose in the House of Representatives to deliver his farewell speech to Parliament after twenty-seven years of service to the nation. Beazley's choice of words were instructive, telling the House "…when you wish to assault democracy, first you attack the unions; when you wish to restore democracy, first you start with the unions." In short, unions matter. Unions are democratic institutions giving voice to the interests of working people. Free and independent trade unions strengthen a nation's democratic fabric and you will find them supporting a host of other institutions that need to be strong in a functioning social democracy.

And unions matter because work matters. Work is a fundamental human activity that provides for personal, social, and economic development. It is central to what makes us social beings and binds us together as communities and nations. Given its inherent importance, work should be structured so that it is productive, safe and above all enhances a sense of self. The programming of work must allow individuals to balance their work with their family and community responsibilities. Such balance, a central focus of all unions, promotes a greater sense of self-worth and provides the capacity to contribute to family, society and builds stronger, resilient communities.

Working people deserve a seat at the tables where decisions about their working lives are made – their unions give them a voice at those tables. In open democratic societies the role of unions must be seen as fundamental and the rights that underpin them must not be delegitimised. Laws should be structured to facilitate the right of working people – freedom of association – to join their relevant union and be represented by those unions. The fight to secure and maintain such rights has been a long one and constant one, because the forces of tyranny know what Kim Beazley knew in 2007 – knock off unions and you knock off a serious opposing force.

How those rights are to be protected is ever evolving. The world of work is never static and technological change has always been a disruptor to the workplace and overall economy. But the lightning speed of current technological change – the fourth industrial revolution – is undermining industrial and social protection far more rapidly than in previous epochs. Norms, laws, and protections that have stood in some cases for over a century are being torn down in a single financial year, with COVID-19 throwing even more fuel onto the fire.

What type of work is being undertaken and where it takes place should not be a factor to remove – or avoid – proper regulation of work practices and the protection of the working people whose labour carries out the work. Accepting practices that were always wrong or illegal just because they have manifested in the form of technology is nothing more than deregulation by stealth. Our industrial relations system – a system that has underpinned Australia's broad prosperity – is currently being gamed by the promoters of indirect employment and platform capitalism. Yet the needs and aspirations of working people have not changed. They want a sense of employment security so they can build a life for themselves and their families – this simple desire is timeless. And it is to that aspiration that the labour movement must speak.

Defence not defiance

In 1834, one of the Tolpuddle Martyrs – the English farm labourers who dared to organise as unionists – said to the presiding Judge, "… if we had violated any law it was not done intentionally. We were uniting together to save ourselves, our wives and families from starvation."

The Judge was unmoved and gave George Loveless and his five colleagues an all-expenses paid trip in prison irons to the penal colony of NSW. Whilst it didn't move the Judge, it did move thousands of agricultural labourers across South West England because his statement resonated with the working families of the day. What united the farm labourers around Dorset were deteriorating wages, poor working conditions and a sense that their work was becoming less secure. Economic depression, growing unemployment and automation were all factors feeding their sense of job and economic insecurity. Throughout South West England some agricultural labourers had rioted but others turned to organising themselves.

Some twenty years earlier similar challenges had seen the Luddites in Nottingham rail against the machines, but their violent responses proved impotent. Their focus on the machines themselves distracted them from the need to protect and advance the interests of those who operated the new machines.

Where the Luddites and the rioters failed, the organisers triumphed. Those who organised and petitioned in support of the Tolpuddle Martyrs had a tangible and lasting impact and the seven-year sentence was repealed after three years. This organising effort also started the long road of organised labour building stronger and fairer workplaces and communities across the UK and across the commonwealth.

Unionism's job is not to, and cannot, hold back the tide or offer false promises – it is to shape the coming world into one that is fairer. Retail workers founded 'Early Closing Associations' in the UK in the early 1840's and retail workers in Melbourne did likewise in the early 1850's. Their objective was to reduce their very long working hours and achieve a better work-life balance. The organising road in Australia was no less rocky than in other jurisdictions. The economic depression of the 1890's and the ensuing shearers' strikes almost extinguished unions capacity to be bargaining representatives for their members but work in the political sphere and with key individuals saw Arbitration and Conciliation powers inserted in our Constitution in 1901. The platform of an independent system where the economic interests of working people could be prosecuted by organised labour had been laid.

On the other side of the world, the extreme left politics of Vladimir Lenin was advocating a different path. Lenin attacked the "economism" of western unions in their quest for improving wages and conditions. He criticised the young Australian Labor Party for being "unalloyed representatives of the non-socialist workers trade unions" (*Pravda* No. 134, June 1913). Lenin dismissed their economic agenda for only being focused on themselves and their children – this narrow focus ignored the creation of a socialist nirvana for future generations. Lenin was wrong then and his apologists are still wrong today. Whereas Lenin's vision of socialism delivered brutal dictatorships and the slaughtering of millions, Australian unions and their political wing would be part of a democratic project that built one of the most open and economically just societies on earth.

The cause is enduring

Unfortunately, growing income inequality – which tracks falling union density – continues to erode the gains of previous decades, but this only makes the union mission more relevant than ever. We must remain focused on the economic security of our members and be part of building an economy that creates opportunity for all.

The approach of early Australian unions was defence not defiance – and this focused approach delivered incredible results. The motto of 'The Sheet Metal Working Industrial Union of Australia' was representative of our young Labor movement – "United to Support, not combined to Injure". This outlook gave strong support to our fledging Conciliation and Arbitration system.

The ground-breaking Harvester Judgement of 1907 set Australian unions and Australian society on a path toward greater economic security and opportunity for working people. Higgins would write in 'A New province for Law & Order II' that "the ideal of the [Industrial] Court is a collective agreement settled, not by the measurement of economic resources, but on lines of fair play". The question he posed in his 'Harvester' deliberations was "what would be the outcome between two parties of equal strength?"

Thus, a uniquely Australian system was forged built on the key principle of fairness. To achieve equal bargaining power, working people must have effective rights to organise. Organised labour deserves proper recognition as the voice of working people and their collective interests, and those collective interests deserve institutional protection. This is not a nice to have, but a must have for any society that aspires to economic justice.

Working people should not be surrendered by the 'powers that be' to fend for themselves against unchecked competition. Companies can and should compete on a range factors, but wages should not be one of them. Everybody should have the opportunity to play their part in the creation of wealth and prosperity and all should have a just share of the fruits of their productive labour. This was not radical in 1890 and should remain uncontroversial today.

This principle drove the Harvester decision, was central to the Hawke/Keating government's Accord with the ACTU and it is what underpins the current fight for a living wage. There is a need to amend existing industrial laws so that they allow the voice of the collective to be heard. The current system is riddled with impediments to achieving good industrial outcomes in a timely manner.

Sharpening the message

Unions have always engaged with the relevant workplace issues of the day and whilst their members might understand this, those outside will be completely unaware of the work unions do. Unfortunately, some 80 per cent of Australian working people today are not engaged with our movement and there are a variety of reasons for this.

Whilst unions are the collective voice of working people, and remain the best vehicle to advance their interests, too many don't see value in the union proposition, too many don't know how to reach us and too many don't even know we exist. Whatever the reason, it is not the fault of the non-member that they have not joined their union – that can only rest with the movement itself. The obligation sits with unions to reach out more effectively, modernise our operations and offerings, and demonstrate our relevance to those non-members.

Over recent decades many unions did allow internal processes to become outdated and many didn't keep up with fast moving changes in communication methods – but change is now well underway. Unions are stepping up and challenging themselves on existing processes, on their priority issues and how they communicate to members and non-members. Australian workers do not exist in a bubble and they expect unions to offer their products to the same standard that any business or organisation might provide in the twenty first century.

A young Delegate to the 2015 ACTU Congress quipped to the audience that "for my generation if it's not on our Instagram feed, it didn't happen". It was jolting for some of us then, but it was true. Today, Instagram itself is becoming dated, but unions are working hard to push themselves to the cutting edge of digital communications with a message as relevant today as it has ever been. It is uplifting to see the blend of young and experienced Officials working together in their unions to drive enhanced communication methods, build stronger member engagement and develop internal processes that are fit for purpose in 2020. The speed of this change in many unions is impressive but there is still much to do.

Tried and tested

Unions have delivered much for working Australians. Be it Medicare, superannuation or Paid Parental Leave it has always been the unions at the centre of the project – giving voice to the concerns of working Australians in the workplace, in the public square and in the corridors of power. To reverse the current economic scourges of insecure work and low wage growth will require a strong union effort and a strong union voice – to fail will be to fail our children. But unions have always been up for the hard tasks.

Australians still turn to unions in a crisis to protect their basic rights. During WorkChoices (2005-2007) it was the Australian union movement that working people turned to. During the COVID-19 crisis again Australians looked to the union movement to protect their safety at work and to protect their long-term job security. It was unions being the voice of their members on the front line that set the COVID safety standards, it was the union movement that called early and loudly for a wage subsidy to get people and businesses through the pandemic.

During the height of COVID-19, even the Coalition Government called a truce and recognised that unions could be a constructive force in dealing with a crisis. It appears that ceasefire is over but, as always, unions were there when the pressure was at its most intense offering workable solutions, driven from shopfloor insight.

Even against the odds, the Australian union movement continues to deliver and continues to prosecute an agenda in the interests of their members and the broader community. The HSU is driving an agenda for better aged care, the ASU/USU is calling for Local Government to be properly recognised as the critical deliverer of essential community services. This is a particularly important issue for regional Australia. My own Union, the SDA, is working in alliance with the AWU and TWU to achieve a sustainable, ethical, and fair retail supply chain in our fruit and vegetable sector. Those agricultural workers harvest the food for our supermarket shelves that we all enjoy, and they deserve better than the shocking exploitation and illegality the current flawed system delivers. The regional communities where they spend their money likewise deserve better and will benefit from a clean and ethical retail supply chain that stamps out unscrupulous operators.

As the pandemic unfolded, it was with great pride that the SDA saw Australians finally recognise retail workers for the heroes they are, providing an essential, frontline service to our community. It was confronting for SDA members to staff the stores in March and April 2020 as panic buying and customer aggression erupted in an environment where medical understanding of the virus was rudimentary and safety measures were still being rolled out. In this pressure cooker of uncertainty, SDA members turned up every day to keep the community supplied with life's essentials. For this we all owe them a great deal and we owe them our respect every time we engage with them. Retail workers know what it means to serve their community with a quiet dignity – and their enduring service thoroughly deserve the recognition it has received.

Workplace COVID Safety Plans, a wage subsidy for Australian workers, paid pandemic leave and recognition payments for essential workers – these were all promoted by Australian unions in the interests of their members and the broader community. Unions stood with their members and the Australian community during the pandemic and are standing with their members and the broader community as we rebuild our economy.

The challenge

Periods of rapid technological change, like the agricultural revolution, the subsequent industrial revolutions and the current digital or fourth revolution, always create social uncertainty. How we order work and how we protect the dignity of those who perform it is always tested.

The gig economy is a social as well as an industrial challenge. An order on a digital platform which must be filled and delivered is work, and those who perform it are no different to any other worker who deserve a fair wage and their safety to be taken seriously. We cannot allow illegality and exploitation to be hidden or ignored behind the impersonality of a phone screen and allowing otherwise would amount to nothing more than a Digital Workchoices. The breadth, depth, and speed of change in the current technological revolution is unparalleled. Governments are challenged to allow the voice of gig economy workers to be heard and offer solutions – not to use it as a tool to undermine industrial and social standards more broadly in a race to the bottom.

Whether it's six farm labourers talking wages under a Sycamore tree in 1834 or six delivery riders waiting for their apps to show their next job or six Amazon employees filling an online order, it is still about a fair day's work for a fair day's pay.

This is the industrial challenge, but the social challenge has always been 'what sort of society do we want to live in?' Low wage countries are invariably poor countries. Australia's relatively high minimum wage has been a deliberate and beneficial public policy supporting industrial and social standards – it is central to who we are and is a redline that must be defended with all our energy. Unions were at the heart of establishing these standards and unions are modernising to defend them – we owe it to our members, our children, and the Australian community to win this fight. And we will.

* * *

Gerard Dwyer is the National Secretary-Treasurer of the Shop, Distributive & Allied Employees' Association. Gerard has been the Secretary-Treasurer of the SDA-NSW Branch (2005-2014), National President of the Union (2008-2014) and SDA National Secretary since 2014. The SDA is one of Australia's largest trade unions and represents employees working in retail, fast food and warehousing. Gerard is currently Senior Vice President of the Australian Council of Trade Unions (ACTU), a member of the ACTU Executive and a member of the National Executive of the Australian Labor Party. Gerard grew up in regional NSW and moved to Sydney at the age of 18 to pursue tertiary studies. He has a Bachelor of Education (History and English (1989)), a Masters of Business in Employment Relations (UTS, 2002) and is also a Graduate of the Australian Institute of Company Directors. Gerard's working life has seen him employed as a shop assistant, classroom teacher, social worker and as a Trade Union Official for over twenty years.

4. A NATION WITHOUT CLASS

Misha Zelinsky

The Australian Labor Party was founded to give political expression to the core desires of working-class people in a small colonial outpost: a fair day's pay and a fair say in the running of *their* nation. History shows those brave union and Labor pioneers succeeded in their mission. Recent history on the other hand tells us that we are failing.

In a disruptive global political era characterised by the rise of identity politics there are two foundational identities that modern Labor has undervalued to its detriment – class and nationhood. For a party consciously named 'Australian Labor', this approach represents a crisis of *self* identity that is hurting us electorally.

If Australian Labor is unable to effectively stand for the Australian nation and the Australian working and middle classes who dwell within its national borders – then what *does* it stand for?

Without an emphasis on these foundational identities Labor routinely loses the key debates that decide federal elections. We are constantly wrong-footed on economic aspiration, while on national security we can fail to project strength.

The result? Six years of government in a quarter of a century.

Being seen to be equivocal on the collective identities of nationhood and class has been as disorienting for Labor voters as it has for the party itself. Today economic and cultural frustration is translating into political anger. But some of these voters are no longer looking to Labor as the natural vehicle to address the challenges they face and express their grievances.

Labor has become far too fixated on the *what* of politics – the big things we want to do; rather than the *who* – the people we must represent and who we must convince to entrust us with government.

This form of bloodless transactional politics leaves voters feeling cold and increasingly attracted to the heat of right-wing populism. More broadly though, the question we must ask – and those who have worked on a polling booth in a regional or suburban seat will know what I mean – why are people in traditional Labor communities so *pissed* at us? Why is it so personal?

Becoming 'aggressively Australian'

COVID-19, authoritarianism and an increasingly aggressive Chinese Communist Party are challenging Australia strategically and economically for the first time in many generations. Dealing with these challenges will require a big vision – a Labor vision – but it will need us to engage with the core identities of nationhood and class.

Fortunately, there is a path to political recovery. National identity and economic class are two powerful story telling frames that are easily understood in policy terms and rich in cultural capital. As part of our DNA they are natural vehicles for Labor's vision and fused together they represent a powerful antidote to right-wing populism.

Politics is the art of compelling storytelling. It's about creating emotion and connection. Studies show that after a speech people rarely remember what the person said, but they can remember how they made them feel. Think of your favourite politician – or scary populist – and you instantly recognise a great storyteller. Instead of digestible stories, Labor has bombarded voters with a dizzying array of technocratic policy. While each policy is beautifully crafted and calibrated to solve a niche problem for one group after the next, the lack of coherence is overwhelming. It can make those who aren't policy wonks – 99 per cent of the population – susceptible to scare campaigns or feeling belittled by barking activists showering them in jargon.

There are varying views as to whether hope can beat fear in politics, but of one thing we can be sure: fear absolutely beats an economics exam posing as a political agenda.

In the words of Paul Keating, Labor must be 'aggressively Australian'. Labor must paint a vivid picture of a strong Australia, sure of its sense of self and confident of its place in the world. We must provide a vision of a nation that provides security, prosperity, and opportunity to its people at home and inspiration for those around the world. We can invite Australians – old and new – to build it with us. This project starts with working out who we are and what we stand for. Only then can we ask Australians to vote for us.

The party of the people?

When societies divide economically, they divide culturally and politically. Obscene inequality numbers and economic insecurity tell us everything we need to know about where we are at globally. In Australia, the trends are more recent and more nuanced – but the direction is clear and stark. The rich are getting richer, the middle is being squeezed and the bottom are locked out of the Good Life.

So, what's gone wrong? Firstly, we aren't alone. Social democrats the world over have found themselves horrified and baffled in equal measure by the rise of far-right nationalism. How can it be in an era of such dramatic economic challenge and polarisation that the people are blaming the parties of labour for their problems? Why aren't they looking to us for the solutions?

History tells us that economic dislocation sets the scene for a social democratic ascendancy – think Franklin Roosevelt's New Deal in the 30s – or a gathering storm of totalitarian nationalism. Whether it's Brexit, the rise of the so-called 'Deplorables' in middle America or the 'Yellow Vest' protests of France – working people are telling parties of the Left that we aren't listening. Our answers and attitudes aren't dealing with their questions or problems.

Using the 'C word'

The Devil's greatest trick, apparently, was to convince us he doesn't exist. The Conservatives' greatest trick has been to persuade Labor that Australia is a classless society; that any reference to the very existence of class represents a capitulation to supposed evils of 'class warfare' or the 'politics of envy'.

No one is suggesting we pit Australians against each another in a zero-sum game. But that doesn't mean there is no value in defining the community on the basis of class. Firstly, it is still how Australians see themselves – with an Australian National University study finding that 52 per cent of Aussies identify as middle class while 40 per cent identify as working class. Secondly, it helps us all work out which team we are on and who is in acting in our interests.

The retreat from class represents a victory by business and capital over the solidarity of the working and middle classes who instead have been splintered into sole traders, precarious workers, and soulless consumers. This makes the selling of big ideas tackling vested interests next to impossible. But while we have increasingly left people to fend for themselves, you can be damn sure that the billionaire class have stuck together and worked in their collective interests. That they've built political coalitions with parts of Labor's natural constituency is on us.

How we discuss small businesses owners – too often described by Labor as 'bosses' – is instructive but also an opportunity. Tradies with vans are working-class people busting their guts. As are shop owners or franchisees. It's also highly likely they're being done over themselves by the billionaire class through unfair business dealings or abuse of market power. Yet as long as we fail to meaningfully reach out to them, we've got no hope of attracting their votes.

COVID-19 has shone a giant torch onto these issues. When crisis struck, we rediscovered the real value in our economy – essential workers. The nation turned to its blue, fluro and pink-collar heroes for help; people who know how to make steel, run oil refineries, and care for someone on a ventilator. The same people we've failed to recognise – and pay decently – for decades. While it's great to see we've discovered the working class as heroes, a pat on the back won't get us back in their good books. They need a pay rise. Now.

The destruction caused by a generation of US workers either left behind through deindustrialisation or wage suppression should give us food for thought in Australia. The Rand Corporation found that had US workers continued their wages growth from the 1970s until now – they'd be earning 100,000 dollars rather than the 50,000 they're currently on. That's a huge pay cut. Over time this represents a wealth transfer of $50 trillion dollars (yes!) from working Americans to the rich. If you're wondering why Americans are so pissed off, look no further. It's how – and where – this anger has been directed that tells part of the story of modern politics.

Perplexingly, as wages have fallen the support for the welfare state and economic intervention through tax and fiscal policy has fallen too. Parties of the Left have failed to see the danger in the collapse of the premium between a good job and being on the food stamps or the dole. Logic tells us that a generous safety net benefits all of us. But this is not how we feel about our own sense of self-worth. Humans need a sense of dignity and belief that their hard work is paying off – that things are getting better today and will be even better tomorrow.

As wages grind downwards, we should not be surprised that the Right can cultivate grievance about 'dole bludgers' and 'big spending government programs' amongst a working poor or a squeezed middle who are busting their arses each day only to see minimal benefit. Working hard and not getting ahead, or going backwards, is incredibly frustrating. Furthermore, we shouldn't be perplexed when those hanging on by the skin of their teeth on the economic margins – those in insecure, casualised work or industries on the brink – get more easily frightened by populist right-wing claims that a Labor Government would destroy the very little they have.

Australian wages – after growing for decades – have started to follow the American trend. Insecure work is up. The danger signs are there. With wages growing at 25-year lows, COVID-19 has demanded we pay frontline workers more. Instead during the months of April, May, and June 2020 – when our essential service heroes manned the forts against the invisible enemy of COVID-19

– profits jumped 14.9 per cent. Worker pay fell a record 2.5 per cent. Some thanks.

On climate change action, despite being the party of industry policy, we find ourselves on the wrong side of job creation. In an economic climate when wages are falling this has proven to be dangerous. The climate wars have been extremely fatiguing for Labor, but the problem itself has not disappeared. The truth is, without a compelling story about job growth, Labor is open to scare campaigns on climate especially in regions that are already suffering from falling wages and rising unemployment.

Once upon a time, Labor and Liberal argued over the rate of pay in a job site or a mine. This made us the natural party of heavy industry workers; we fought for a better deal at work and safer workplaces. Under electoral and policy pressure from the Greens, today that distinction is less clear. If the electoral choice for a blue-collar worker is no longer about the quality of your job or payrate but whether your job should exist at all, then it should be little surprise if they choose to send their vote elsewhere.

Those in regional communities understand the value of a good job and the good life that it brings. They've had front row seats for what happens when things close in the name of progress – the jobs never return and often their mates or parents never work again. The town shrinks as kids go elsewhere for opportunity and the crisis deepens. Make no mistake; the working class in the regions understand the threat climate challenge and they want it dealt with – but not if it means they alone bear the consequences.

How to fix this dilemma? Calling people idiots, oddly enough, is probably not the solution. A loud debate – from either side – serves nobody well. Labor must be the party of long term, sensible climate action *and* blue-collar jobs. If it isn't, Labor can't hope to win. If we lose, nothing gets done.

Queensland Labor and Joe Biden provide some hope in a balanced approach.

After Federal Labor's 2019 electoral shellacking in mining regions, the Queensland Labor Government quickly approved the Adani mine. During the Queensland election, Premier Palaszczuk cut the ribbon on a metallurgical coalmine while launching a $500m renewable energy future fund – proving to resource communities Labor wouldn't abandon them as it transformed the energy market. The result? Labor kept its central Queensland mining seats. Interestingly, the ideological Greens Party went backwards, winning a single seat from Labor thanks to the Liberal Party's cynical decision to preference them.

On climate change, Biden said: "When Trump hears it, he says hoax – I say jobs."

A lifetime of credibility as 'Working Class Joe' from Scranton, gave blue collar workers confidence that Biden was not hostile to heavy industry as he promised a huge investment in green energy. As proof, Biden refused to support a ban on fracking as others attacked the gas industry during the primary race. It meant a trickier path to nomination but made Biden much more electable with heavy industry union workers in Michigan, Wisconsin and the gas state of Pennsylvania. Biden's domination of blue-collar states might have included Ohio if progressives hadn't demanded Biden go against his strategic instincts and harden his gas position late in the race.

Traveling around Australia in my capacity as a union official, it's amazing how many working Australians I meet who remember which factory or mine site closed, how many people it employed and – most critically – who they blame for the closure. While we are right to celebrate the legacy of the Hawke-Keating economy, we'd do well to remind ourselves there were some communities that were upended that bore deep scars. This should give us clues as to how we manage this economic and environmental engineering challenge. We need to do it over the long run and with heart. Promising 'green jobs' some day in the future won't be enough to win votes if it means closures today.

A focus on economics – while critical – won't solve this emotional dissonance entirely. Class is more complex than that. Class has as much to do with how you spend your time or what your interests are as it does with your job or income. In other words, class is cultural. This is why Labor is sometimes staggered when a blue-collar worker on more than one hundred and fifty grand objects to being called 'rich'. Rich people live in big cities, not regional towns. They go to Europe, not down the coast or Bali for a holiday. They go to the theatre not the footy. They go to yoga on the weekends, not to church. And they prefer a wine bar over a cold one at the pub.

The working class can sense this divide that, at its worst, has inner-city types mocking them for who they are. This cultural divide has allowed the Right to drive a wedge between Labor and its base. And if we aren't careful, it will be permanent.

Ask yourself, if the party of the working class, appears to no longer call itself one, sounds like it wants to close down your industries and is filled with the sorts of people you probably wouldn't have a beer or dinner with – would you vote for it?

Of course, this shouldn't be an excuse to fetishise the working class as some in Labor make the mistake of doing. There is no cloth capped worker eager to remain in his or her station in life, nor are they wild animals to be observed or studied. Neville Wran was right; the best part of the working class is getting out and Labor is and – always will be – the party of aspiration. But aspiration does not mean the acceptance of hyper-capitalist neoliberalism through the prism of a meritocratic falsehood. Labor aspires to provide the Good Life to all, and while we want to give people the best opportunity in life regardless of how they start out, we do not believe in 'rags to riches' societies. Australian Labor doesn't succeed when anyone become a CEO; it succeeds when you can have a good life regardless of the job you do or the cards you've been dealt. A big, growing middle – that's real aspiration.

Giving a free kick to our opponents

As a starting point we must accept – and believe – that patriotism is positive. It is a not a right-wing value or 'the refuge of the scoundrel'.

Being proud of your country is a good thing. The problem with vacating the field on nation and class is that it leaves two enormously powerful identities uncontested but not idle. It doesn't end the argument – if that's the intention – but leaves fertile ground for either the Coalition or far right nationalists to tell their own stories uncontested. Sitting on the bench allows positive virtues like patriotism and community to be metasitisised into jingoism or ethno-nationalism. And the bad guys are making hay.

Despite being responsible for the cultural and economic alienation of working people, thanks to their promotion of unfettered hyper-capitalism, the Right have somehow been allowed to walk away from their policy fetishes of the last four decades. Parties of the Left have been made answerable for the smashed and dislocated communities, despite having their best interests at heart and policy solutions at the ready.

This political victory has allowed the billionaire plutocrat class and their paid acolytes to label inner-city progressives as 'elites' with a straight face while pretending they're on the side of the working class. Drawing the Left into fighting culture wars has allowed the Right to continue to pursue its economic agenda on the quiet. This political jujitsu would be galling enough if some on our own side didn't load the gun for them. This problem expressed itself best in Hillary Clinton's mocking of the so-called 'Deplorables' in 2016 and the surprise outcome of Brexit.

Unable to solve the economic pain or soothe the cultural alienation felt by their voting base – and cocksure of the superiority of their arguments – the US Democrats and British Labour found themselves as the defenders of a technocratic status quo, of predatory financial capitalism, while a shonky huckster from New York and a wanker from London were able to steal the working class from underneath them.

The problem is there are some on our side who don't understand the working class. They don't visit where they live and socialise, they don't watch their sports, they dismiss their religions and are hostile to their industries. Working people have detected this and voted accordingly. The fault is not with them, it is with us. Joe Biden's election may have us believing that all is well. Such a belief, while comforting, would amount to a false positive. 'Working Class Joe' outperformed the Democratic Party in the House and Senate precisely because he is not a modern day progressive. He won 'Never Trump' Republicans and working-class democrats in the Midwest for that exact reason. One should remember the relentless attempts to kill off Joe Biden's candidacy by the Left of his party and the fact that had Trump managed to act competently during the pandemic and not self-immolate, it's quite possible he would have won.

It's perhaps unsurprising that the Elite Left consensus answer to hyper-capitalism – a borderless, cosmopolitan internationalism overseen by unelected technocrats – has left us unable to communicate to two of the most profound drivers of self-identity, class and nation. There has been no seat at the table in Davos for the production worker tethered to their worksite in a regional town. These same trends are emerging in Australia whether we like them or not – and they represent an existential threat to Labor. While it is easy – and even comforting – to dismiss 'Hansonites' as racist, and no doubt some are, we might ask ourselves how a former leader of our great party now sits atop a nationalist party fielding coalminers as candidates in Labor strongholds.

While there is a special place in infamy for Labor 'Rats', the answer to this dilemma cannot be that everyone is wrong but us or that people have been 'tricked' into voting in ways we don't like. Such arrogance has seen the disappearance of social democratic parties around the world and it can happen here too. Could it be that right wing charlatans have moved into a juicy space that we've vacated for them?

An aggressively Australian Labor Party

The COVID-19 crisis has taught Australia two powerful and timely lessons – you can't run a nation state like it's a convenience store. And that while we need to choose our friends wisely, we need to be able to stand on our own two feet. Sovereign capability – the ability to produce the things you need, when you need them – is a little more complex than having milk, bread and the daily papers dropped to your door every day. And the consequences of not having critical products when push comes to shove are dire. Next time the shortage might be more serious than face masks.

The stress of the pandemic has exposed pre-existing problems in our economy and foreign policy. COVID-19 will speed up changes already underway and there will be no turning back what an inflexion point in history this crisis represents. Australia finds itself economically and geo-strategically challenged for the first time since the end of the Cold War. A more assertive, totalitarian Chinese Communist Party – increasingly prepared to weaponise its centrality to global supply chains – and a hollowed-out economy have made Australia more vulnerable than ever before. A future Labor Prime Minister will need strong answers to these questions. We need to be clear we will stand for a strong Australia.

While unchecked patriotism can be dangerous, a pacifist approach to nationhood or a far-left belief that nations are mere constructs inhibiting a 'global humanity' cannot be a remedy. Nor will they be accepted by Australians looking for political leadership. If nothing else we should understand that elections, after all, are conducted in nation states by citizens – so it would do us well to be clear that we represent those people unabashedly.

For geostrategic reasons, Australian cannot return to a presumptive open and non-hostile global world order under which we have grown rich since the 1980s. Doing so would not only be dangerously naive but would not be supported by an increasingly wary public. A more forensic assessments of trade deals and a concerted focus on diversification will be demanded by voters who worry about all our economic chips sitting in Beijing. A good example is the fact Australia has become the world's largest exporter of natural gas, without putting in place a reservation policy for domestic use – something all other gas nations have. This has left Australians in the bizarre situation of paying much more for our own gas than we charge our overseas customers – putting our manufacturers to the wall and threatening hundreds of thousands of jobs. Likewise, Australians wanting to know their sovereignty still matters will expect a more assertive approach to foreign multinationals avoiding tax and big business or digital platforms trying to smash our industrial relations protections.

Furthermore, the advent of Chinese state capitalism means we can no longer assume an even playing field for Australian products. Chinese industrial scale cheating means we need to be clear eyed about economic tradeoffs and how best to create manufacturing and high-tech industries from our natural resource bounty and our innovative ideas. Digging and shipping isn't good enough to meet these challenges.

The crisis provides the reset that Labor desperately needs. It provides an opportunity to recast the Australian economy and the Australian nation in a Labor image. We can define the Australian economy and the Australian nation on our terms. We can define a positive and patriotic vision – a nation where Aussies get a fair go at the Good Life and the nation is capable of protecting itself from those who mean us harm. But only if we try. The last time Labor attempted to contest and modernise the Australian identity happened under the Keating Government embodied by his project for a Republic and Reconciliation. Projects that incidentally remain unfinished.

It's time we tried again.

To win government in, we must own the economy and own the Australian identity. We cannot be a passionless assembly of technocrats in blue suits or a hide behind a bible of policies. We must confidently tell the story about Australia's future, the Labor way. Australian Labor can fuse together an economic and national security story that expresses a strength in the present and a confidence about the future.

But to excite people to share in our plans, we must connect with who they are.

5. Digital Inclusion

Michelle Rowland

The Land of the Fair Go 2.0

In the twenty-first century, world-class connectivity isn't a choice, it is an imperative. Digital transformation demands online participation for basic government services, banking, shopping, and entertainment as well as work, education and social interaction. Yet too many Australians face barriers to access, affordability, and the ability to use digital technology.

The COVID-19 pandemic has accelerated the dependence of society and the economy on digital connectivity and online services, and those who are not participating digitally have more to lose than ever before. Just as the pandemic has thrown a spotlight on connectivity, the recession has drawn focus to nation building. It now almost goes without saying that communications infrastructure, as well as the skills and confidence to use digital technologies and services, are critical to our recovery and ongoing prosperity.

Australia's trillion dollars of debt underscores the importance of investing public funds wisely – once borrowed and spent, we don't get those same dollars back. The growing connectedness of our economy and society demands connected policy. On the cusp of the fourth industrial revolution, Australia deserves and requires policy ambition that links inextricably the digital inclusion of its people with the success of the nation; that harnesses our strengths to rebuild out of recession stronger, fairer and more secure to meet the challenges of the networked era of high disruption and deep transformation.

The original Labor vision for the National Broadband Network (NBN) had a deep logic that joined up its policy architecture, political values, broadband pricing, and the economics of a fibre network to make it work. A connected logic informed by engineering and economics. A plan that addressed the expectations of the Australian public on connectivity, fairness and opportunity alongside which ran Labor's *National Digital Economy Strategy*, which translated the implications of the physical network into tangible goals for people on digital literacy and skills as well as teleworking, with a roadmap for implementation. The features all joined up to address two dominant ideals of modern Labor – one, advancing access and equity; to break down the barriers of disadvantage and improve the lives of working people. And secondly, to promote fairness and prosperity in the broadband enabled world.

Generally, the idea that something is unfair offends the sensibility of most Australians – be it on the sports field or the school ground or workplaces. Communications policy is no exception. But in the land of the fair go, fairness is not self-executing. The multi-technology-mix devised by the Liberal National Party from Opposition to 'demolish' the NBN was a mess that means that how someone fares in Australia's download speed lottery is still a frustrating matter of luck. Their decision to abandon fibre was never about cost, it was always about the politics – and it is Australians who have paid an unnecessary price.

Fairness is a value that must be guarded, embedded, prioritised, and realised. The NBN speaks to the value Labor places on economic growth and prosperity – as well as inclusion – when it comes to the digital economy. One can only imagine a COVID-19 scenario without the visionary steps taken by Labor to commission the NBN and shudder at the prospect.

The Great Dividing Range 2020

Inequality is not just immoral; it is economically irresponsible, and in the 21st century, inequality has a digital dimension. To be digitally included means being able to access, afford and have the ability to use online technologies to participate in society and the economy and, in turn, help realise the benefits of the digitally connected world across all spheres, including health, education, government, business and community services. To be digitally excluded, on the other hand, means not being able to participate owing to barriers, and not contributing as a result, while being left further behind – at an escalating pace – with each new development in the rapidly evolving digital landscape.

Too many Australians are being left behind in the offline world, and this carries over into the online environment – with each disadvantage compounding on the other. The latest release of the *Australian Household Use of Information Technology report*, published by the Australian Bureau of Statistics in March 2018, shows a digital divide reflective of larger social, economic, and geographic inequality in our country. Across the nation, Australians with low levels of income, education and employment are significantly less digitally included, and the gap between the city and the bush hasn't narrowed over time.

The *Australian Digital Inclusion Index 2020* (ADII), undertaken by Telstra, RMIT and Swinburne University of Technology with data from Roy Morgan, shows that a substantial digital divide exists in Australia, and that the gaps between digitally included and excluded Australians remain substantial, and have even widened slightly in some groups. This is particularly true for Indigenous Australians, older Australians, and Australians with a disability, as well as those not in the labour force or with less than secondary education. The ADII provides a comprehensive picture of Australia's online participation by measuring three key dimensions of digital inclusion: Access, Affordability and Digital Ability. This year it finds some improvement in some areas, but also reveals that the rate of improvement has slowed and for Indigenous Australians has stalled. For a country in recession, the digital divide may slow down economic recovery and will exacerbate the pain for those already doing it tough.

Although internet infrastructure is available to almost all Australians, the ADII states that more than 2.5 million remain offline with affordability a key challenge. This is likely to be exacerbated by the COVID-19 economic slowdown, with those already on the economic and digital margins likely to be the most impacted by the tidal wave and then backwash of the COVID-19 recession. The ADII confirms that Australia's affordability score has increased only marginally since 2014 despite the cost of internet data having gone down because households are spending more on internet services due to greater usage. Expenditure on online services has generally increased faster than household income.

The digital divide translates into a myriad of hardships, compromises, and risks. It can mean deciding between the purchase of certain groceries or mobile phone data. It can mean having to find a public Wifi spot, possibly at night, to access Centrelink online or to meet a deadline. It means students not having a suitable device on which to do their homework and it spells social isolation and loneliness for the elderly or disabled, especially during the pandemic.

Over the course of history, cycles of inequality have oscillated with the upheavals wrought by new technology, from the steam engine, to electrical power, to electronics and digitisation. New fault lines are emerging with the advent of 5G, because of the range of new services it enables and the same challenges of access, affordability, and capability that they will bring. The troubling irony is that the very people in greatest need of the benefits that 5G promises, risk being the most likely to be excluded. The rollout of 5G-enabled smart grids could save households hundreds a year on energy by assisting consumers in choosing where they buy energy, for example, yet low income households will least be able to afford and use the new technologies and services that could assist in paying the bills.

Similarly, analysis by academics at RMIT and Canberra Universities finds that people over 65 years of age are the heaviest users of health care, yet just over one in five people in this age category access online health services – substantially below the national average of two in five. Meanwhile the potential benefits of digitally delivered healthcare over 5G would be transformative for regional Australians but the cost of providing 5G access to those in rural and remote areas is a significant barrier. The Bureau of Communications, Arts and Regional Research is not yet settled on whether mobile wireless technology itself or 5G in particular is a 'general purpose technology' typically associated with industrial revolutions. But the Information Age has equipped us to recognise and respond to inequality as it emerges, and it is imperative that we take steps to promote fairness when we do see it and before it entrenches itself.

Connected country

Just as Medicare and superannuation once were radical concepts which later became mainstream, so too are measures evolving to address the digital divide. Just look at the recent backflip the Government performed on fibre, after seven years of criticism and $51 billion in expenditure on older technology. There isn't just a digital divide in this country; there is also a wide gulf between what the Liberal National Government says it's going to do and what it actually does, or fails to do, as the case may be. There is a gap between policy and practice; between rhetoric and reality; between photo ops and the outcomes on the ground.

From envisioning the NBN, to the kind of society we want to be with 5G, AI and the Internet of Things, to seriously utilising technology to address digital exclusion amongst Indigenous Australians, older Australians, and Australians with disability – the only way governments can make technology work for its citizens and consumers, rather than against them, is with a joined-up, long-term approach. This is the Labor way of governing.

Make no mistake: as I move around my electorate, it is the absence of long termism and coordinated policy vision that frustrates people the most. From over-development in our outer suburbs, train stations made inaccessible by inadequate commuter parking, to purchasing 27,000km of new copper to build a supposedly 21st century broadband network: people are frustrated because it's their quality of life that is impacted by such short-sightedness.

The Liberal National Government's record in communications and the digital economy is characterised by neglect, delay, and short-termism. This government, now into its eighth year, has failed to produce a Communications Policy Roadmap to guide the transition of the sector at this time of change, despite acknowledging the need for one and claiming to have started work on it years ago.

They have failed to produce a digital economy strategy, a 5G strategy or a digital inclusion strategy. There is no sign of a strategy on the future of broadcasting in view of standards evolution and the advent of 4K and 8K TV. A Government with a coherent vision for its industry, consumers and citizens would signal its intentions and lay out its program and linkages – particularly in a sector with such high value benefits at stake.

In government, Labor delivered and then updated the *National Digital Economy Strategy* in 2011 and 2013 – setting the goal of Australia becoming a leading digital economy and laying out the roadmap for delivering Labor's 2020 vision. The strategy prioritised digital skills – second only to physical infrastructure – as one of the key enablers of a leading digital economy and noted the need for a comprehensive approach to build digital literacy. In contrast, we have seen this Government try and rebadge 'digital economy updates' and 5G direction papers, without any roadmap, targets, or plan to coordinate industry with stakeholders who seek to bridge the digital divide. This is what happens when governments make announcements only for the media release, but not because they believe in what they are trying to achieve.

The NBN is a project that is very important to the Labor Party and, for us, has always been a values proposition. Not simply because we started it – after all, no telecommunications network is an end in itself – but because the original mission is the embodiment of our core values: Access; Opportunity; Improving quality of life. The NBN has never been an end in and of itself. It was always a means to an end. That end being the consumer: the student, the entrepreneur, the small business owner, and the broader social and economic benefits to the nation at large.

Labor is a movement of and for the future. This is why we invest in human capital through education and childcare. It is why we back renewable energy. It is why we backed investment in world-class broadband infrastructure. We believe that investing in people and the productive capacity of our economy is the way to drive inclusive economic growth that is built from the bottom up. These investments are not just policy measures in isolation. They represent value judgments that become the broader narrative about the society we aspire to be.

The Communications portfolio is an instrument to help create a smarter, more modern, and more inclusive Australia. An Australia where connectivity and content enriches our quality of life, educates us, informs us, and empowers us to fulfil our potential – whatever that may be.

The Lucky Country

Donald Horne wrote his book, *The Lucky Country*, which suggested a new way of looking at, and understanding Australia. Commonly misquoted since, Horne's idea of 'The Lucky Country' was not an affirmation of praise; rather, it was an ironic dig, intended to shake Australians out of their complacency and start a national conversation about the future. Horne wrote: "Australia is a lucky country, run mainly by second-rate people who share its luck". As ANU Professor of History Frank Bongiorno put it: "Horne's message was that while Australia had been lucky, he was doubtful whether it deserved its luck and was worried that, unless it lifted its game, its good run would not last".

So where are we now, over half a century later? Before the COVID-19 pandemic and the recession, the Australian National

Outlook 2019 was released by the CSIRO and National Australia Bank. A landmark report, two years in the making, it states unequivocally that: "Australia is at a crossroads – stride towards a more positive future outlook filled with growth, or face a slow decline". The ANO looks out to 2060 and signals that Australia may face a 'Slow Decline' if it takes no action on the most significant economic, social and environmental challenges. It acknowledges that Australia has enjoyed nearly three decades of uninterrupted economic growth, but that: "there is no guarantee that this good fortune will continue into the future. The world is changing rapidly and Australia will need to adapt to keep up".

Australia is now in recession in the midst of a health pandemic. We need all the smarts at our disposal to climb out of it. Government, industry and civil society have new tools, including behavioural economics, 5G, IoT, AI and big data, at their disposal to shape policy development, as well as a rich global network, and comparisons, to draw from. The recent announcement that CSIRO and NBN Co will use data-derived insights to direct investment to support business and consumer use cases is an example, however it remains to be seen what values this will serve or whether it will result in meaningful improvements to digital inclusion.

Addressing inequality and improving the lives of working people is Labor's defining mission. A key part of that mission is to promote fairness and prosperity in a disrupted, broadband-enabled world. To achieve that requires a connected, long-term vision for a better Australia. Australia must build on its luck to date, and make its own luck going forwards, using communications as a tool to foster growth and innovation in step with inclusion. As Labor Leader Anthony Albanese's Budget-In-Reply 2020 said:

> We can make this once-in-a-century crisis the beginning of
> a new era of Australian prosperity and Australian fairness.
> With the rights plans, the right policies – and the right
> leadership – our country can make this moment our own.

Strength and fairness. We can beat this recession, we can launch a recovery and we can build a future where no-one is held back and no-one is left behind.

There is no time like the present to build the future.

* * *

Michelle Rowland was elected to the House of Representatives in 2010 as the Member for Greenway. Prior to entering Parliament she was a senior lawyer specialising in competition and regulation in the telecommunications, media and technology sectors. In 2013 she was appointed Shadow Minister for Citizenship and Multiculturalism, and Shadow Assistant Minister for Communications. In October 2015, Michelle was elevated to the Shadow Cabinet and appointed the Shadow Minister for Small Business and Shadow Minister for Citizenship and Multiculturalism. Michelle was appointed Shadow Minister for Communications following the 2016 Federal Election. Michelle was re-elected at the 2019 election and re-appointed as the Shadow Minister for Communications. Michelle has served as a Councillor and Deputy Mayor of Blacktown City Council, Chair of Screen NSW, and a Director of the Western Sydney Area Health Service.

6. The Best Deal for Australia

Bill Shorten

The federal parliamentarians leading Australia in the year 2070, half a century after these words were written, will remember the strange period when their primary school years were disrupted by a small matter we called coronavirus.

The Victorians, in particular, will remember days spent learning at home, playgrounds cordoned off with hazard tape, people bumping elbows in greetings, parents abiding by curfews, empty sports stadiums, shuttered shops and closed state borders.

They will remember the time a nasty novel virus, thought to have jumped from animal to human in the Chinese city of Wuhan, disrupted the world, killing more than a million humans, infecting millions more, and plunging nations into recession.

What may be remembered too is the revelatory nature of the coronavirus: how the pandemic revealed weaknesses in economies and societies, frailties that had previously been papered over and obscured. And the Australian people and their parliamentary leaders will rightly ask: what did we do?

Out of luck

From the sheep's back to the mineral boom, Australia has indeed been a lucky country in the real Donald Horne sense of the phrase. But relying on endless waves of good luck is no plan and certainly no plan worthy of a great nation.

Too often our economic strategy has involved taking the path of least resistance, following the latest wave of luck and pursuing only the easy money. We Australians stopped making things. We became a service economy. We decided to play tour guide to the world's holidaymakers. (Again, relying on the inherited luck of world class beaches and natural landmarks.) And we never wondered what we might do on a day when history conspired to remove the incoming planes from our horizon.

The lesson of the coronavirus is that the globalist fantasy of the world's nations acting in sync like a Swiss watch with perfect supply chains and free flowing capital making all the major decisions, is just that – a fantasy. Or, perhaps, a dystopia. The arc of history tells us that we are first a collection of nation states. Nations can of course cooperate to achieve beneficial global ends. But national ties and interests have proven time after time to have a stronger pull than any other. We are compatriots before we are consumers. As Australians, we know this intuitively. But for so long we have been led as if we are contingent on the world, just so fortunate to have a seat at the table, and not able to stand on our own two feet. Our economic worldview had become one of cultural inferiority, necessarily reliant on others. The pandemic reminded us that we are a large nation and an island continent of twenty-five million resilient, self-sufficient people. It reminded us that for better or worse our fate was in our own hands. It always had been. We had just forgotten.

Out of stock

Local production of masks, sanitiser and ventilators was not something Australians thought of very much before the coronavirus hit. But the pandemic brought the mysterious National Medical Stockpile – a strategic reserve containing drugs and personal protective equipment (PPE) for emergencies – to the forefront of people's minds. The Royal Australian College of Physicians stated several times that specialist physicians – the frontline against the pandemic – were unable to access PPE from the stockpile. Many hospital workers were having to buy their own inferior masks. The Australian Medical Association and Catholic Health Australia joined the clarion call on PPE. At least one cancer clinic had to resort to making their own hand sanitiser. Surgeries were cancelled out of concern about risks to medical workers. Quizzed by the Senate the Chief Medical Officer revealed:

"Masks aren't made on site in Australia to any great extent … One of the challenges has been that one of the biggest production sites for PPE in the world is the city of Wuhan – and that was locked down." We publish how much fuel Australia has at any one time, how many battleships we have. But the Government refused to detail the size of the stockpile.

To do so would have been to admit there was insufficient local industry, and that the magical global supply chains had let us down. The answer, it seems, when reality does not match myth, is to look away. At the same time, some Chinese-backed companies in Australia were rounding up locally sourced PPE and exporting it back to China. One report estimated in just two months, China amassed 2.4 billion pieces of protective equipment, including more than two billion masks. This prompted the Morrison government to eventually ban the non-commercial export of PPE.

Let's make a deal

Australia's approach to trade and industry should not be dogmatic. It should be neither ideologically protectionist and nationalist nor ideologically neo-liberal and free market. Rather Australia's leaders should, on a case by case basis, determine which policies and which international agreements are in Australia's interests. In our history we have too often seen extremes of both protectionist and free market approaches that leave Australia with fewer options and fewer opportunities. Overly subsidising industry often simply delays an inevitable day of reckoning and can artificially obscure the very real need to adapt and innovate. But it is similarly hazardous to conceive of the global free market as a fair and omniscient force that ensures the biggest benefits flow back to the nations that make the greatest sacrifices. (The biggest benefits of course go to the nations who make the best deal for themselves.) This view has also, for years, absolved the nation's leaders of the requirement to lead, to be our nation's chief negotiators.

The recent history of the car industry in Australia tells the tale.

In November 1989 automobile manufacturing including parts employed 80,200 Australians. In August 2020 it was 33,700. From 1970 Australia undertook significant trade liberalisation, reducing tariffs and quotas as part of its commitment to the General Agreement on Tariffs and Trade. As a result of this loss of protection various Australian governments pursued often contradictory policies on the car manufacturing industry, none of which saved it from vanishing from our shores.

With domestic protections removed and incentives to export introduced, the Australian car industry repurposed itself sufficiently to increase its sales into the world market throughout the 1990s and early 2000s. A low Aussie dollar – below half a US dollar in 2001 – clearly helped. Having traded the domestic market for the world market, things changed at the end of the decade when the dollar regained its value. And in the meantime, Fords and Holdens were being undercut domestically by cheap imported Hyundai's and Kia's.

This is not entirely a partisan parable. (Whitlam lowered some tariffs. Fraser increased some.) But there was a speed and ideological ferocity with which later Liberal Governments vanquished what remained of the Australian car industry. In the early 2000s, despite being squeezed by foreign imports in the small car and prestige car categories, locally made Falcons and Commodores were still dominating the upper medium vehicle category. In 2005 John Howard presided over the reduction of the motor vehicle import tariff from 15 to 10 per cent and signed free trade agreements with the United States and Thailand that ensued a further later reduction to 5 per cent.

It is convenient, and absolves the culpability of some, to think of the death of our car industry as a steady inevitable decline since the 1970s due to changing consumer tastes. But it was much more recent, much more sudden and very much connected to decisions taken by national leaders. The total number of cars made in Australia declined by almost 50 per cent between 2004 and 2012. Slashed in half in eight years. The cause? Even the Productivity Commission which had urged the industry policy changes attributed as one of the key causes "a shift in vehicle manufacturing capacity toward regions with lower costs structure". With the FTAs signed, the multinationals moved their works to the cheapest forum, civilised labour laws and minimum wages be damned. The fairness umpire of the free market – the one which rewards the nations who rush down that route the quickest – must have been off sick that day. You hear much less about the 'regions with lower costs structure' than the 'dusty old industry couldn't keep up' narrative. The answer it seems, when the reality doesn't match the myth, is to look away. The Abbott Government intensified the dogma tub-thumping about "ending the age of entitlement to the auto industry." Treasurer Joe Hockey got up in Parliament and dared Holden to leave the country. Emboldened by the mining boom, struck with the latest dose of 'lucky thinking' the Liberals essentially said: 'Hello resources and services, *Sayonara* car making'. The death warrant was signed. There would be no preserving even the thriving parts of the industry, no transformation to electric vehicle manufacturing. Ford Australia closed its engine and vehicle plants in October 2016 and the Holden and Toyota Australia factories closed in late 2017.

Think global, make it local

The lesson of the pandemic is to fight for and retain a strong national economy of diverse industries. Not to drop everything for the next bright shiny bauble. That is the curse of lucky thinking. We need to lose the day trading approach and embrace long-term strategic planning. Struggling industries need smart solutions. They cannot and should not be promised eternal subsidies. But tactical support can preserve industries while they evolve to changing needs. There is pragmatic gradual removal of subsidies and protections and then there is ideological pull-the-rug-out vandalism. They are two very different things.

Around the world national governments are indulging in what

Liberals once regarded as the cardinal sins of 'picking winners' and financially supporting local industry. Canada, who incidentally have retained their car industry, has focussed on six areas for government support with targets for expansion: advanced manufacturing, agriculture/food, clean technology, digital industries, health/bio sciences, and resources. Only in the wake of the pandemic, after abolishing Labor's strategic manufacturing plan in 2014, did the Coalition slightly change tack and identify sectors for investment. Six years of wasted opportunity.

In the UK, Tory PM Boris Johnson co-opted social democrat language of 'A New Deal' for his policy of bringing forward five billion pounds worth of infrastructure projects. Germany, which counts three car manufacturers in its top four companies, has a 'National Industry Strategy 2030' which overtly recognises state intervention in the market is sometimes necessary "because a company has its sights set on its own advancement and not that of the entire country." Germany's response to COVID-19 was to buy stakes in companies threatened by the pandemic. The German government now has authority to block foreign purchases for "potential interference".

In Canada there are growing calls urging the Government to embrace a new industrial policy due to concerns over potential disruption in the global supply chain. One of Canada's largest news sites editorialised: "Canada can no longer rely on others for certain vital goods. (It needs to rebuild its) industrial base and be prepared to rely more on (its) own resources in the future."

Australian exceptionalism

Australia is a great society because of what have been described as our three inheritances – our original indigenous culture, the institutions of democracy imported from the United Kingdom, and our tremendous migrant success story. We are a great society because of the resulting character of our people. We are not an overtly patriotic people in the American model. But our egalitarianism, larrikin cynicism and lack of deference to authority informs our view we can do things as well as the inhabitants of any other nation. As we emerged from the infantilising shadow of Mother England on the world stage of the two major twentieth century conflicts, we found ourselves a distinct thing, as seen through the eyes of others. In World War Two with our Pacific comrades in arms such as New Zealand, Fiji, and Papua New Guinea, we found we could fight as smart and as hard as any other. In World War One an Australian general with verve and genius, cut through the nepotistic dross of English military leadership so potently he ended the bloodshed of that war at least a year earlier than otherwise would likely have happened.

Australia is an exceptional society. Even compared to similar western democracies, our common sense often results in a better community. We don't assassinate our leaders. When we had a terrible spree killing, we enacted firearm reform. We don't have school shootings. If we did, we would take whatever actions necessary to prevent more. During COVID-19 our citizens and our leaders have acted maturely, responsibly, with intelligence and altruism, and so we have not seen the death tolls experienced by other nations. And in a world looking for national solutions to global problems we have so often led the way, punched above our weight, and continue to do so.

And yet against this background of Australian progress – I do not hesitate to call it Australian exceptionalism – we have been constantly told by forelock-tugging conservative governments to know our place. We have been given the impression that we have no agency, we are a cork bobbing on the ocean, a plastic bag being blown around the barren carpark of the international free market. Australian Prime Ministers and Treasurers have absolved themselves of being patriots, lever-pullers, and deal-makers. They have become like neo-liberal voodoo priests scanning the weather for signs of how many virgins must be thrown in volcanos to appease the invisible hand.

It remains to be seen whether there is a return to this in the post-pandemic world. But the silver-lining of the pernicious virus that has disrupted and destroyed so much, has been the demand it has placed on national leaders to act like they are indeed leaders of a nation rather than, say, like CEOs of JPMorgan. We have seen conservative governments dip into their ideological grab-bag and find the usual tools of 'supply-side economics', 'blame the victim' and 'cost-cutting austerity' completely useless for the job at hand. With pegs on their noses they have had to become latter-day Keynesians and rely on social security safety nets established by Labor governments to avoid utter disaster. Parties of labour have had the last laugh (albeit a pyrrhic one given at the time of writing they were in Opposition in the UK and Australia.) This does not signal the final triumph of Labor philosophy, of social democracy, and what Francis Fukuyama might call the end of history (in our favour.) But we should not underestimate how big this ideological capitulation by the forces of neo-liberal conservatism has been.

It has allowed people to look behind the curtain and see the dangers of Australia acting like a craven global outpost, the dangerous holes in sovereign capability, the places where dogma is stretched paper-thin over yawning chasms. We have seen who fronted up for their neighbours and who fronted up for themselves. We have seen the federal government refuse to buy a stake in an airline to save it. And we have seen the public-turned-private national airline take the opportunity to offshore jobs and race toward the prospect of monopoly status. The pandemic allowed people to see communities come together to act in their own interests, and to act in a self-sacrificing way for the common good. Much of that will not be unseen.

* * *

Bill Shorten is the Shadow Minister for the National Disability Insurance Scheme and the Shadow Minister for Government Services. He was leader of the Australian Labor Party from 2013 to 2019. Bill joined the ALP at 17, then the Australian Workers' Union as an organiser in 1994. He has been secretary of the Victorian branch and AWU National Secretary. He is credited with reforming and reviving the AWU, and while there led the fight against WorkChoices.

During the Beaconsfield Mine collapse in Tasmania 2006 he acted as a union advocate for the workers at the mine and their families. As Parliamentary Secretary for Disabilities and Children's Services he was a key architect of the NDIS. He has also served as Assistant Treasurer and Minister for Financial Services and Superannuation, Education Minister, Minister for Employment and Workplace Relations and Minister for Financial Services and Superannuation. He was elected the Federal Member for Maribyrnong in 2007 and has held the seat ever since. He lives there with wife Chloe, their three children and two bulldogs.

7. The Future of Labor

Jim Chalmers

It is for Australians to decide what our future economy and society looks like, and for Australian Labor to determine what role we play in shaping it. We know where we have been, what we are going through, but we do not yet know with any surety what the future will bring our country. We do know why we need to be more ambitious than our political opponents – so that Australians have something meaningful to show for all the sacrifices they have made during the COVID-19 pandemic.

The alternative is to wake up in five- or ten-years' time, when the worst of the crisis has passed and the COVID wards are empty, and we tell our kids that we went through this remarkable event and we learned nothing from it. That we did nothing different afterwards than before. That our highest priority was to fast-forward back to the past – when we know people weren't faring that well in a broken economy defined by insecurity in the lead-up to this crisis, which left us vulnerable to it.

This is a defining moment for modern Australia. We have a tremendous opportunity as a country, and yet we might miss it. The Liberal Government shows all the signs of making the mistake analysed so compellingly by the author Jared Diamond, who examined the failure of nations over time and came up with a key conclusion: that the most damaging thing you can do is assume your nation has peaked at some point in the past and that's as good as it gets. That's what the Liberals and Nationals think. But it's not good enough for Australia, or for Australian Labor.

Learning the right lessons

For many Australians the year ahead might look like a recovery but still feel like a recession. The next election will be partly about that – about what's happening in the labour market and how the Government has dealt with it and is dealing with it. But primarily it will be about the future. By then, the Coalition will be asking for 12 years in office, pretending to be middle-road pragmatists when in reality they want to relive past ideological obsessions ill-suited to the challenges of the 2020s. It will be about whether the best Australia can hope for is a 'snapback' to the insecurity of the past, or an economy and a society stronger after the pandemic than it was before.

For Labor this is natural territory. We've always seen change as our guiding mission. Sometimes we drive that change. But – just as often – it's our responsibility to manage change thrust upon us, to make change serve the interests of our people. Not to slow the pace of change but to find a place for people in change.

In this coming contest, Labor's only path to victory is as the party of the future. We will not succeed as a throwback party, nor have we never succeeded as the party of the past. Each time we've won from opposition since the Second World War has been primarily because Gough Whitlam, Bob Hawke and Kevin Rudd and their Labor teams had a vision of the future vastly more compelling than their opponents.

Fresh thinking is required and it should be natural territory for the centre-left

Instead of this fresh thinking, many parties around the world have turned to ideas of the past. There's no shortage of politicians channelling discontent that liberalisation has failed to address inequality, has promoted financial bubbles over real economic growth, has introduced new volatility into our economy and has reduced the role of the state – and they're right to point all that out. But their diagnosis is weakened by proposals which draw from a grab-bag of defunct ideas.

This is a dead-end for Australian Labor. Not for us the 'Austalgia' for politics past, or for the policies of the 1980s or earlier. Our task is not just to celebrate a long list of Labor achievements but to lengthen it. Not to retrace the steps of our heroes but to walk forward and further in their direction. Not to pretend we can alter the pace of change but to find a place for people in the changes imposed on us. Not to resist that change but to ensure more people can harness and flourish and prosper from it.

At a time of substantial personal, family, national and economic anxiety, we need a national government prepared to move deliberately and purposefully and re-imagine a role for itself as a constructive, creative and strategic enabler of good jobs, shared growth and future opportunity. That can only be a Labor Government. But to rise to this occasion and reclaim focus, definition, purpose, and clarity – we need to apply the right lessons of recent history to the future.

The Global Financial Crisis exposed deep flaws in neoliberalism; COVID-19 is exposing the deep flaws in right-wing populism; both crises savagely exposed ineffective government. Yet the foundations of the political contest are still largely undisturbed because the wrong lessons have been learned and because our opponents are in a rush to retrofit old agendas onto the post-COVID world.

For some decades now our economic policy debates have been dominated by the drive to liberalise the economy. Some time ago these reforms did address some of the challenges of the 1970s and 1980s when economic performance was hampered by centralised state domination, over-regulation of certain markets, and rigidity. Today's problems are different. Three decades of liberalisation made our economy more flexible, but brought those new challenges of financial instability, job insecurity and income and wealth inequality. Unchecked liberalisation can't address this.

But the answer to neoliberalism is not permanent big-state socialism; just as the antidote to right-wing populism isn't left-wing populism, and the antidote to failures of leadership is not bloodless technocratic status quo centrism. This is not a contest between our ideology and our opponents', but between their ideology and the jobs and security that the Australian people need and deserve to get ahead

71

and not just get by. In many ways that means it's a contest between the past and the future.

Longstanding insecurity

This COVID-19 crisis is the defining moment for the 97 percent of the global population born after World War Two. More than a million lives have already been lost and tens of millions more have been infected. Australians, though spared the same magnitude of mass casualties, have felt the devastating economic consequences of our most damaging recession in almost a century. Our labour market is weak, unemployment and underemployment could be unacceptably high for an unacceptably long time, and the nation's future is deeply uncertain.

In Australia, some of the early second wave of the virus rallied in Melbourne's public housing towers. The catastrophe there was transmitted – in part – by precarious work, financial insecurity, lousy training, SMS alerts from labour hire companies, no sick leave in normal times, and no pandemic leave. By dint of too many forced to choose between doing the right thing by family, or by workmates. By the hollowing-out of public services crashing into the hollow heart of vulture capitalism.

That is why it's a mistake to separate the health aspects of this crisis from the economic or to pretend pre-COVID conditions had nothing to with the recession that followed. For all the talk of 'unprecedented' times, it's the economic problems that preceded this crisis which will weigh heaviest on our nation's capacity to emerge as a stronger and fairer country, and to embrace the future with confidence.

This crisis has revealed just how many Australians endure insecure work, their incomes are inadequate and too many of their basic workplace conditions have been stripped away. Yet these are the same people we counted on to carry our economy while we stayed home: truck drivers who kept the wheels turning; people stacking shelves in our supermarkets; hospital cleaners; farmers; and small business owners.

The pandemic has entrenched the disadvantages of age, geography and education and exposed problems with an industrial framework which promotes casualisation, job insecurity, stagnant wages, financial pressure and extreme household debt, and contributes to structural weaknesses in growth, investment, dynamism and productivity. While the most vulnerable have been the hardest hit, the middle has not been spared. The magnitude of the pain has intensified but so has the multitudes at risk. These problems existed before COVID, have been accelerated and exacerbated by the crisis, and their solutions, Labor solutions, need to endure long after it is over.

We risk countenancing a dangerous alternative: every government action framed as a short-term response to an impossible-to-predict emergency, every idea caveated as a desperate measure for a desperate time, all the while squandering the chance to dig deep and find big answers to big questions, with lasting benefits spread across society. The real risk of this intellectually, politically lazy approach is that its only legacy could be saddling generations of Australians with a lifetime of new debt paying for a return to the inertia, inequality, immobility, and insecurity of the past.

Snapback to the past

2020 has reminded us of the good that government can do. Wage subsidies kept many in work. Increases in transfer payments saw hundreds of thousands of Australians lifted temporarily out of poverty. Childcare and early education was treated as a social and economic good, not an expensive privilege. Frontline workers were respected, valued – literally applauded – for their contribution to our communities.

Yet the Liberals will disown and dismantle this as quickly as they can. They want Australians to believe that helping people in a crisis was just a phase, an aberration, and not deeply ingrained in our national psyche. They rely on a false yet powerful nostalgia to obscure a return to a dangerous right-wing agenda.

Whereas this pandemic is a timely reminder that our primary purpose is to look out for each other, and not just during crises, the Liberals seek a convenient excuse to make work more precarious, attack superannuation and retirement incomes, diminish higher education, and weaken consumer protections – all making Australians even less secure and less prosperous than they were before.

Instead of learning the lessons of this crisis, the conservatives are actively promoting the failed policies that left us vulnerable to its worst effects: flexibility as code for workplace insecurity, active suppression of wages, disinterring the old false choice of a secure retirement or fair pay in the here and now. Prime Minister Morrison even coined a term – 'snapback' – to describe this return to the pre-COVID economy.

A snapback to neoliberalism, protectionism, tribalism or nativism is a recipe for a deeper downturn, longer unemployment queues and more pronounced and enduring social and economic dislocation – cruelling the recovery before it gathers pace.

To respond adequately to the perils of a post-COVID world we need parties and leaders capable of empathy, compassion and understanding; a sense of aspiration which comes from experience and comes from the heart – not from focus groups; a perspective on the national economy from outside the Sydney-Melbourne-Canberra triangle; and, perhaps most importantly, with a grasp of the future. Parties and leaders whose primary purpose is to extend the opportunities of a growing, inclusive, sustainable economy to more of our people now and in the years ahead.

The fear that keeps us awake at night is that today's spike in unemployment could concentrate in communities and cascade through generations, that a new lost generation is sacrificed to the deepest recession in our lifetimes, accelerating social dislocation and economic immobility, cruelling opportunities for our kids, and theirs.

Choices made by centre-left parties and leaders will matter so much in the months and years ahead. This is our moment, and our mission: to respond to the recession, kickstart the recovery and reimagine our economies in ways that maintain a focus on jobs, security and the future and prevent the worst consequences of unemployment, social dislocation and intergenerational disadvantage.

Future generations will wonder what it was like, will look back at these days and guess at how we felt and try to imagine what we feared – in much the same way we look out the doors of Parliament House down Anzac Avenue to the War Memorial in Canberra and try to picture the nation that saw bombs fall on Darwin and sent its young people across the world to die for the cause of freedom.

Australia emerged from that global conflict with new ambitions, with a new vision for what our people and our government could do – in science and infrastructure and energy and health care and education. We discovered a new confidence to innovate in policy, chase full employment, reduce underemployment and speak for ourselves in the councils of the world. Now our nation and our generation can emerge from this global pandemic with a vision for better than we had before.

The long lens

As we Australians respond to the immediate crisis, we need to make sure our approach to jobs is forward-looking and relevant to the megatrends bearing down on us. Our decisions today need to take account of big forces set to play out over years and decades; from rapid changes to technology and digital innovation, the longer lives of our population, the shifting economics of Asia's rise, and the strong possibility that the effects of this crisis may be felt for a prolonged period of time.

The American economist Nouriel Roubini, for example, anticipates a 'decade of despair'. His prediction of a 'Greater Depression of the 2020s' is based on ten "ominous and risky trends" including unsustainable company and household debt, leading to mass defaults and bankruptcies; ageing societies requiring a greater proportion of public spending on health and social security; a collapse in commodity prices; currency debasement; digital disruption and automation; fragmentation, protectionism and de-globalisation; a populist backlash against democracy and its institutions; the geostrategic standoff between China and the United States; a new cold war and the associated risks of cyber conflict; and environmental degradation including climate change and worsening health outcomes and outbreaks.

We can't pretend-away these future challenges, nor can we assume that all the damage done by conservative governments or by the pandemic itself can be immediately fixed. People will understand and accept big things done slowly, but not big things down quickly (or small things done slowly). There's an important role for priority-setting, and for honesty that not every problem can be eliminated overnight.

Today's jobs crisis has been caused by intentional policies in response to an unexpected health crisis. But tomorrow's jobs crisis is likely to be caused by an absence of policy in response to foreseeable crises like labour market scarring, long term unemployment and underemployment, and cascading and concentrating disadvantage.

Technology

Where this type of policy thinking matters greatly is the impact of emerging technology on work and in society. There is a tremendous upside to technological change. It has the potential to improve lives and wellbeing and help overcome challenges to a good life in a thriving society. But people's real fears about where – and whether – they fit in workplaces increasingly dominated by machines should not be lightly dismissed, especially in today's very weak labour market.

We need to find new ways to turn aspiration into opportunity for more Australian workers and their loved ones. 'Back to the future' politics won't cut it as an answer to the challenges of the new economy. We need to seize the opportunities of new technologies and ensuring broad participation in their benefits. We need to recognise the possibilities for information technology, big data and the internet of things to lift the quality and efficiency of public services, transform transport, education and health, and take a new approach to markets.

We should be putting power back in the hands of citizens by ensuring they have rights over their data and get more value from it, and control over their digital presence. We should be thinking differently about the role of government. In education, using technology to identify learning gaps before kids fall behind; in health using new data to identify warning signs before people get sick. We should intervene earlier and more effectively to ward off disadvantage, using technology to update the social democratic state's egalitarian purpose and method.

Putting these pieces together, we have part of a new way of governing: use technology to improve the quality and efficiency of public services; use public services to prevent not just treat social problems; and extend opportunity in the new economy.

A future Labor government could apply developments in technology to economic policy in at least five new ways. First, by facilitating investment in new technologies that create, store, and distribute cheaper and cleaner energy and promote energy efficiency in ways that lowers business costs, incentivises investment and creates jobs. Second, by co-investing in new technologies that generate sources of new growth and jobs and to maximise the opportunities in areas of traditional economic strength. Third, by teaching and training for technological change so that digitisation can be embraced and not just feared. Fourth, by leveraging research and development to better turn Australian ideas into Australian jobs. And fifth, by using data to enhance place-based approaches and interventions, empower local leadership, and develop more effective and more targeted jobs programs for the most disadvantaged areas, and by better tracking progress by measuring what really matters in our society and economy.

This is how we could create more jobs in the recovery, avoid a lost generation sacrificed to this recession, and turn aspiration into reality for more of our people. It's how we can invest in mobility in all its forms: social; economic; intergenerational – how we create a forward-looking society, an outward-facing country, powered by an upward-climbing economy – in a nation which leaves nobody behind and holds nobody back. Where we celebrate people doing well and getting ahead because we want more people doing well and getting ahead. That's the whole point of the Labor Party and it's the test of where we endure as a party of government or opposition.

In *Upheaval: How Nations Cope with Crisis and Change*, Jared Diamond wrote that "the challenge, for nations as for individuals in crisis, is to figure out which parts of their identities are already functioning well and don't need changing, and which parts are no longer working and do need changing". To do that, "they need the courage to recognize what must be changed in order to deal with the new situation. That requires the individuals or nations to find new solutions compatible with their abilities and with the rest of their being". This is as true for Australia as it is for Australian Labor. The future of our Party and our country depends on it.

* * *

Jim Chalmers became federal Labor's Treasury spokesman in 2019 after three years in the Finance portfolio. Prior to his election to the House of Representatives in 2013 he was Executive Director of the Chifley Research Centre and, before that, Chief of Staff to the Deputy Prime Minister and Treasurer. Jim has a PhD in political science and international relations and a first-class honours degree in public policy. His first book, Glory Daze, *was about Australia in the Global Financial Crisis and published in 2013. His second,* Changing Jobs: the Fair Go in the New Machine Age, *was co-authored with Mike Quigley and released in 2017. He represents the same suburbs of southern Brisbane and Logan in Queensland where he was born, grew up and where he and Laura are now raising Leo, Annabel and Jack.*

8. Australia's Social Democratic Moment?

Chris Bowen

In politics as in life, there is the conventional wisdom and there is the truth. Sometimes they are the same thing, but often they are not. More than ten years ago, the conventional wisdom was that the Global Financial Crisis would lead to 'the social democratic moment', as voters around the world saw the failings of laissez faire capitalism and the benefits of sensible progressive intervention.

History tells us this didn't happen. What was meant to be the social democratic moment became the right-wing populist moment. In the decade since, around the world, the election of social democratic governments has been very much the exception. Right-wing populists have been more effective in giving voice to the visceral frustration of working people at the damage done by the global recession, growing inequality and job insecurity. In fact, parties of the broader Left have been torn apart by the political and societal developments of the last decade. As disappointed as we all are by the result of the last federal election, we in Australian Labor can take some comfort from the fact that we have avoided the fate so common that it has a name: 'Pasokification', which refers to the decline in the vote of Greece's main centre-left Party Pasok from 44 per cent of the vote in 2009 to a mere 5 per cent in 2015, a decline which has been replicated in several countries.

Now, the conventional wisdom is that the aftermath of COVID-19 will provide a new opportunity for centre-left parties. That the massive government actions and interventions necessary to flatten the COVID curve, and the death and tragedy unfolding in countries where governments have stood idly by and declined to use the levers at their disposal, will remind people of the power of government.

That the increased importance of health in the public discourse will benefit social democratic parties that are more trusted on health. That the reminder of the importance of workers in the care economy will help social democratic parties prosecute our agenda for better pay for essential workers and investment in key sectors like aged care. That the newly refreshed emphasis on the importance of community and the collective will help progressive parties. That the mantra of debt and deficits is harder for conservatives to run as they rack up trillions of dollars of unprecedented debt.

This conventional wisdom might turn out to be true. But only if we make it so.

Great care and precision will be necessary to ensure we capture the mood of the community in these troubled times. Simply assuming the times will suit us or a mood for change will sweep us in with the tides is a sure-fire recipe for disappointment. We must make the case as to why Labor – and only Labor – must be trusted with the job of rebuilding Australia. Of course, it is the case that COVID has changed everything; but not absolutely everything. The ideological contours of policy and political battles are changing – but those contests must still be won in the public realm. It is down to us to shape the new terrain to maximise our chances of success, and success for the millions of Australians who rely on Labor governments. The battle lines of previous elections, including recent ones, are less relevant to future contests because COVID has been such a disruptive political influence – which means that in 2021 or 2022, federal Labor must fight the next election, and not the last one.

Lessons for Labor from COVID-19

As Labor considers our place in this new battlefield, we can take some of key lessons from COVID-19 to help inform our framework. Firstly, don't boil the ocean. It is undoubtedly true that the power of government has been shown during the crisis. A few examples are useful. Australia went into this crisis with 2000 intensive care beds, numbers amounting to fewer per head of population than Italy.

Concerted efforts by governments state and federal saw that number climb to more than 7000 in quick time, meaning we had a much greater capacity to cope should a wave of COVID hit us.

Another example is homelessness. Governments were concerned that homeless people would become a vector for the disease. Massive efforts were put into housing homeless people, such that around 5,000 of the 8,000 rough sleepers in Australia were accommodated in hotels in the early months of the crisis. Likewise, in the United Kingdom, the Government's five-year target of reducing homelessness by 90 per cent was met in just 48 hours.

These and other examples are an important reminder of the power of government to act and act decisively. There *is* an opportunity for parties like ours to argue that big problems shouldn't be confined to the too hard basket. Imagine if the same force of will was applied to Indigenous disadvantage, domestic violence or any of the myriad of social ills for which precious little progress has been made for decades. Imagine if governments applied the same 'fierce urgency of now' approach to difficult issues that had previously been relegated to the realm of the intractable.

But here is the rub: part of the reason for the success in doing these things is that governments have been focussed on very few priorities. A laser-like focus on COVID-19 has meant policy success. If bending the curve had been one of a long list of government objectives, it would be sitting unloved and unimplemented on a shelf full of white papers and reports. This is worth reflecting on for a party as ambitious and impatient as Labor can be.

The lesson out of COVID-19 is not just the power of government action: it is the necessity of focus and prioritisation. This is a particular challenge for social democratic governments, whose inclination is intervening whenever they see a problem or a social-ill. But if we try to boil the ocean, we will fail – if not at election time, then perhaps in government in the way Whitlam's government's ambition gave way to a frustrated chaos born of a generation on the opposition benches. If we compartmentalise our agenda into more realistic tranches, then success is more likely. There is a role for the moderate wing of the party here. Not to call for less ambition. On the contrary: to demand more focus, to increase the prospect of that ambition with proof points of success.

Voters attracted to populist right-wing parties aren't voting for less change: they want more. But by the same token, they can understandably find a dizzying array of complicated policies concerning. But an ambitious agenda focussed on a small handful of agreed priorities is likely to be less disconcerting and has the advantage of being easier to explain as well as digest. Such an approach also reduces the capacity for scare campaigns to sow doubt or distrust with our agenda and allows us to more readily address these head on in discrete battles rather than defending a broad front.

A second lesson from the COVID-19 crisis is the importance of essential workers. Conventional wisdom is that the rise in status of this workforce in the general community is to the disadvantage of conservative parties, who don't support pay rises for blue collar workers and routinely seek to undermine industrial protections. Properly understood, there are matters for the Labor Party to reflect on here. There has been much debate since the last election about how Labor needs to re-connect with workers in traditional industries; the blue collar-high vis sector. This however is of course not an homogenous group. Miners in high vis are important, but so are nurses, teachers, and factory workers. We need to think about how we prioritise our policy offerings and our how we frame our rhetoric with regard to all who would regard themselves as working voters looking to the party of workers for leadership.

We also need to think about how our offerings and language are perceived among the group of Australians who used to be regarded as 'rusted-on' Labor voters.

We can't assume that financial offerings to low-income workers is going to cut the mustard. When I was growing up in a fibro house in suburban Smithfield, a salesman turning up at the door offering something for nothing would have been given short shrift by my parents, despite the fact we did it fairly tough at times. People who work hard for a living know that something for nothing is likely to be too good to be true. Voting decisions are much more complicated than that, anyway.

Some people lament that working class voters might vote on so-called 'cultural issues' against their own financial best interests, while celebrating higher income voters who vote against their own financial best interest because they support the 'greater good'. Our Party *does* have to reflect on how our rhetoric, positioning and prioritisation on matters as diverse as faith and freedom of religion, education and recreation have been received by voters who were once regarded as a reliable support base.

This brief chapter is not able to conclude such a conversation. But hopefully it provides some opportunity to progress it. Some thoughts on those questions. For decades, a key element in Labor's offering has been improved university funding and an emphasis on the importance of equity in university admissions to improve social mobility. Now of course, this *is* important. From the Dawkins reforms of the 1980s converting Colleges of Advanced Education to universities to improve access, to the Bradley reforms under Education Minister and Prime Minister Gillard, important progress has been made. But Labor must guard against the perception that our main pre-occupation for the working class is simply to improve the means to get out of it.

The term 'Meritocracy' was coined by philosopher and British Labour Party activist Michael Young. He did not regard it as something to aspire to. Of course, positions should be filled on merit and people and university entrance should be as equitable as possible. But Young projected a world in 2033 in which those who 'made it' were privileged over those who didn't in such a way that the left-behinds rose up in a populist revolt. Perhaps he got the year wrong by a decade or so.

A majority of the Labor Caucus (including myself) and many Labor activists were the first in our families to attend university. We've lived the journey of improved social mobility. And while Labor has also promoted good policies to improve investment in TAFE, this has often over the years been relegated in terms of our rhetoric , especially at the federal level, where it has generally been secondary to our commitment to improved university funding. Again, I emphasise that this commitment to universities and education more broadly is an important part of Labor's ethos. But we also need to find ways of emphasising we are not merely interested in providing pathways to improved social mobility, but also improving the lot of those who can't or don't want to take that path. Life must not be so miserable at the bottom or the middle as to demand a mad scramble out of it.

In 2013, I suggested in my book *Hearts and Minds* that the key for Labor was to embrace "growth and opportunity". I still believe that today. Growth to lift people out of poverty and turn aspiration into reality. Opportunity for people to grow to their full potential. I still believe that today. But we must guard against opportunity being seen narrowly as only through university or earned for those at the very top. Opportunity involves the capacity to have a fulfilling, secure job with agency in one's life – not subject to the vagaries and callousness of the gig economy. It involves the opportunity to get a trade. It involves opportunity to live free of chronic disease which ravages lower socio-economic communities. Put simply, it's about a good and meaningful life.

And nor is it just about Labor. While our opponents are quick to argue Labor's parliamentary gene pool is narrow, this misses the point. As Mark Bovens and Anchrit Wille argue in their book *Diploma Democracy*: "Most contemporary democracies in Western Europe are governed by a select group of well-educated citizens. They are diploma democracies ruled by those with the highest formal qualifications." Bovens and Anchrit go onto point out that 90 per cent of the members of the House of Commons are graduates, as are 86 per cent of the members of the Bundestag, 97 per cent of the members of Dutch Tweede Kamer and 99 per cent of the members of the US Senate.

Generally speaking, Labor has been more successful at the state level than the federal level in recent decades. Take Queensland as the starkest example. Labor has governed Queensland for all but six years in the thirty-one years since 1989. Over that time, only once has Queensland returned a Labor majority in its delegation to the House of Representatives. There are many and varied reasons for this discrepancy. However, the ability of Labor at the state level to emphasise their support for working families through investments in essential services which benefit all is one of them.

Labor is partly a victim of its own success here. People sometimes pose the question: could Ben Chifley win Labor preselection today? I respectfully point out the better question is: would Ben Chifley vote Labor today? Today's Ben Chifley, because of Labor reforms, would have gone to university, probably been a lawyer and moved to Sydney. His income would encourage him to vote Liberal. The confluence of his comfortable existence and social conscience might encourage him to vote Green. 'Chif' is of course to be revered and his spirit to be honoured, but my point is that his demographic profile as the son of the working class has gone through great change. Just as the Chifs of the 2020s are probably university educated, support from those who've remained in manual trades has been fought over by the LNP and One Nation, meaning our electoral path to a majority is increasingly fraught.

I'm confident universities will always be better off under a Labor Government than a Tory one. But we need to find better ways to tell the story of our commitment to working people – and it can't just be that we will make it easier for the children of the working class to get out of it.

The compact

The final lesson out of COVID-19 is a reminder that the challenges of our times can't be ducked. A combination of climate change and rampant land clearing around the world will make pandemics more likely as habitat changes see animals and humans interact more regularly. Even discounting that possibility, climate change and land clearing is regarded by the WHO as the biggest public health threat of the twenty-first century, leading to an additional 250,000 deaths each year through increased malaria and heat stress. This figure doesn't even include more bushfires and natural disasters. An increased focus on public health and respect for science quickly leads to the call for action on climate change.

It's not Labor's way to duck challenges like this. But nor is our way to ignore the concerns of workers concerned that their jobs and communities are already insecure enough without the added insecurity caused by action on climate change.

We can draw on the past. Hawke and Keating didn't duck the challenges of their time: declining national income demanding the shaking off of the chains of a sclerotic economic framework. But concerns about insecurity in the face of climate change action mirror the concerns many had about floating the dollar, tearing down tariffs, competition policy and financial deregulation (some of which occurred during a recession).

And yet Labor won election after election. The key was that Hawke and Keating made sure concerned voters knew there was a compact in place, with concerned Australians at the centre of that compact. Yes, economic reform was necessary. But Australians were re-assured they would receive the dividends of that reform, by way of Medicare, universal superannuation, improved school retention rates and other improvements in community standards.

Conclusion

The aftermath of COVID might yet prove to be the 'social democratic moment', in which our Party is able to recast the debate, to remind people of the importance of the Labor mission of improving the living standards and lives of all Australians. It comes down to offering inspiration and aspiration – with a workable plan that people trust. Inspiration for a better, fairer country with the aspirations of the millions of Australians who want for more security and more reward for their families as a result of their labours at the very centre. It means rooting our offering and messages firmly in the improvements of the living standards of those who have always looked to us to do so but have been looking elsewhere in recent years. It will mean hard work – but Labor has never ducked a challenge yet and we must not now.

* * *

Chris Bowen entered Parliament in 2004 and has held a wide range of portfolios including serving as Treasurer, Minister for Human Services, Minister for Immigration, Minister for Financial Services, Assistant Treasurer, Minister for Competition Policy, Minister for Small Business and Minister for Tertiary Education. Chris has been responsible for a range of significant policy reform programs in these portfolios. He served as Interim Leader of the Labor Party and Acting Leader of the Opposition following the 2013 federal election and served as Shadow Treasurer. He is now the Shadow Minister for Health. Chris served on Fairfield Council for nine years, was a former Mayor of Fairfield Council, and former President of the Western Sydney Regional Organisation of Councils (WSROC). He has a Bachelor of Economics, a Masters Degree in International Relations and a Diploma in Modern Languages (Bahasa Indonesia).He lives in Smithfield with his wife Rebecca, children Grace and Max and his Labradors Ollie and Toby.

9. Australia Safe

Kristina Keneally

Labor Prime Minister Bob Hawke and Treasurer Paul Keating are rightly lauded for their sweeping reforms that modernised Australia's economy. But Hawke should get just as much credit for reforming our national security agencies and creating the modern national security architecture on which Australia relies to this day.

The two most important political claims for the 'right to govern' in Australia are sound economic management and keeping Australians safe. For all the bluster from the Liberals about their supposed superiority in these areas, it is undeniable that the Australian Labor Party under the leadership of Hawke and Keating created the modern framework of economic growth and national security that underpin Australia's success as a democratic, multicultural and prosperous nation.

Hawke and the hawks

Within months of Bob Hawke's election in 1983 he faced a crisis of confidence not only in his government, but also in the Australian Security Intelligence Organisation (ASIO). The context for the crisis was decades in the making. Australia's intelligence agency was created by the Chifley Labor Government in 1949, but by the time the Hawke Government came to power in 1983 ASIO had developed a reputation for partisan interventions in Australia's democratic processes, strategic leaking, suspected collusion with other nations, and intelligence failures. Many groups and individuals in civil society were the targets of ASIO's partisan actions throughout the term of the Menzies' Government, and many were openly critical of the agency. In 1972 Labor's national conference came close to passing a motion supporting the abolition of ASIO.

In 1974 Gough Whitlam called a Royal Commission into Australia's intelligence agencies, appointing NSW Supreme Court Justice Robert Marsden Hope as commissioner. Hope produced eight volumes recommending the rules, processes and oversight that should apply to Australia's intelligence agencies. But the main focus of Hope's findings was his scorching assessment of ASIO and his recommendations for significant changes to its operations. However, change did not come quickly for ASIO. Despite some attempts at internal reform, ASIO continued to leak and act in particularly partisan ways throughout the period of the Fraser Coalition Government.

As a newly elected prime minister, Hawke faced two competing challenges: to show the Australian people that he could be trusted with national security and could work well in a strategic partnership with the United States, and to respond meaningfully to public criticisms of ASIO and calls for the agency to be abolished. Hawke knew that Australia needed an agency like ASIO, but that ASIO needed to gain the public's trust in its operations. Hawke asked Justice Hope to undertake a second Royal Commission into the operations, conduct, performance, control, and accountability of the intelligence agencies, including ASIO. But before the inquiry could be announced, another scandal broke: ASIO identified a Soviet diplomat, Valeriy Ivanov, as a KGB operative and established he had been cultivating David Combe, a former ALP national secretary. The Ivanov-Combe affair became the top priority for Hawke's new Hope Royal Commission.

The Ivanov-Combe hearings were a media sensation. Justice Hope adopted an open courtroom style examination of the Ivanov-Combe affair and the Australian media covered the hearings as if they were a criminal trial. (Professor Peter Edwards, writing in ASPI's The Strategist in 2019, provides a terrific account of these hearings.) The Ivanov-Combe hearings effectively turned into a trial of Hawke's ability to manage national security. Hawke took the audacious decision to appear as the government's first witness across three days of evidence. For a sitting Prime Minister, it was high risk, high stakes, and – ultimately – highly successful.

Hawke triumphed in the witness box, thereby strengthening his position to manage Australia's intelligence and national security operations. When Justice Hope handed down a report justifying the need for an intelligence service like ASIO but recommending significant reforms to its oversight and operations, Hawke was able to ensure that Hope's recommendations were implemented with the broad support of the ALP and the wider public. As with much of his prime ministership, Hawke took Australians with him and, in turn, they trusted him.

These recommendations still shape Australia's intelligence framework today: an independent Office of the Inspector General of Intelligence and Security (IGIS), an ASIO Act, rigorous internal rules for ASIO to protect individuals' privacy, protocols for communicating security intelligence to partners and government, and clarification of ASIO's role in supporting other functions of government, such as immigration and transport security.

Another significant and enduring change Hawke introduced was a joint parliamentary committee to oversight ASIO. This committee was the first iteration of the contemporary Parliamentary Joint Committee on Intelligence and Security (PJCIS). Hope recommended against such parliamentary oversight, preferring the IGIS model alone, but the Hawke Government argued:

> Further improvement (to oversight and accountability) can be obtained by directly involving the Parliament – on both sides and in both Houses – in imposing the discipline of an external scrutiny of the intelligence and security agencies quite independent of the Executive. While the Government has been conscious also for the need to carefully protect intelligence and security information, it believes that appropriate arrangements can be made to ensure that a small but informed parliamentary committee would operate effectively in the public interest.

Stronger together

By establishing a parliamentary joint committee, Hawke created the basis for the bi-partisan compact that exists in Australia today in relation to national security. Bipartisanship does not mean immediate agreement. Rather, Australia's unique bipartisan compact on national security means a sober analysis of the policy and security questions before the parliament and eschewing partisan electoral calculations in favour of the national interest.

Federal governments of all persuasions have upheld the convention of this bipartisan compact and looked to the PJCIS for resolution of sensitive or complex national security matters. Today the PJCIS provides scrutiny to a wide range of national security agencies, considers the listing of terrorist organisations, and holds inquiries into national security legislation. The PJCIS provides a framework for a 'small but informed parliamentary committee' to recommend, in a bi-partisan way, how national security agencies and national security legislation can and should best operate in the national interest.

In recent times the Morrison Government has further expanded the PJCIS' scope by referring non-legislative inquiries to the Committee for consideration and report. The media freedom inquiry is one such example, arising from raids conducted by the Australian Federal Police on the home of a NewsCorp journalist and on the ABC in response to stories about national security matters. The PJCIS made bi-partisan recommendations significantly improving the process and contestability of warrants issued for journalists and media organisations.

Anyone who doubts the ability of Australia's major political parties to work together for the benefit of all Australians should look no further than the work of the PJCIS. Yet, this bipartisan compact on national security is a Labor legacy from the Hawke Government, but Labor must always acknowledge the compact only endures with the support and cooperation of our Liberal counterparts. The compact benefits Australia, and Australians, in important ways.

One, the compact ensures that the overriding national security objective for the two parties of government is the national interest and not partisan politics. Two, the compact provides space for genuine conversation and non-partisan contestability between parliamentarians to consider how the national interest is best served. Three, it delivers resolutions that are usually heeded by the government of the day.

One example occurred earlier this year. The PJCIS unanimously resolved that a Government bill to create and maintain facilities for the sharing of facial recognition data lacked appropriate safeguards and should be withdrawn and re-drafted. In other words, the PJCIS sent the bill back to the drawing board. As a result, the bill did not proceed.

The Australian bipartisan compact on national security has been stretched and strained, though it has yet to reach a complete breaking point. The Morrison Government's decision to ignore the PJCIS' bi-partisan recommendations on the 'encryption laws' and ram the legislation through parliament at the end of 2018 was certainly a political fracture within the compact. The government further cracked the compact by refusing to facilitate passage of the PJCIS' amendments in early 2019.

This compact on national security is one of the most important, successful, and unique features of Australia's national security approach. Labor should always value it, but not stay silent if or when our counterparts put the compact at risk. In the case of the encryption laws, Labor regularly voices its strong criticisms of the Liberals' rejection of the PJCIS' bipartisan amendments and moved our own legislation in the Senate to make clear our support for the committee's recommendations.

The encryption laws aren't the only example of a creeping partisanship in relation to national security under the last seven years of this Liberal Government. Tip-offs to media of AFP raids and leaks of intelligence assessments, such as during the parliamentary debate on the Medevac laws, are a worrying echo of the politicisation of national security agencies during the Menzies era. Such incidents show that Labor cannot take for granted that our Liberal counterparts will always value the compact as they should to benefit the national interest. Likewise, the compact does not mean that Labor should remain silent in the face of emerging and legitimate national security concerns. Labor always puts the safety of Australians first, and we must be alert to the rapidly changing national security landscape.

New threats

For the past twenty years national security threats have been largely understood in the context of traditional military conflicts and in relation to Islamic extremism and jihadist terrorism – with good reason. Today, those risks are still present, but we also face an evolving, complex national security environment that will require new approaches, new technological solutions, new community engagement, and quite likely new laws. As a party of government, Labor is now, and must continue to be, robustly engaged in keeping Australians safe in facing these new threats. We need to shed light on these threats, discuss how to combat them, and just like Hawke did in the early years of his prime ministership, take Australians with us as we work with together to keep our nation safe.

Global pandemics, widening economic inequality, increasing nationalism, and climate change pose new kinds of security risks for Australia. The economic and social upheaval created by a global pandemic has the potential to create chaos and requires us to re-think the role of the State in ensuring national stability and safety. The large-scale movement of populations, such as one million Rohingya out of Myanmar into Bangladesh, or the potential for wholescale evacuations of Pacific Island nations in the face of rising seas, is also a challenge to the economic and security stability of our region.

Australia also faces a rapidly accelerating threat from violent right-wing extremism. We are not alone – most Western nations are witnessing a surge in far-right extremist propaganda, growing numbers of citizens joining right-wing extremist groups, and violent attacks attempted or carried out by right-wing extremists. Australia's success as a multicultural nation cannot be taken for granted: ASIO says that some 40 per cent of its counter-terrorism operations now focus on right-wing extremists. Australia has not yet had a proper conversation about the extent to which the violent right-wing extremist and Christchurch terrorist Brenton Tarrant was radicalised in this country. Australia remains the only Five Eyes nation that has not listed any domestic or international right-wing extremist groups as terrorist organisations – lagging behind our allies in the USA, the UK, Canada and New Zealand.

Foreign interference in Australia's democratic processes and institutions, as well as in the private and public sector, is at a scale and scope never before seen in our history, including at the height of the Cold War. Our national security agencies require investigatory tools to detect interference and the technological, personnel, and legal capacity to disrupt it. We also must engage the Australian public to assist them to understand what foreign interference is and what it is not, how it can affect our economy and our community, and what steps each one of us can take to make Australia resistant and resilient to such interference. The experience of elections overseas suggests that one of our most urgent tasks now is to safeguard Australian democracy from misinformation campaigns, disinformation on social media (e.g., deep-fake videos), and protect our democratic institutions – including political parties as well as agencies like the Australian Electoral Commission – from foreign interference in our electoral processes. Australia's independent electoral system has strengthened our democracy and national security, but it must never be taken for granted or neglected.

Enhancing Australia's cybersecurity capacity relates to the threat of foreign interference, but also responds to broader demands. Labor must continue to push for a fit-for-purpose cybersecurity strategy that meets two of our most pressing challenges: developing a domestic workforce with the skills to build our own cybersecurity defences, and taking a 'public-health' approach to cybersecurity across the community to create an online environment that resists and repels many forms of cyber-attacks, including on our critical infrastructure.

In addressing these new national security challenges, Labor must uphold its commitments to our democratic principles: the rule of law, freedoms of association, speech, religion, and media, the right to privacy, and transparency and accountability in government. Just like Labor's legacies of building Medicare, superannuation, and the National Disability Insurance Scheme, we must stake our claim – and ability to govern – on the bedrock of Hawke's modern national security framework.

Labor must uphold the Hawke legacy by holding firm to our principles of proportionality, oversight, and protection of our democratic values. In practical terms this means ensuring there are checks and balances in relation to our national security laws, supporting continued parliamentary oversight as well as independent oversight of our national security agencies, and insisting on independent authorisation of extraordinary or intrusive powers.

Finally, wherever possible, Labor should seek to preserve the bi-partisan compact on national security gifted to us by Hawke, as it has served the best interest of Australia and Australians. It is an important Australian innovation and an effective and appropriate convention to assure the Australian people that our national security laws and our national security agencies are serving the national interest and keeping Australia safe.

* * *

Kristina Keneally is the Shadow Minister for Home Affairs, a Senator for New South Wales, and the Deputy Leader of the Labor Party in the Australian Senate. Born in the USA to an Australian mother and an American father, she grew up in Ohio. Kristina worked in a fibreglass factory to put herself through university and was a member of the Teamsters Union. Kristina moved to Australia in 1994 and joined the Australian Labor Party. A member of the NSW Parliament from 2003-2012, Kristina served as Premier of New South Wales from 2009-2011 and is the first woman to hold the office. After leaving state parliament Kristina hosted a daily program on Sky News Australia and contributed to the network's coverage of Australian and international politics. She was elected to the Senate in 2018. Kristina is married and the mother of three children.

10. Getting to Work

Clare O'Neil

In 1978, Mick Young – the shearer, trade unionist and Labor icon – wrote a book called *I Want to Work*. In it, he argues that government's principal economic role is to create full employment, so that Australian prosperity can be fairly shared through work. For a policy book, it's deeply humane: a compelling description of the cost of unemployment, but also of the heartbreaking destruction of the human spirit that goes with it.

I Want to Work was written in a difficult period for Labor. After 23 years in opposition, we had won government in 1972, only to suffer a gutting defeat after just three years. The party could have turned on itself, as it did during the split of the 1950s. Instead, between the devastating election loss of 1975 and Bob Hawke's euphoric victory in 1983, Mick Young and a group of leaders across the union movement and the party led Labor to do something hard: to evolve, to transform, to renew.

Renewal is difficult. But the philosophy and approach developed in this period led to Labor's longest-ever period in Federal Government. It led to the longest running period of growth experienced by any country in modern history. It made Australia one of the wealthiest countries in the world. And between Bob Hawke's election and the end of the Gillard Government thirty years later, the standard of living of Australians across the income spectrum more than doubled.

Every Labor member stands proud of these achievements. And every Labor member knows that we cannot achieve reforms like this from opposition. Our mission is long periods of Labor government, which govern in a Labor way, and leave Labor legacies. Labor legacies like millions of kids getting a better-quality education, and generations of Australians benefitting from free healthcare. When Kevin Rudd was Prime Minister, his government raised the pension rate and a million Australians were lifted out of poverty overnight. That's the power of government.

Jobs for all

Mick Young's prescription for Australia was for everyone to have a job. Today, we again face high unemployment. But work – even when we have enough of it – is no longer doing a good job of fairly sharing prosperity. Inequality has grown significantly since Bob Hawke was elected Prime Minister, but the problems have become particularly acute since 2009, when wages growth slowed right down. Over the last decade, our economy has grown, but the average Australian household has seen no discernible increase to their disposable income. And we wonder why so much of the electorate is disengaged, and increasingly sending their votes to the minor parties.

Part of the problem is that Australia's economy is over time delivering greater rewards to those at the top of the income spectrum than at the bottom. Since the 1970s, Australia has seen strong growth in high skill jobs, intermittently strong growth in low-skill jobs, but a declining share of jobs that are middle-skill, and middle-income. Australia is edging towards a two-class economy – where highly skilled workers do better than ever, and workers in lower skill jobs struggle to get by.

In the old days, you either had a job and you were doing OK, or you didn't, and you were suffering. Today, the situation is more complex. Underemployment and casualisation are rife. Job quality is a life-defining issue for many Australians, especially for women. Try paying the rent and feeding a family as a $21-an-hour casual in aged care, with no security and few entitlements.

Companies across the economy have found new ways to avoid paying hard-fought conditions to workers. More than a million Australians today work in the largely unregulated gig economy, and the federal parliament has done nothing about labour hire. In some industries, underpayment for workers is a part of the business model. On the promise of jobs that never eventuated, penalty rates were cut, leaving many thousands of Australians worse off for no reason. Working people – not just individually, but as a collective – are not getting a fair share of economic growth. There is a long run trend underway which is seeing owners of capital – machines, real estate, equipment, companies – get more benefits from the economy than people who own only their own labour.

Australia's first recession in thirty years is set to make each of these problems worse. With high unemployment and underemployment, wage earners will find it even harder to bargain for a pay increase. Workers' share of the benefits of the economy is the lowest it has been for 61-years. The Reserve Bank has foreshadowed that wages will increase 1 per cent in 2021, and that wages growth will be stuck at 2 per cent for years beyond the pandemic.

Conservatives may argue that some of the shifts I describe are the inevitable consequence of our transition from the goods-oriented, more closed-economy of Australia of the early 1980s, to the services, knowledge and machine-oriented economy of today. But I don't agree. These changes are the predictable consequences of economic change which was not sufficiently partnered with thoughtful, significant policies to help the benefits of those changes be fairly shared with Australians.

Labor governments have done their bit. Hawke and Keating created superannuation, Medicare, and created massive increases to the standard of education of young Australians. Rudd and Gillard boosted education, created the National Disability Insurance Scheme, and created Australia's paid parental leave scheme. But Labor has governed for just six of the last twenty-four years. In times of Coalition rule, very little has been done to improve the quality of life of Australians through better service-delivery – let alone help prepare Australians for economic change.

Working nation

So what is the answer? As Mick Young knew, it all comes back to work. Work is about so much more than financial security. It is fundamental to who we are – shaping our days, giving us purpose, connecting us to community and making us feel valued as human beings.

Some have argued that the answer to some of the problems I have described is a permanent universal basic income – that is, an amount of money paid to each Australian every year, no matter how wealthy they are. It would represent a profound shift away from one of the most successful and targeted welfare systems in the world. Estimates of the policy run into the hundreds of billions, significantly expanding the size of the whole federal budget. Who would pay? And it's a problem in search of a solution. The mass unemployment impact of technological change hasn't eventuated. The number of hours worked per employee has not changed greatly in the last generation – even as women have joined the workforce in massive numbers. We need work to be a means of fairly sharing national wealth again.

In today's economy, better rewards and choices are flowing to better educated and skilled workers. So, a clear route to getting Australians more choice and control is to boost skills and education. This is not a pitch for more Australians to go to university. I'm more concerned with the many Australian young people who are not sticking with school through to year 12, and the many who do not have access to quality skills training. This is not a small problem: still today, a quarter of Australian young men do not finish high school and millions in the workforce did not get the chance for the skills training they deserved.

The biggest single issue here is the state of the skills sector in Australia. The savage cuts to skills, education and training have probably done more to undermine the life chances of young Australians than any other single decision of this current government. The Abbott/Turnbull/Morrison governments have cut

$3.6 billion from trades training. There are 140,000 fewer apprentices in training today than when the Liberals took office. And we know the systemic problems: quality of skills training is patchy, access is terrible, young people don't have quality information about what their best pathway to solid employment.

I've said that the economy of the future will continue to provide outsized rewards to skilled workers. That's true, but we are not completely unable to shape how our economy grows. We want to live in a country where quality jobs exist for everyone. And that's why the discussion about reviving manufacturing is so incredibly important. To help our country on the path to strong growth in the 2020s, we need to get as many high skill jobs of the future in Australia. The next push of global productivity growth is going to come from innovation, technology, manufacturing and science. It doesn't mean that all future Australians will wear lab coats to work or sit all day in front of a computer screen. It means that innovating and inventing are going to be integral to how wealthy a country we are when my children are parents themselves. And in all these areas, government investment and good policy are critical.

Every Australian deserves quality work. And clearly, we are way off that right now. We want Australian jobs, at every skill level, to be jobs that workers can count on. A big part of this is getting the Parliament to step up on core industrial issues like labour hire, wage theft and the gig economy. We need stronger laws, and better enforcement. And, there are huge gains to be made for the whole community in looked at the way work in the care economy is rewarded, and making sure the social value of this work is properly expressed through fair wages and conditions.

The policy issues touched on here are areas that everyone in our party will get behind. The challenge for Labor Unity is for us to ensure that these problems are the front and centre of our agenda. We win elections when we focus on core business: a growing standard of living for Australians, quality work for everyone, more families in control of their destiny, a fair Australia where everyone gets a go. Our job is to ensure our party gives these aspirations issues singular focus.

If there is less well-tilled soil here, it is addressing the issue of owners of capital getting outsized benefits of economic growth. We can fix all the problems we face with work, but structurally, a fundamental inequality is likely to exist between those who own only their labour, and Australians who own assets. One option could be to tax capital a good deal more and redistribute those proceeds – but I do believe that thinking is out of step with the desire of so many working Australians to get the control over their lives that comes with ownership, and indeed who want to benefit from assets growing in value over time just as rich people get to do.

One critical area of focus here is housing: both because it is so *intensely* important to Australians and their sense of security in life, and because, according to the RBA, the increasing return on housing wealth is one of the primary reasons why capital owners are getting outsized benefits in today's economy. While house prices have gone up, so too have rents: the average price of rent in today's dollars is about double what it was in 1960. Unsurprisingly, it is low-income people who are most affected by an out-of-reach housing market. Working-class Australians are today about half as likely to own their own home as they were in the 1980s. This is a profound change to see over just one generation, and a problem that needs our urgent attention.

COVID could give us a unique opportunity to crack open the problem. Interest rates are at all-time lows, our immigration rate will be zero or negative for a period, and we have a community of underpaid people who have done more than anyone else to get Australia through this crisis (think nurses, and childcare educators). Plus, we have on our hands a generation of young people who were doing it tough well before COVID, and who will probably suffer more from the current economic crisis than any other group of Australians.

Government could play a role as developer, as funder, or as coordinator, for large-scale rent-to-buy schemes. Partnerships between local, state, and federal governments could assist in securing land. Super funds have shown a strong interest in projects which provide a reliable long-term income stream, and which help solve profoundly important social problems. We have a chance, here, to do something meaningful and important about this core driver of the quality of life of Australians.

Housing is not the only reason why capital owners are getting more out of the economy than they were before. Another driver of the growing returns to capital is that a small number of highly profitable businesses are getting to be a bigger and bigger part of our economy. It means that the better chance Australians have to share in the spoils of hi-tech, hi-profit sectors like finance, the better.

In this, of course, we have the ultimate run on the board: the superannuation system. Labor people are well-versed at speaking about superannuation as a retirement incomes policy. But super is so much more than that. Hawke, Keating and the union movement built a society where the vast majority of working people owned some capital. Genius at the time, even more genius now. The argument for 15 per cent superannuation is compelling for this reason, and needs to be explored further, especially in a period where wages growth will be under huge pressure given the dire underemployment and unemployment situation that is likely to persist in Australia for some time.

I think, too, it's time to have the discussion about how Labor might help more people into their own business. It's an aspiration of many working people, and the work done by the Transport Workers' Union to represent owner-drivers shows how this model, in some sectors, could really benefit workers. It would also be a chance for us to build a stronger connection with this growing, critical share of our economy.

In Mick Young's day, work did a good job of distributing the rewards of the economy. Today, work isn't doing the job we need it to, and the next Australian Labor Government needs to focus – really focus – on this core issue in the lives of Australians.

Work is not broken because it has to be. Work suffers from policy neglect. Reforms to help Australians benefit from economic change have not kept pace with the change itself. And we know this for sure: when the economy grows but ordinary people aren't getting better off, the model is well and truly broken.

Fixing work – through helping Australians get fair access to education and skills training, through ensuring new jobs are created across the skills spectrum, through making sure good rules exist and that they are enforced – should be the crucial first objective of the next Labor government. As a party, I want us to debate, too, about how we can help working people own capital. It's a part of the puzzle we need to put together to ensure that as our economy changes, so too does how we think about sharing its rewards.

* * *

Clare O'Neil is the Member for Hotham and the Shadow Minister for Innovation, Technology and the Future of Work. She has been a Labor Party member since she was 16. Clare has Arts and Law degrees with Honours from Monash University, and a Master of Public Policy from Harvard University where she studied as a Fulbright Scholar. Clare is a former Mayor of the City of Greater Dandenong and a World Economic Forum Young Global Leader. Before entering Parliament, she worked in the private sector. She co-authored a book, with fellow MP Tim Watts, entitled Two Futures – Australia at a Critical Moment.

11. THE PROSPERITY DIVIDEND: PAVING THE WAY TO A BETTER AUSTRALIA

Richard Marles

This was the year our nation reminded its government that we stand together in crisis not apart, with businesses and workers coming together during the uncertainty that has defined 2020. Now, more than ever, we need a new narrative of shared prosperity to grow jobs and the economy. The dividend of investing in innovation – the strength of our ideas – to grow a more diverse economy is the prosperity dividend this nation cannot afford to miss. It is what grows productivity, profits, and wages alike. In this moment, as we face the biggest reimaging of Australia since the Second World War, we need a government that is not simply reactionary but has the courage to seize this moment and put us on a different path.

Labor has always understood the importance of embracing innovation as a path to prosperity and invested in it. We focused on turning ideas into action. Innovation is the key ingredient in any kind of serious economic reform, and it is the pathway to higher economic growth. It can help unlock the path to prosperity for the nation. Our country needs that full potential embraced – we can't keep letting these opportunities pass us by.

Innovation potential

Australians believe in aspiration. That is what makes us great in-novators – we see and seize opportunities. We deserve govern-ments that will reform and innovate to keep the economy growing and diversifying. The coronavirus pandemic has led to innovation on almost every front, but it has also exposed a serious deficiency in our economy – the absence of economic and productive complexity. Our economy does not reflect the depth of our collective skills. And that holds us back from fulfilling Australia's growth potential.

We've forgotten how to turn our best ideas into better businesses – and this amnesia is hurting our economic potential. During this crisis, this is a willful laziness we can no longer afford. It wasn't always like that. Our nation's moments of advancements have been many, and more often than not they have come at the hand and will of Labor Governments. After the Second World War, the Chifley Labor Government built what is still to this day the largest renewable energy project in Australia – Snowy Hydro. Under Whitlam came economic reforms of universal health care, free university education, and opening the Australian economy. Then Hawke and Keating floated the dollar, protecting our economy from economic shocks, boosted labour productivity through the Accord and sparked the genesis of the superannuation system. Rudd and Gillard added to the Hawke-Keating legacy with the national disability insurance and the vision to deliver a truly national broadband network. Growing the economy out of one the deepest recessions we have seen in decades requires a new narrative. Our previous economic reforms were built around innovation, and now we need the next wave.

The innovation challenge

Well before the 2020 pandemic, economic growth per capita had fallen through the floor, wages growth was stagnant even though business profits were growing, and household debt had hit record levels.

Where Labor's legacy has been reform, the alternative has been stagnation. Tony Abbott oversaw the decline of manufacturing and along with it, successive Liberal leaders have let productivity languish, resulting in stagnant wages and working conditions for most Australians. This happened because the Liberals do not understand what shared prosperity is and nor do they care to.

The economy became less diverse when they literally goaded the car industry to leave Australia. As one of a handful of nations that could make a vehicle from design to finish, car manufacturing had been the most high-tech complex manufacturing undertaken in the country. The moment Australia stopped doing it we significantly reduced our national industrial capability. This massively hurt our innovation capacity. The effect on other parts of the manufacturing sector was devastating.

Labor understands that growing the economy is about more than just transactions. It is about people and how they experience the economy. The problem facing the economy and workers is a question of where and how growth could be restored. The answer is there if you simply look at the composition of the economy.

Today we need a government that will tackle this productivity challenge through technological innovation that does not pit jobs against profits. And one that understands innovation does not just happen, it is created. That is the prosperity dividend. And only a Labor Government can deliver it.

Productivity is the heartbeat of the economy. It is the value generated in the economy and by extension is an indicator of the standard of living. Labor has always asserted that the economy is not just about growth. It must be about the shared prosperity that sees employees as the biggest asset to a business not its biggest cost.

What does innovation mean for the economy?

If all government seeks to do is recreate what existed before the pandemic, Australia will have missed an historic opportunity. Labor is best place to have a genuine conversation about how we reimagine a more prosperous Australia.

But more complex economies are more resilient. They grow more. They innovate more. When we talk about innovation, we should be asking two questions. Do we have the enabling conditions for innovation and is our economy diverse enough to capitalize on that innovation? This will answer the productivity challenge.

Immediately prior to the pandemic our innovation system was weak and that meant Australia's prosperity was in decline. Over the past five years, seven out of 18 industries went backwards in labour productivity despite growing value in profits. Australia's innovation system is broken. Australia has dropped out of the top 20 most innovative countries in the OECD. If Australia wishes to remain a rich nation, it must not just get back into the top 20 but aspire to the top 10.

An example of this is our tech sector. While WiFi was invented in Australia, our technological sector forms a smaller part of our economy than most OECD countries. In fact, we are second last just ahead of Mexico. We are also behind our OECD peers in digital innovation, a key driver to unlocking Australia's potential across the economy. Shockingly, Australia is the worst commercialiser of public research in the OECD – our ideas sit on the shelf or worse, go overseas to become productive and profitable businesses for foreign nations.

Arresting this decline requires a new culture that embraces innovation and puts science at its heart. That means turning the tide on a long running decline in the proportion of students pursuing STEM subjects in their education. Until we embed science as a factor in our thinking and decision making, Australia has little chance in achieving the economic reform we need to climb the technological ladder and come out of COVID-19 not just in recovery, but on a path to prosperity. Australia is now at a crossroads in our conversation about work, technology and productivity. Labour and multifactor productivity were in decline before the pandemic. Complex problems, but no excuse for doing nothing.

Culture and institutions shape innovation

Innovation that results in prosperity is as much about the institutions and entrepreneurship as technological change. Innovation begins with research and educational institutions, stems from a culture that encourages risk taking, and manifests where there is the political and industrial maturity to cultivate it. Our universities are innovation engines and should be funded like economic drivers. These world-renowned institutions have drawn the ire of the very government that should have been rewarding them. The CSIRO has 200 fewer scientists now than when Labor was in government seven years ago. Spending on research and development has fallen by around 15 per cent since Labor was in office and is behind the OECD average. In a globally competitive environment, this disdain and Australia's underspend on research and development inevitably leads to a national brain drain.

Increased casualisation which has left more workers vulnerable to economic shocks has been frighteningly demonstrated during the coronavirus pandemic with casual workers accounting for two-third of those who lost their jobs. To grow government must think about how it supports more investment in human capital, not less.

The pandemic is a change point in our history

For most Australians, 2020 will be remembered as one of the most challenging years of their lives. Along with the significant health impact, Australia's economy has also been battered. The pandemic has meant for many families, aspiration has taken a back seat to just clutching at economic survival. This is the year in which the number of Australians without a job reached 1,000 000 – enough people to fill the MCG ten times over.

Australia was officially in recession in June 2020 for the first time in a generation. The worst economic shock since the Depression. And unlike the GFC, this is a crisis that has impacted working people almost from the outset. What started as a health emergency quickly turned into a jobs crisis because of the fault lines that existed in our labour market well before anyone had heard of COVID. Think of the removal of penalty rates, stagnant wages, underemployment, casualisation, increasing household debt all as tectonic plates that buckled under the pressure of a pandemic. All of the economic trauma of the pandemic just added to the load.

Yet for all the astounding changes to our lives, the pandemic has reminded us that the show must go on. The parameters of public policy are wider. If it can be done, then it should be. The gravity of the situation demands action, and in action comes opportunity. Public services and institutions across the world have innovated at an unprecedented rate, taking on new technology and software and completely redesigning the way they work in ways that may have taken years without forced impetus of COVID. That innovation offers a road to prosperity of a different kind – one rooted in economic security and health – but only if we take it.

Innovation means change which is why people can be reluctant to embrace it when they know government is unwilling to provide the type of support and environment that gives them the courage to take a chance. It is Labor's task to make this innovation an opportunity, not a cost and to ensure that the dividend is spread widely and that dislocations do not occur disproportionately. Yet, in this current, highly uncertain environment, dramatic change has become mandated. It is in these sink or swim moments that innovation is at its greatest as caution is thrown to the wind and focus narrows on the outcome needed. Innovation which can deliver for our country the inclusive growth we have been missing will pave the way to prosperity if government is open to supporting people to do this more and spreading the benefits fairly.

Becoming a country that builds things again

In 2019, the idea that making surgical masks was a matter of national importance would have seemed laughable. The pandemic has reminded us of the importance of sovereign manufacturing capability. By April 2020, engineers from the Australian Army were in Shepparton ensuring that all the machines in a private factory were working 24/7 to ensure a supply of surgical masks to the country could be maintained. The sense of essential industrial capability being central to our sovereignty suddenly became clear to everyone, not just policy makers.

For Australia to have a modern diverse economy fit for a G20 nation it must include manufacturing. In turn Australian manufactured products must be able to compete on the world stage. Competition can only occur based on price or quality. And we are unlikely to be a country which makes cheap low value goods at a globally competitive price when one considers the nature of manufacturing in the developing world. The manufacturing that makes sense in a first world setting is the making of high value, high-tech products. The global benchmark here is the way manufacturing occurs in countries like Korea and Germany. Again, to achieve this and unlock the prosperity and opportunity it offers we need science to help us climb the technological ladder. A government can outline reform, but our economic talent pool is the key to achieving policy success. An environment where entrepreneurship thrives requires a government and country that embraces risk. Australia must radically change its cultural attitude to trial and error that comes with taking risks – we must accept that failure is sometimes a necessary precondition to success. Setting the right economic conditions will allow the ambitiousness that leads to prosperity.

While Australia performs well at early stage entrepreneurship, we struggle at the commercialisation of ideas which lead to sustainable jobs. This last stage is critical to a broad based, innovative economy. Compare this with Israel, a country that commercialises research well and consequently has a more complex economy that is expected to grow at well above our economy over the next six years. This has been achieved by building the relationship between vocation and research. There are incentives for researchers to commercialise. Promotion is tied to patents. Businesses are embedded in research institutions.

The way forward

The way forward starts by recognising the value in our universities and research bodies like the CSIRO as economic institutions and the bedrock of our innovation ecosystem. That means appropriate funding and certainty. As a critical economic reform, the Australian government must start to actively foster this environment of collaboration in Australia, rather than simply relying on good intentions. This would go some way to addressing intellectual property disputes that so often are an impediment to the commercialisation of an idea.

The United States has a much more complex economy than Australia because it actively cultivates one. This stems from much larger technological, medical, and pharmaceutical sectors – but also their interrelationships. Integrating business and research institutions plays a big part in the success at commercialising but a critical factor is thinking about innovation as a system rather than an add on.

Canary in the coalmine

Falling productivity growth comes from a lack of innovation and a lack of diversity in our economy. Recent trends showing a decline in productivity but an increase in hours worked make clear it is time to rethink how we talk about our economy. It is also a time to innovate how we engage with business and employees to develop a more complex and resilient economy. That task must be purposeful and bold like the Accord. Only Labor can do this. Australians are working harder, we have not yet advanced our thinking about how we work. To become a better Australia, we will need to work smarter. Casualisation of work and flat wages are both canaries in the productivity coalmine that attest to this failure of imagination.

Innovation is more than the just invention. It means changing the way businesses and labour are structured. It begins with leadership and manifests in culture. Changing the productivity trajectory means changing the attitude government has to workers. Australia needs to have a mature conversation about how we improve job security, grow profits and diversify the economy. That means talking about how we grow the economy together not erode working conditions at the expense of consumer confidence.

All through this, the dialogue between science and government must become functional. Investment must be seen as just that – government investing in the future where a return for the macro economy is seen as a net win. And the place of embracing science in our economy must be seen as the most critical piece of microeconomic reform facing Australia today.

The prosperity dividend

As an economic priority, Australia must seek to create a culture that embraces innovation, risk, and science. That is how we become the destination of choice for the world's best scientists and engineers and grow jobs and our economy. That is how we climb the technological ladder. It is how we boost productivity and grow prosperity.

In the past, the cutting edge of modernity has been in Australia – and that modernity has been defined by our standard of living and economic enterprise. Today, modernity lies elsewhere in places like Seoul, Silicon Valley and Shanghai. But Australia can pursue these goals again through much needed economic reforms. Australia's aim must be to become the most modern country in the world. For where lies modernity lies its most precious dividend – prosperity for its people.

* * *

Richard Marles is Deputy Leader of the Federal Opposition. Richard was elected to Federal Parliament as the Member for Corio in November 2007. He was raised in Geelong and educated at Geelong Grammar School. He has a LLB (Hons) and BSc from Melbourne University. He began his career with legal firm Slater and Gordon, before going on to become the Federal Assistant Secretary of the Transport Workers' Union. In 2000, he became Assistant Secretary of the ACTU. Richard has previously served as Parliamentary Secretary for Innovation and Industry, Parliamentary Secretary for Pacific Island Affairs and Parliamentary Secretary for Foreign Affairs, Minister for Trade, Shadow Minister for Immigration and Border Protection and is currently the Shadow Minister for Defence.

12. Generation Lost?

Amanda Rishworth

It is the politician's lament – why aren't young people turning up to community meetings or involved in political parties and other institutions? In the media young people are often categorised as apathetic, disengaged, and even selfish. On the more extreme end of public discourse, they are accused of living superficial lives full of screen time, selfies, and smashed avocado on toast.

But is any of that actually true? This one-dimensional analysis of young people actually reveals the real problem – their views, actions and experiences are not being understood, which only serves to make the situation worse. The truth is that on almost every metric young people are ramping up their participation, yet this continues to go largely unnoticed.

To get a better understanding of how engaged young people are in politics we not only need to compare their current participation with older cohorts, but also examine how this has changed over time. A good place to start is the Australian Election Study which has been running for 30 years. The data shows us that 18-24-year olds' interest in elections has actually been increasing – more young people now care 'a good deal' about who wins the election than the rest of the population. Similarly, while the share of young people who discuss politics during election campaigns has traditionally been around the same as the average for all age groups, in 2019 it jumped up to 83 per cent compared to 74 per cent for all ages.

The one credit young people do get from their elders, although sometimes as part of a dismissive comment about 'slacktivism', is for their online advocacy. What is less appreciated is that young people are just as likely to attend political meetings, volunteer on election campaigns, and donate to a party or candidate. Outside of elections, the number of 18-24's who are 'a good deal' interested in politics has trended upwards since 1987; starting at 15 per cent and now at 36 per cent – four points higher than for all ages. While young people were previously less likely to contact an elected official, over time that gap has almost closed. Young people really are pulling their weight when it comes to political engagement and perhaps that should have been apparent from their passionate involvement in campaigns on marriage equality and climate action.

Breakdown of the generational compact

What is driving young people to get more involved in politics, and why didn't we notice it sooner? The short answer is that young people harbour growing unease about their future, and they don't see the current political scene doing anything about it. Only 32 per cent of Gen Zs in Australia expect to have a better standard of living than their parents. According to the Museum of Australian Democracy, Gen Z is also not convinced that delivering a good economy and lifestyle is an achievement of our democracy. Only 14 per cent picked that as a top positive feature, compared to 43 per cent of Baby Boomers.

If you're wondering why you haven't heard too much about the issues facing young people, it's probably because as a society we haven't been listening. The 2019 Mission Australia Youth Survey found that 52 per cent of young people felt they have a say 'none of the time' in public affairs. Despite this, the percentage of young people enrolled to vote has been steadily increasing and reached 89 per cent at the 2019 election. It's crucially important for politicians and the media to take note of this and start seriously considering the views and acting on the concerns of young people. If our inaction continues despite their increased advocacy, we risk leaving an entire generation behind and permanently eroding their trust in our democracy.

While every younger generation though history has felt misunderstood, there is currently good reason that young people feel their interests are not being represented. A key component of the fair go in this country has been a compact that each generation could grow up to be better off and enjoy a higher quality of life than the generation that came before them. It is becoming increasingly evident that this social contract is fraying; deep structural challenges have emerged, and the Liberal party's response has been one of ambivalence. Young people are faced with declining wages, increasingly insecure work, plummeting rates of home ownership and increasing housing stress, mounting personal debt, and an environment in decline. Generational progress can no longer be taken for granted.

The Australian Actuaries Intergenerational Equity Index shows that both the relative and absolute wealth and wellbeing of the youngest age band is lower now than at any other time in the past two decades. This is backed up by a recent Productivity Commission paper which found that 15-35-year olds experienced a lost decade of income growth following the GFC. Firms offered lower starting wages, young workers had to turn to part-time work and roles that did not use their qualifications, and long-term youth unemployment and underemployment rose. The full extent of this is highlighted in a 2018 Australia Institute report, which found that the erosion of the standard employment relationship has been experienced most painfully by young workers – 55 per cent of employees under age 25 are now in casual jobs. This phenomenon of insecure and insufficient work has a negative impact on social and emotional wellbeing, career progression, and future income growth.

Generation Gap, a Grattan Institute report, found that the average equivalised net wealth of households headed by a 15-24 or 25-34-year-old has barely shifted over 12 years, while all others have increased significantly. Some posit that the simple remedy of inheritances will resolve this problem, but evidence shows the biggest beneficiaries of these are those aged over 55 and the already well-off. The report goes on to note that younger Australians are now less likely to own a home than in the past, despite cutting back on non-essentials and saving more, simply because prices have increased so quickly as against wages. ABS data shows 67 per cent of 30-year olds owned a home in 1981 and by 2016 that dropped to 45 per cent.

Young Australians also recognise that their current economic challenges sit alongside the long term challenge of a changing climate which not only threatens ecological disruption, but also presents a major threat to economic security in the future where younger generations will be saddled with the increasing costs of extreme weather events, population displacement, and increased global security threats.

It should now be clear why young people are losing trust in government. In recent elections this has led to a pronounced increase in the number of under 25s looking towards the Greens. This trend is not an inevitability though, as a party of government Labor is the natural home for young people who want to make sure their aspirations can be realised. To turn the tide, we need to respect their increased political participation, offering genuine consultation and new policy approaches that address their concerns.

Investing in young people

On a fundamental level, Australians of all ages care about each other. Parents and grandparents regularly advocate for changes that would improve the lives of their children and grandchildren on issues like jobs and education. Equally, it's not uncommon for Gen Zs to raise concerns about issues facing their parents and grandparents. However, when we get into the public debate about how to improve the fortunes of younger Australians, it all too often descends into rhetoric about generational war. The fact is, the longer this discussion revolves around an argument over who had it tougher, who is more deserving of help, and wealth redistribution, the more unproductive and electorally harmful the outcome is. This is not a battle we can win, nor is it useful.

To create real progress that has buy in from all ages we must follow the Labor Right tradition of investing to generate new prosperity and economic growth for each emerging generation and not narrow our focus to fighting over what we already have. In fact, the only way to ensure successive improvements to living standards generation after generation is to provide young people with opportunities to create new value through economic growth. Treasury acknowledged in the 2015 Intergenerational Report that improving participation and productivity in emerging generations is key to economic growth that generates more prosperity and improves the budget, yet we are still heading in the wrong direction.

An OECD Forum report, *Give Youth a Chance*, highlights the compounding damage youth unemployment and underemployment can cause. Those who do manage to find work after being unemployed at the beginning of their working lives will earn around 8 per cent less and suffer weaker career progression across their whole working lives than their peers who enter the workforce directly. Importantly, it also makes clear that young people don't just need any job – in order to avoid economic stagnation and growing resentment they need quality jobs that fulfil them and continue to advance our economy. If we start to approach the success of Gen Z as an investment to grow our economy and benefit society for many years to come then it not only makes improving the fortunes of young people all the more urgent but also encourages us to ensure we are fully realising the potential returns when we do make investments.

The most obvious area for investment is education. Accessible quality education and training is essential to unlocking young people's potential and building new wealth through economic growth. It is crucial that our efforts don't end there though, we need to make sure the skills developed by that education are utilised. We can do far more to support young people through the bumpy transition stage between study and their careers.

Despite considerable expense, youth labour market programs often fall short on delivering the outcomes they promise. All too often these programs are about short-term job churn and don't fully utilise the skills or fulfil the aspirations of young Australians. It is in the interest of young people and the economy to look at the kind of work being done – we need to ensure young workers are able to reach their full potential in the economy and not simply be satisfied that someone has been placed in precarious employment that only lasts as long as the government incentive does.

We must do more to build mentorship, industry links, and workplace-based training into all types of education to foster the relationships and experience that smooth the transition into relevant and secure employment. That includes a massive effort to expand the number of trainees and apprentices as well as promoting cadetships in sectors that have not traditionally taken advantage of such recruitment pathways. Of course, these programs will need to be meaningful and not simply lead to exploitation; the whole system should be focused on setting up young people for long term success in their careers. Business should see taking on a young person as an investment in human capital, not simply a cost to be offset by government subsidy.

Young people are also brimming with ideas and often willing to take a risk while exploring new ways of working – so long as there's reasonable conditions and an adequate safety net. One example, the young entrepreneur who has created a program where, within 16 weeks of training and mentorship support, disadvantaged young Australians are generating seed funding, starting their own businesses, and creating economic opportunities for themselves. Young people are willing to take a punt, but we need to support them when they start out as well as when it doesn't work out. Take the young magician who was able to make a full time living in a job that he loved and where there was demand in the market for his talents. But when Coronavirus hit the safety net didn't catch him. The same goes for the young DJ and so many more in the arts and entertainment industry which disproportionately employs the young, the creative and the risk takers. Government failures like this put a serious handbrake on future entrepreneurship and we can do much more to encourage and support young people on this path.

Investing in our young people and supporting entrepreneurship will not only increase their opportunities, but also drive participation and innovation. We should also ease up on moralising about failure – there is nothing wrong with the learning and growth that come from rough patches. Factors like poor housing, mental illness and discrimination must be tackled concurrently to ensure we realise the returns on our investment. Providing holistic wrap around support will break cycles of disadvantage, allowing young people to take up opportunities and reach their full potential.

Access to safe, stable, and affordable housing is crucial in enabling young people to remain engaged in education, build their career, stay healthy, and participate in their community. Our superannuation and aged pension systems also effectively assume home ownership in order to provide a comfortable retirement. Yet home ownership is decreasing, rents and mortgages are going up, and according to a Mission Australia survey one in six Australians experience some form of homelessness before they turn 20 – a figure that should shock us. Investments in this space would relieve significant resources from the flow on effects of housing insecurity. As well as a focus on social housing, we could look at how to encourage well-regulated build-to-rent-to-own models that help improve the supply of affordable rentals, as well as provide a path to home ownership.

Another crucial element to unlocking potential is fostering mental wellbeing. According to the seven-year study *Can we talk?*, young people were experiencing a long-term increase in psychological distress before the COVID-19 pandemic. In recent years governments have made efforts to further resource the mental health sector, particularly clinical services, but we should also turn our minds to how we can build resilience – including by fostering community-based initiatives. The investments we make to improve the material conditions of young people are crucial to decreasing stress and promoting good mental health, which again reduces cost to government and delivers economic returns.

Forging a new path

The challenges and opportunities that young people face are all interrelated and will require a coordinated response that works to understand that complexity and simultaneously ease all the pressure points. The best way to navigate this path is to use the voices of young people. Young people are valuable participants in our society and economy now and in the future and they deserve genuine input over the issues that are shaping their lives. Bringing young people into policy making isn't just about respect, it's about outcomes. History has shown us time and time again that when governments implement policy solutions on cohorts from the top down they rarely work.

Young people also bring fresh thinking. Our old ways of doing things aren't working and the ideas of young people can drive innovative changes. Some one-off focus groups won't solve these structural problems though, this work requires ongoing and iterative co-design where a diverse range of experiences are represented and there are mechanisms to coordinate a whole-of-government response. Young people are engaged but our current system isn't fully capturing that within policy making. This will continue until there's structural reforms to how government interacts with young people. Three foundational pillars to meaningful and constructive inclusion are needed in this space; direct engagement, professional advocacy, and infrastructure within government.

The first pillar, direct engagement, is about short-circuiting the traditional barriers young people feel, and creating a compelling invitation from government to real participation. The most comprehensive historical example in Australia was the Australian Youth Forum that ran from 2008 to 2013. It was a genuine attempt to foster mass involvement of young people and create links with policy makers, but it wasn't around long enough to fully embed into the way we do things. In the 2020s we can utilise advances in technology and social media to build mass involvement more quickly and authentically.

The second pillar is professional advocacy – from youth-serving organisations and peak bodies, to organisations representing youth workers. These organisations often have deep roots within a diverse range of communities, particularly those facing disadvantage. They provide support services, build skills and capacity, foster community and much more. Importantly, their direct interaction with young people of varying experiences and levels of engagement means they hold valuable knowledge about the wellbeing of young people and the challenges they face. It is important that we support not only their continued provision of services, but also their research and advocacy as a complimentary avenue to bringing the experiences of young people into policy making and public debate.

Infrastructure within government is the crucial third pillar to bring it all together. While the first two are broadly about listening, this pillar is about having the resources and coordination to respond. Young people are affected by decisions made across almost every portfolio and the inter-related problems they face require a holistic response. Rather than youth engagement being an afterthought or duplicating functions across departments, it is important that there is an appropriately resourced unit within government to feed in the contribution from young people and advocates, improve and harmonise policy across government, and ensure government is communicating effectively with young Australians. Current practice is that any government bureaucracy for youth, if it exists at all, sits in the department where the relevant Minister's other portfolios sit. If we are serious about developing and retaining youth policy expertise in government then the bureaucracy dedicated to youth should have a permanent home. The Department of the Prime Minister and Cabinet seems the most obvious place for a unit that coordinates across government and already hosts the Office for Women and the National Indigenous Australians Agency.

Reform is rarely easy but with a renewed commitment to engaging with and investing in today's young people we can make sure they remain a part of the Labor project for the long term. By changing the narrative from generational wealth transfers to investments that generate new prosperity, cementing the role of young people in decision making, and supporting their aspirations we can get good economic returns and win back their trust in government. Putting the Labor ideals of opportunity, fairness, and inclusive economic growth at the heart of youth policy would serve our nation and its young people well.

* * *

Amanda Rishworth was elected as the Federal Member for the South Australian seat of Kingston in 2007 at 29 years of age. Amanda graduated with a Bachelor of Psychology Honours from Flinders University and a Masters Degree in Psychology from Adelaide University. After graduating, Amanda practised as a psychologist working with general practitioners in the delivery of mental health care to the community. While studying, Amanda worked in a range of occupations including within the trade union movement, both as an organiser and an occupational health and safety trainer. Amanda is a member of Federal Labor's Shadow Cabinet, serving as Shadow Minister for Early Childhood Education and Development and Shadow Minister for Youth. Amanda lives in Hallett Cove with her husband Tim and their two young sons, Percy and Oscar.

13. NORTHERN AGENDA

Jenny Hill

Townsville is the largest city in Northern Australia with a population approaching 200,000 people in an area of 3,700 km sq, but it is the second smallest local government area in North Queensland. Cook Shire is the largest local government area in Queensland at 105,700 km sq but with just under 5000 people. Belgium would fit into this area three times. The Shire covers most of Cape York to just outside of Port Douglas on the east coast and comprises eleven Indigenous councils. It's more than 2,500km between the Cape's main town of Weipa and Parliament House in Brisbane, and 3200km to Canberra. Reliable internet and mobile phone access is a wish that comes true only during certain times of the day. Do not expect rapid delivery from Australia Post. It already takes five days for a letter mailed from Brisbane to get to Cairns, add at least a few more for people outside this area.

There are a couple of big mines in the Cape, but there is according to government statisticians 26 per cent unemployment in the region and in places like Hopevale, Aurukun, and Lockhart River it is probably closer to 50 per cent. Community Development Employment Projects (CDEP) is the only reliable employment in these indigenous communities, but people are seeking more. Unemployment of course has contributed to a raft of community and social problems that are well known.

So why is unemployment so high in an area with some of the biggest bauxite mines in the world? If opportunities can't be realised for Indigenous people in these resource rich areas, is 'Closing the gap a dream? Housing in Indigenous communities remains a major issue and for some reason the Federal Government does not believe it has a role to fund this important infrastructure. Without adequate housing the schism between indigenous and non-indigenous health will never be breeched. And it's not just a problem in these more remote indigenous communities, but is even in places like Hughenden, four hours' drive west of Townsville, and other communities beyond the divide, housing is in crisis. If Australia is serious about nation-building, then we must urgently tear down the North vs South divide.

Them and us

On 18 June 2015, the then Prime Minister Tony Abbott launched the Northern Australia White Paper. To quote: "The White Paper is a vision to unlock the great potential and opportunities of the north. It focuses on building priority roads, developing water resources, removing red tape, building a sustainable workforce, and ensuring effective governance arrangements." Five years on unemployment is unacceptably high in Northern and Western Queensland, clean water is not necessarily available in many of these communities and telecommunications is not at a level we in urban areas would accept. Governments believe that Australians can easily use the internet to communicate with them, but not so in places like the Cape.

The feeling of 'Them vs Us' has grown, not subsided, over the last few years. While the Northern Australia agenda began with great support from Canberra, roads seems to be the only real investment the Federal Government will commit to. The North Australia Infrastructure fund (NAIF) has not been the economic activator that the Federal Government had hoped. The potential that is Northern Australia is still untapped and the population movement needed to sustain the northern part of our country is still a dream. Tony Abbott, Warren Truss and Andrew Robb promised so much, the policy was a breath of fresh ideas, but like with most strategies, where the secret is in the execution, it has largely failed.

Population decline is the new threat to Northern Australia as the youth of the north drift from their communities to places like Cairns or Townsville, relieving boredom, seeking education, or searching for a job. Many then drift to Brisbane and other southern capitals because there are better universities and more employment prospects. Yet there are jobs in the regions like Townsville, Cairns, Mackay, Emerald, Bowen, and Mt Isa. Would you want to move into these areas? Even in Cook Shire, Weipa has work for trade qualified people, doctors, nurses, and cleaners, but it is hard to find people and then to connect them to these positions.

In many places around the world, countries create tax zones that allow major companies to set up industries in these regions. We are told due to the Constitution that this is not possible in Australia. The Productivity Commission with its bureaucrats based in Canberra says it won't work anyway but doesn't offer real reasons why. Perversely the tax system has allowed the drift away from remote and regional communities. Apparently mining companies are exempt from paying Fringe Benefit Tax for the provision of flights, meals, and accommodation for mining staff.

Previously mining towns would spring up where big projects occur. Towns like Mt Isa, Moranbah, Emerald. During the mining boom of the 70's and 80's people flocked from Melbourne and Sydney to make a life amongst the big money that was mining. They would travel home each day after work, schools shopping centres and other community facilities sprung up in these areas. Their children would often train and work in the same industries as their parents. Local governments had funds to pay for services in these communities, and we saw a healthy population growth outside the golden boomerang of Melbourne, Sydney, and Brisbane.

Flying out

The next boom in 2000's saw a need to improve productivity and to attract workers with more than just high wages. This led to the development of fly in-fly out (FIFO) workforce. There are a number of papers, government reports and surveys by the mining industry and unions describing the pros and cons of this method of employment. Long shift hours, little ability to communicate with family, and child bullying issues are just a few of the topics dealt with in these studies.

Fundamentally it is not a lifestyle for everyone, and it is a method of employment that has contributed to the near death of many a remote community. And the FBT exemption for FIFO workforce has encouraged this type of employment. Workers are flown from all over Australia, Perth to Cloncurry, Sunshine Coast to the Cape, and my fellow mayors in these communities continue to ask why?

In July 2019, Mt Isa had an unemployment rate of just under 10 per cent. Local politicians complain about the use of FIFO workforce and the lack of real support to train locals to fill the roles especially in the mining industry. Mt Isa is a mining community built on the back of a migrant workforce that moved to the region in the 1920's and 30's to mine copper. In its heyday it was the most multi-cultural community in Australia with more than eighty ethnic groups identified living and working in a town 900 kms west of Townsville with more than 25,000 people. Today it has declined to 18,500. What would happen if the FBT exemption was removed from FIFO workforce but FBT exemption was given to companies who provide housing in these communities?

The story of population loss in the North is just not a story of Queensland. The Northern Territory Government has run a major campaign in the last six months to encourage business and people to move north. The introduction of the Covid-19 pandemic is a new layer of opportunity. With little to no cases of Covid-19 in Northern Australia can we unite to use this pandemic to our advantage? Many FIFO workers in areas such as Mt Isa, have purchased homes – 155 homes in fact since the start of the pandemic so they can stay safe and continue to work. Home prices have increased but unemployment particularly in youth and indigenous communities remains stubbornly high. The local mine once had well over 100 apprentices alone training at the local TAFE, but today about twenty apprentices can be attributed to the mine from the total of sixty students.

This decline in training has rung alarm bells. It has been easy, pre-pandemic, to fly in the staff you need, rather than spend the time to train. Bob Katter's mantra about "them vs us" rings true for the voters in the North where politics is as much about parochialism as it is personality. Thus, while Canberra talks about growing Northern Australia, the mayors of North Queensland see stagnation or decline. In a carbon neutral world how does the North growth and spread the economic benefit to all? There are significant opportunities in North Queensland, but it will take leaders with political courage and the ability to accept risk to take the first steps.

Northern lights

We have a bold plan to develop a manufacturing and industrial precinct powered by renewables. With more than 320 days a year of sunshine in cities like Townsville, and the ability to harness pumped hydro from Kidston we have companies and banks looking to invest. Sending renewable power 2000kms plus to the southern capitals from the North is just not feasible, the network is fragile. There is a simple solution, why not move industry to where the power is generated? Why not run a refinery or a lithium battery manufacture using this type of energy with a behind the meter solution? Solar farms produce far more energy in the North than we can use, we have a viable pumped hydro project that needs industry to secure its viability and there is a gas fired power station in the city as well looking for customers.

Melbourne was the home of Australia's manufacturing for more than seventy years and its decline is related to the increase in electricity pricing. Melbourne was once the home of aircraft, vehicle, clothing, and electronic manufacturing. When migrants came to Australia, they often had their first job on an assembly line polishing shoes or placing a windscreen in a new car and Melbourne grew with these post World War Two migrants and refugees. My parents migrated to Australia in 1954 and worked in those factories and gave us a safe home and the opportunity for a tertiary education. However, I took the opportunity to move North with my husband as we saw a great opportunity. The decay in Melbourne began not long after we left. The closure of clothing and shoe manufactures was the first part. Motor car manufacturing decline and closure, especially in Melbourne and Geelong, had a massive ripple effect.

Today the pandemic has shown how fragile our supply lines from foreign manufactures, items such as masks, gloves, and gowns just to name a few. Voters are asking why don't we manufacture in Australia anymore? The Queensland Government has supported Townsville City Council with our push to establish an Advanced Manufacturing Hub on a site owned by Council that will be powered using renewables. Behind the meter provision of power is the answer to cost, land available near enabling infrastructure such as roads, accessible fibre cable, gas, rail, and a port is the clincher. This area has also been nominated as a hub for hydrogen production as part of the Queensland plan to produce 'green hydrogen'.

I believe the opportunity is now there for Labor to lead with its support for industry and support the reestablishment of manufacturing in the North. Ostensibly the workforce in the regions is skilled or semi-skilled and is looking to remain in this part of the country often for the sense of the outdoors, we call BCF, boating, camping and fishing, it is a lifestyle choice. The ability to catch a barramundi from our river is commonplace, locals love it. Their job allows them to enjoy life, work to live not live to work is the chant from our supporters. National Australia Bank is backing one of the projects proposed for the Hub and like local and state members they are willing to put their name and reputation to support this audacious plan.

Speaking on RN Breakfast in early September of this year, Paul Keating said Australia's vast pool of super savings – close to $3tn – was vital to fund nation-building. I doubt much of that pool of money is spent north of Rockhampton. Superannuation funds are risk adverse and many are more likely to invest in projects offshore, local manufacturing is not high on the investment ledger. Thus, the role of the Federal Government is to act as the final enabler for the establishment of these industries. The pandemic gives the north the opportunity to attract people out of the major cities and encourage them to re-establish a life here, and to stop the stagnation. The Federal Government needs to recognise this opportunity and act fast to facilitate the flow of people and money to the north. Establishing a policy to support and grow the north with meaningful employment, not just tourism or health, but genuine blue-collar employment will be welcomed. The benefits to the rest of Northern Australia would be substantial, if Townsville establishes green heavy industry, then this could be replicated in Darwin, Mt Isa and maybe Weipa.

Really closing the gap

With these insights in mind, I come back to 'Closing the Gap'. From Torres Straits to Mackay, Mt Isa to Townsville, indigenous and non-indigenous are connected by family and friends. Children from these remote areas wishing to continue their education board in Cairns, Townsville, or Mackay. Strong educational establishments in regional centres ensure that these children are not too far away from family and support. Whether it is completing secondary education or learning a trade, education is a fundamental plank that can be completely delivered in a major centre. Housing and clean water must be address in remote Australia and this is a Federal issue. Why would you return to your home in remote north if you are sharing a home with ten other people, that you may get clean water and your mobile connection to the rest of the world is limited. This happens 70 kms from Townsville at a place called Palm Island, and it is commonplace in both indigenous and non-indigenous communities right up the Cape.

Today State and Federal bureaucracy are constantly telling their political masters that everything can be done over the internet. That's fine if you are living in cities like Cairns, Darwin, or Townsville, but what about Hopevale, Lockhart River or Doomadgee. At the recent LGAQ conference on the Gold Coast I listened to a number of Mayors and councillors from the Cape and Gulf regions speak.

Internet access is limited and not reliable. Populations in these communities are fluid, but with around 1000 people living in a place like Lockhart River, and unemployment around 50 per cent. Accessing training via the internet is difficult, dealing with government agencies is impossible. The cycle of unemployment, overcrowding in housing and violence continues. FBT exemption for FIFO allows companies and contractors to employ from as far away as Western Australia, while those people, a couple of hundred kilometres away, in communities with extraordinarily high unemployment and no training sit idle.

I don't want a divided Australia but the advantages of life in a first world country is not shared beyond the boundaries of capital cities. The Northern Australia policy is the start of the conversation, but its time Labor owned it. Gough Whitlam, Bob Hawke, Paul Keating, and Julia Gillard invested in the North, and it's time again for Labor to take the initiative and turn their attention North again. We still remember how the Hawke-Keating government decentralised federal departments, Townsville benefited from this policy implementation. Fortune favours the brave. Will Labor be brave enough to tackle the issues and opportunities North? The State Labor Government just won an election on the back of a recommitment to Northern Australia. Big announcements and commitment such as support for Glencore. There is no doubt this steadied the ship post Adani and it has paid dividends with an increased vote. There was no way Annastacia Palaszczuk was going to win the election with the regions. She backed them and they backed her. The same commitment from Federal Labor could just win them the next election.

* * *

Jenny Hill was born and educated in Melbourne, Victoria, and graduated from LaTrobe University with a Bachelor of Science in 1981. The following year she moved to Townsville with her fiancé who was enlisted in the Australian Army. She has 23 years' experience as a scientist with mining companies, the Department of Primary Industries Animal

Research, and Medical Scientist at Townsville Hospital. She has also completed a Masters of Public Health and Tropical Medicine at James Cook University. In 1982 she joined the Army Reserve, first serving in the Royal Corps of Australian Electrical and Mechanical Engineers (RAEME), maintaining and recovering defence vehicles. In 1987, she graduated from the Officer Cadet Training Unit (OCTU) as a General Service Officer (GSO). After 12 years' service in local government, in 2012, she was elected the first female mayor of Townsville.

14. Australian Laborism: The Way Ahead

Wayne Swan

Success for Australian Labor will require not the growth of inequality and a shrinking middle class, but shrinking inequality and a growing middle class. This is the heritage and the heartbeat of the Australian Labor Party. It is the essence of what I call Australian Laborism as outlined in my 2012 essay "The 0.01 per cent – the power of vested interests in Australia." While the Federal Liberal coalition prepares to snap back to classic neo-liberal policies of tax cuts for the wealthy and wage suppression for Australia's working people, we are going to have to pursue our Labor values and our traditional policy frameworks with pragmatic idealism and ruthless organisation.

The same powerful vested interests that hounded the Gillard Government from office are pushing their tired but aggressive neo-liberal agendas to drive higher inequality, wage suppression, deregulation, tax cuts for the wealthy and a smaller public sector. How different things would have been in this pandemic if Labor had won the 2019 federal election. Labor's campaign review points our way ahead. We have to dramatically improve our campaign machine and we have to get much better at winning the battle of ideas. Just having the better ideas is clearly not enough. We must be ruthlessly and relentlessly fixated on winning government – not because government is the end, but because without the power of government Labor is powerless. In 2019 we failed to convince working people we would protect and lift their living standards. We heard their fears and their priorities, but our campaign left them wondering if we had really listened. Protecting the living standards of working people is how Hawke, Keating, Rudd and Gillard campaigned and won election victories. We did it by adapting Laborism to suit the times and to win we must do so again.

In a book published late in 2019 academic Elizabeth Humphries argued that Labor's agenda was no different from the neo-liberal agenda of Reagan and Thatcher, and that the unions were complicit on this path. To call the Hawke-Keating agenda neo-liberal is to squint at it through one eye. If Hawke and Keating were merchants of neo-liberalism they wouldn't have resurrected Medicare, nor raised a capital gains tax to rein in the excesses of the financial sector. They wouldn't have delivered a social wage which included greater funding for health, education, child care and welfare for those who the "let it rip free" market might have left behind.

The Hawke-Keating economic reforms should be more appropriately described as Australian Laborism, and nothing like the Third Way ideology embraced by some US Democrats and some in British Labour. We were first. And we did it our way, the Australian Labor way. We led the way, forcing the conservatives into policy retreat and to fight the battles on our turf. Australian Laborism showed that when the circumstances are right policies that produce a competitive economy delivered in conjunction with policies that taper the excesses of market capitalism can provide economic benefits for working people. The ethos of Laborism guided the Rudd and Gillard governments ambitious reform program: a price on carbon, the national broadband network, the national disability insurance scheme, all appreciated that equality could not take a back seat to the pursuit of economic growth.

We can take some comfort from the list of those epoch-making reforms – Labor ideas stand the test of time. Medicare is a national icon, the NDIS remains entrenched and the conservatives have finally conceded the value of the NBN after a decade of petulant vandalism. And just as the coalition has embraced activist fiscal policy after more than a decade of denial, carbon pricing will one day be forced upon them by a global community tired of post-fact Trumpian antics.

The conservatives in this country are forever in revolt against the future, and forever falling back trench by trench. But dishing out humiliation in the battle of ideas is not enough – must never be enough – for Australian Labor. Forcing Liberal Governments to adopt Labor policies under sufferance will never deliver on our sacred mission. To deliver Labor policies we must be in government. As Labor has long recognised, economic equality must be a driver of prosperity. Strong working and middle-class households are a *source* of growth not merely a *result* of growth. The IMF has shown conclusively, when the benefits of growth are concentrated overall growth is weaker, when growth is more fairly shared overall growth is stronger.

When the GFC arrived, Labor's response recognised this and was swift, sweeping, substantial and most importantly, stunningly successful. It was the very antithesis of the trickle -down vision of neo-liberalism, which is why the Murdoch media was so frenetic in its attempt to demonise stimulus and the role of governments in markets and society. In contrast, Australian Laborism provides a guiding light. A dynamic public sector which pursues activist fiscal policy and honours a commitment to full employment is entirely compatible with the pragmatic heart of Laborism.

Listening to the people

The last decade, while a trying one for Labor, shows that we can still set the terms of engagement on policy – but to win, we must meet people where they are and put their interests first. When we lose sight of the people, we cannot hope to win. Laborism's defeat in 2013 owed as much to our internal disunity as it did to the powerful vested interests that mobilised to install Tony Abbott and his survival of the fittest ideology. Bill Shorten's remarkably narrow loss in the 2016 federal election, with a traditional Australian Laborist platform centred around the fight for Medicare, gave us all hope for the future.

Yet sadly since then social democrats here in Australia in 2019, and in the United States in 2016 suffered narrow, cruel and unexpected defeats. In 2019 British Labour was trounced in an environment where victory should have been certain – an example of policy ambition and preoccupation with non-core issues overrunning connection with working people in their communities. What is clear for progressives in Australia, the UK, the US and recently in Scandinavia, is that the rise of the populist right is hollowing out centre-left voter support among working class and lower income earners. These defeats have brought forward the predictable debates that policy agendas have either been too radical or too conservative, and the usual debates as to whether policy or leader electability has been the culprit. There is no question a robust economic message is a pre-condition for winning back working-class votes, but it doesn't clinch the deal. British Labour's dreadful loss demonstrates that.

A party of government

We must remind ourselves that Labor isn't a pressure group, nor a policy seminar, or a wine and cheese society. Labor is a vehicle to win government and to govern, or it's nothing. To do so, Labor must have a message that gives voters comfort if it is to be handed the keys to the car. We are living in a world where the right's success in demonising the whole political class depletes the reservoir of voter trust progressive parties rely on to shape and win a mandate for change. In a world of diminished voter trust, progressives must start with a core set of saleable intelligent reforms that begin to turn back the tide – reforms that build political capital for the next tranche of reforms and the one after that.

That doesn't mean we shouldn't adopt a bold policy architecture, but it does mean we must adopt a policy architecture which can be used to win the votes of our traditional supporters as well as the increasing body of people in the community who are not aligned with any of the traditional political parties. We must not allow our enemies to wedge our own people, working people, against one another. We need visionary policies that convince our base and the middle that we hear them and have their backs. In 2019 Labor made the campaign miscalculation of having *too many* progressive policy solutions which enabled the conservatives to argue they would surely wreck the economy and people's lives. The clearest lesson from the campaign is that good old-fashioned scare campaigns work and the conservatives were successful in demonising our tax and climate change policies.

In 2019 the core conservative argument was that Labor lost because it pursued the politics of envy, namely removing tax loopholes that delivered huge tax benefits to higher income-earners and corporates. The Liberals characterised these as tax increases for all which would hit lower income earners and stoked fear in those living on the economic margins with the most to lose. Ironically, the conservative attack that Labor's program was aimed at curtailing middle-class aspiration delivered an unexpected result. Swing voters in middle-income areas stayed with Labor. Upper middle-income earners shifted toward Labor. Meanwhile, lower income voters in regional and outer suburban areas shifted to the conservatives. In other words, lower income-earners who were the principle beneficiaries of Labor's program moved away from Labor, while the people who may have lost through our proposals held or swung towards us.

Getting the basics right

So where did we fail? First, Labor didn't do enough to defend our vulnerabilities on taxes. Our policies were ruthlessly demonised by the 'surround sound state media' of the Murdoch press and a $80 million spending spree by a single plutocrat, Mr Clive Palmer – one of the biggest in the modern history of Western elections. The combined expenditure of the Liberals, the Nationals and other minor parties saw Labor outspent six to one. Labor had a knife in a gun fight.

In 2019 the Liberals persuaded Australians with low incomes and in insecure work to go with them, often for the first time. This is a cause for concern. If you're a truck driver in Logan city or a steel worker in Wollongong you are constantly told to work harder for lower wages and more insecurity while Liberal tax cuts go to the top end. Too frequently the underlying economic issues of these workers are lost in the noise of wider moralistic and identity issues, leaving them to think their priorities of jobs and wages and a better life are not on the agenda. When your primary concern is economic insecurity of your family, hearing constant debate and conflict over social issues makes you feel like you don't count. So, if we have learned anything about the last election it's that we cannot assume economic discontent will push support our way. In fact, it may be the opposite. We must consider the fact that Liberal fuelled economic insecurity and scare campaigns are a potent combination in driving fear into those who need the most help but have the most to lose when policies change or recessions hit.

In life and politics, loss aversion is a real thing. When things are tough, gambling with the future is often a risk not worth taking. In 2019, it is clear working-class Aussies felt that, while it would be nice for things to improve, the chance of things getting worse under Labor was real. In short, the scare campaign worked. Unstitching this dilemma requires policy, campaign and messaging focus and will not be a fight won easily. To prevail, Labor must always have a strong message centred around growth and jobs.

For Labor members of Parliament and Labor members more generally, nothing should spur our imagination and activism more than matters of economic democracy – how wealth is created and distributed fairly, wage setting, the power of monopolies – the list is long and frequently our voice is not heard loud enough or drowned out. We must have a robust economic agenda to capture the imagination of Australians in language they understand because bold sounding bad ideas will often triumph over better ideas that seem hedged, timid, or technocratic.

Avoiding false contests on climate policy

It is here that the right's *cause celebre* of climate denial smashes fairly and squarely into the scientific and political imperative of zero net emissions by 2050, the biggest social and economic challenge for our generation. Clearly in parts of the country our climate agenda cost us support in some working-class, resource and regional communities as surely as it won it in the broader community. Make no mistake. Morrison has no climate policy, but as you would expect from a marketing guy, he does have a clearly articulated PR strategy to use climate as a wedge aimed not just at coal miners but working people more generally and particularly the elderly.

It *is* possible to support blue collar jobs *and* reduce emissions across our economy but proposals that talk about shutting down the export coal industry or demonise entire sectors instead of focussing on the hard and tough policy which includes reducing emissions across the whole of our economy are entirely counter-productive.

Australian Labor has an historic opportunity to show how an inclusive, fair clean energy economy can be achieved and doesn't leave working people fearful of the future but leaves them confident they fit into a world that is de-carbonising rapidly. They need to see their elected politicians are talking straight to them and have solutions not just slogans. Those of us who accept the science of climate change, support blue collar jobs and are seeking a way forward to reduce emissions across the economy have had no support from either the right or the extreme left, with Labor often left in the middle of a firing squad from all sides.

Over the next twenty years there will be a dramatic reduction in fossil fuel production delivered by the market. As Ross Garnaut has pointed out through this, we can rediscover our zest for innovation and re-industrialisation. Fortunately, we are one of the few developed countries with access to the most bountiful store of renewable resources on the planet. As a nation we can successfully achieve strong industrial development and rapid climate transition.

This is something that Labor has been good at in the past and needs to be good at again. It is about getting into the communities most exposed to job losses and change, organising politically and industrially, deciding together on the new opportunities that can genuinely replace the jobs at risk and then using the tools of

Government: incentives, subsidies, grants, industry and community development to smooth the path between the present and the future. In short, we need to do what the Germans have done; that is a strong dialogue between government, industry and the unions operating on the principle 'no-one gets left behind'. If it sounds familiar, it should – because its old fashioned Australian Laborism put in place during World War Two by Curtin and Chifley, Hawke and Keating during the rebuilding of Australia into a modern economy, and our government during the GFC.

The cause of Labo(u)r matters

While we are a progressive party open to idealists from all parts of society, we are, and must remain, a party of working people – it is after all the reason we were created some 130 years ago. We can't be that voice for working people unless we maintain a strong voice for the representatives of working people – their trade unions. That's what makes us Laborists and makes our party uniquely special amongst the parties of the world. Put simply the task for Australia for the rest of the twenty-first century is to do what our forebears did in the last century – massive economic and environmental reforms that will drive future economic prosperity and social cohesion.

We must also acknowledge that the task of winning power has got harder in Australia in the last twenty years. The power of big corporations and big money in politics, backed in by the surround sound of the Murdoch empire and the disappearance of balanced journalism across many platforms has made it difficult for our voice to be heard. At the same time, it has gotten easier for our opponents to run massive under the radar social media campaigns of Trumpian proportions. In much of regional Australia, where Labor's fortunes floundered in the last campaign, independent media has disappeared to be replaced by Sky After Dark. The $80 million spend of Clive Palmer in the recent federal election is but a foretaste of what is to come as more and more plutocrats join the assault on Labor and on our democracy.

For Labor, persuasion of the non-aligned and the disaffected has never been more difficult nor more urgent. We have an obligation to reach out to the broadest possible coalition and building as many allies as we possibly can, some of whom we might have disagreements with on matters that are important but, for now, not as urgent. We must organise with the new tools at our disposal and rethink ways to raise money through small donations in the method undertaken by Democrats to compete with the forces massed against us.

More than fifty years ago, one of Australian Labor's greatest Prime Ministers, Gough Whitlam, said, in a call to party members to campaign pragmatically for Labor values that "only the impotent are pure." There is nothing more disloyal to the sacred mission of progressives in defending the interests of working people than the heresy that says achieving power isn't our most fundamental responsibility. There is nothing gained by winning the argument but not government. Winning power to put in place the building blocks of economic prosperity and environmental sustainability is what Laborists must focus on. This is the path to shrinking inequality and growing the middle class. It is the path to a better Australia.

* * *

Wayne Swan served the Australian community and the Australian Labor Party for over 24 years as the Member for Lilley, Treasurer of Australia for six years, including three years as Deputy Prime Minister. He was awarded Euromoney Finance Minister of the Year in 2011 for his "careful stewardship of Australia's finances and economic performance" during the Global Financial Crisis. He was instrumental in the introduction of Australia's Carbon Price and Clean Energy Package. Wayne is the author of The Good Fight: Six Years, Two Prime Ministers, staring down the Global Recession (2014). He is a member of the International Commission for the Reform of International Corporate Taxation and President of the Australian Labor Party and has been a member of the Australian Labor Party for 46 years.

15. Northern Dreaming
Is not a New Gig

Robbie Dalton

Who am I?

This is the question we all ask ourselves and where all our stories start. I am an Aboriginal man who grew up on community in Kalkaringi or Wave Hill until I was eleven years old, and subsequently moved to Katherine for High School and then later to Darwin for university studies. I have a Bachelor of Arts with an Anthropology Major and a Political Science Minor. I have served in junior and senior roles in Land Councils and the Northern Territory (NT) Government and have been fortunate enough to serve in various high-level senior roles at a national level. Most of my roles have been focused on promoting Indigenous economic development. I have at various times focused my professional and personal efforts on buffaloes, crocodiles, carbon, bioprospecting, regulatory compliance opportunities and ultimately Government services as economic drivers in remote areas of the NT.

My background has led me to think deeply about the nature of the modern Australian economy. The gig economy, insecurity, deindustrialisation, centralisation, wage theft, automation – those threats will impact us all, but they have a special meaning in the context of the modern 'Northern Indigenous' political and economic landscape. Some of these themes challenge the historically accepted model of the Australian way of life – what we have understood until now to be the 'fair go'. The notion of a fair day's work for a fair day's pay is under attack. But perhaps for one of the first times since the Harvester judgment of 1907 – the principle attack comes not from the usual suspect, a hostile Coalition government. The erosion of pay and conditions we are seeing via the on-demand employment sector – the so-called gig economy – is attacking our way of working in ways not seen since the industrial revolution. And the consequences of this are profound.

Not all pain is fair or equal

But as with all issues impacting on Australia – there is how they impact on us all. And there is how they impact on First Nations peoples. What do these challenges me for me and my people? Are we to be part of the shared Australian experience? Or remain apart still? Will COVID-19 'change everything' – or will for too many of us, will we remain strangers in our Country.

It is a fact that the Gig Economy is disproportionately impacting on the skills, industries, and occupations that Indigenous Australians disproportionately rely on. And this has profound consequences for a people already doing it tough and starting from behind. But the Gig Economy – if managed appropriately – can also offer a pathway forward for remote Indigenous communities in a way that was not previously conceptualised. It is important that in pursuit of the perfect, we don't let that perfect become the enemy of the good. There is a risk of overregulation of the gig economy that could – if not managed appropriately – lead to more pain and suffering in regional, remote and Indigenous Australia. These are profound questions that we must grapple with.

To undertake this journey fulsomely, readers must start at the beginning. We must begin with the incontrovertible proof of Australia's harmful colonial history and the harm principally incurred by the original owners of this Land – the Aboriginal people. Having assessed this, we can begin to layer into the compounding inequality of education, employment prospects and remoteness and the benefits that immediately accrue to middle class, non-Indigenous Australians living in major metropolitan centres on the South Eastern Seaboard of our continent.

The invisible hand of the Sydney-Melbourne model

Australia is the twelfth largest economy in the world with a very small population in global terms. Thanks to our inhabiting of a continent – Australians have access to prosperity and welfare most global citizens can only dream of. Australia rightly offers a high standard of living for the majority of its citizens and residents – the fabled 'Good Life' – and we should expect that those standards extend that offer to all Territorians and all Australians. Let us consider then how we arrived that this standard.

Australia has followed an extraordinarily successful socio-economic model – which we will term the Sydney/Melbourne model. We will see how early momentum can compound into a lifetime of success. It is worth reflecting on this model, because up close it can seem almost invisible. And yet like an invisible hand, it is there, guiding you upwards and onwards. The chances are that, regardless of your ethnicity, if you are born in Sydney or Melbourne then you will born into a high-functioning economy bursting with opportunity.

Your life course most likely features English as the main language at home, and you probably have been guided by some mentors and role models who are born into, innately understand and can – most crucially – operate within the Sydney-Melbourne model. You will have enjoyed early childhood learning either at home, if Mum and Dad have made that call, or via the highly regulated and well-structured Australian mainstream early learning industry (which is not without its problems) that generally operates efficiently. You will have gone to a pre-school, leading you to the best school your parents can afford. You then most likely go onto a well-funded primary school, and if your parents have reasonable access to funds, a school with better numbers and even better result. You will go to a primary school that will lead to a better performing high schools.

Truth be told, I am not versed and am not in a position to argue about the merits of elite private schooling; but if there is anything has ever earnt the label of 'First World Problems' it is the general jockeying that occurs over what schools you may attend. Chances are you will then achieve your Year 12 Certificate, or you might go on and earn an apprenticeship. If you are well off, you will probably end up in a full-time white-collar role. If you are not so well off, you will more likely end up in a blue-collar role – and to be absolutely clear from the authors point of view, neither are an accurate label of your potential success in life or your worth as an individual.

Either pathway, you probably will work a minimum 37.5 hours a week and will have a pretty decent standard of living for which we can thank the trade union movement – the stability and security at work it fought for is and was an outstanding effort in global terms. If you have your act together you probably bought a house somewhere along the line, you will pay off the mortgage and then work until you retire, collect your superannuation, and you will probably find yourself in an aged care residence of some description.

While Australia is fortunate to have avoided the dog-eat-dog, rampant commercialism of the United States, the Sydney/Melbourne model remains ascendant, as people transition through the life stages outlined above. To be clear, I am not trying to paint an overly bleak picture. I am more than cognisant that the standard of living that has been delivered from this socio-economic model is one of the better ones in history. The invisible hand of Sydney and Melbourne was with you the whole way – keeping you safe and secure. Making sure someone was there to guide you, to pick you up if you feel and to hold your hand if you were in trouble or felt worried.

Unless of course you are Indigenous. Or from up north. Or, most critically, both. This is a model worth celebrating. It has given so much to so many and the good life is everything we aspire to as the Australian Labor Party.

The gig is up: a model under threat

It goes without saying that the Sydney-Melbourne model doesn't exist up North – which in of itself is a concern. But, perhaps more concerning than our inability to translate the wealth and ease of success taken for granted in the Sydney-Melbourne complex; is the fact that it is on the wane. If we can't protect it, then we most certainly can't expand or replicate it. Most critically, the Sydney/Melbourne model depends on you working for 37.5 hours a week until you are of retirement age.

The Sydney-Melbourne model has never been immune to globalisation and in 2020, there is a major threat to its ongoing viability. Nevertheless, Australia's relative remoteness and its relative abundance has allowed it to endure even major periods of global or economic dislocation in relatively good shape. Apart from the Depression – which hurt everywhere – Australia has had more boom than bust. More good times than bad.

The rise of the gig economy represents a seismic change to traditional employment that is rapidly emerging in mainstream economies across the globe, and the Sydney- Melbourne model is under as much pressure from its impact as anywhere else.

Broadly relatable examples of the gig economy include creative endeavours – music, art, sport, customer service and relations, and any other 'cottage industries' that allow people to make enough money to suit their needs but to also opt out of 37.5 hours a week, superannuation and the rest of the model. I am not suggesting that no one should have the option of opting for the gig economy or alternatively that it is the optimum economic model. But the gig economy clearly doesn't work for too many working people and their families or meet their needs and circumstances. The law shouldn't be optional and nor should be a living wage. This stealthy creep of technological driven change represents a relentless and secretive opt-out of steady, full-time work. And while it can be painted as 'flexible' or 'romantic', the truth is the benefits are largely one sided; with the returns accruing to those at the top or those best able to demand a premium for their services.

While it's true that some individuals who opt out of the Sydney/ Melbourne model in favour of gig work are rejecting the concepts of a prescribed life path and 'end of life return on investment' – I can't think of too many people that wilfully wish to struggle. Poverty isn't fun; even the starving artist can only starve for so long.

The economic model in remote Northern Australia

Now we turn to almost a different universe, remote Aboriginal Communities in the Northern Territory. A place so different, that it might as well be a different country. A place where the guiding hand has gone on strike, if it ever indeed existed. A place where the only thing that compound is disadvantage. If you are born in Maningrida or Yuendemu, the chances are that you are born into a life of poverty and extremely low levels of government service delivery. Early childhood services may or may not be available. The chances are that English is well down the list on the languages that your family speaks (but which the education system mostly delivers). You might grow up in a family where education and employment are desirable, but without a strong and functional economy and job market for you to transition into, your family and your mentors can only do so much.

Almost across the board, you will educationally underperform against your urban peers and most certainly against your Southern urban peers. Year 12 will be difficult but not impossible, and most usually you will need to board in an NT urban centre, away from your family and support networks. On seeking to enter the workforce (if that is still your aspiration) it will be extremely difficult, if not impossible for you to find and hold a 37.5 hour a week job – if they exist, they are likely fleeting. If you have done vocational training, you may have a number of qualifications that are probably not backed by an existing industry or even a project in your local community.

If you accept this scenario, then the rest of the Sydney-Melbourne model is obsolete. Your disadvantage (if it hasn't already) will immediately being its compounding. Home ownership, superannuation (if you live long enough to enjoy it – a serious contemporary issue for Aboriginal Australians), retirement and aged care? In remote Northern Aboriginal remote communities? Some communities and some individuals, certainly. Enough for a sustainable economic model that delivers the Good Life to the majority? Absolutely not. Many of my fellow Aboriginal people have opted out of the Sydney-Melbourne model for many of the same reasons that many especially younger people resident in the Sydney-Melbourne model also have chosen.

Many Aboriginal people aspire much more strongly to the gig economy model that supports immediate lifestyle needs but more broadly, cultural or family needs. Aboriginal economic development more often not represents industries and activities supported by the gig economy such as creative industries: I think here of arts, crafts, sports, music that feature a flexible production model and are based on specialist refined knowledge and skill-sets; but also land and sea management; and finally situational and seasonal management of natural resources on the Aboriginal Estate according to traditional expert ecological knowledge. These are the types of skills that the Sydney-Melbourne model has always undervalued, and the Gig Economy is particularly assailing.

So then how to marry this cultural and regional predisposition to gig employment in a way that delivers the greatest good to the greatest number? How can we overlay a Sydney-Melbourne model in the twenty-first century into the regions? If managed correctly, the gig economy model then is, rather than a threat to Northern Aboriginal economies, more of an opportunity. Thus, there lies the potential in the Gig Economy that political parties – particularly progressive ones and governments of any particular political persuasion should embrace to a much stronger degree than previously.

What should governments do? Governments and political parties must shy away from an all or nothing model that depends on full time jobs or no jobs at all. Those of us in regional Australia know that a zero-sum approach such as this will mean zero jobs. Gig Economy jobs can be improved – but attempting to corralled them into the 37.5 hour week is a lie that cannot be achieved in fulness and may lead to worse outcomes than we currently have. Government must look much closer at FTE equivalents within in a more flexible workforce model as a measure of success in socio-economic model that suits that measure and better match community aspiration.

I am not asserting that no Aboriginal person on community wants a 37.5 hour week and the financial rewards it brings – those individuals should be recognised and supported to pursue their ambitions (and will likely acquire the level of work they seek from one source or another if the general hours are available). We must be ultra-cautious in thinking through the potential harm to vulnerable socio-economic groups when we seek to determine macro solutions. We must be particularly careful when we develop macro-solutions for those living on the East Coast and seek to drop them on top of communities in which those solutions may not fit, or worse, may cause bigger problems.

As I have shown – not everything is equal. Including our answers to problems.

* * *

Robbie Dalton is a proud Mudburra man whose home country is Top Springs in the VRD region of the Northern Territory. He currently works in Aboriginal Policy in the Northern Territory Government and has served as member and Chair of the Indigenous Advisory Committee to the Federal Environment Minister. His previous national level roles include time spent as a Policy Adviser to the Indigenous Water Policy Group and as a former member of the First Peoples' Water Engagement Council. Robbie nominates a brief but 'eye-opening' stint in the NT Office of Women's Policy in his early career as a defining moment. He has also worked as an Industry Development Manager and spent a substantial portion of his career as a Policy and Research Adviser for the Northern Land Council. Dalton holds a Bachelor of Arts featuring an Anthropology Major and a Political Science Minor.

16. "Do Not Go Gentle into That Good Night"

Helen Polley

Australians are being forced to fight for an aged care system that will give them dignity at the end of their life. Australia's ageing population is well documented, Our ailing aged care system has been a talking point around many kitchen tables due to the Royal Commission and COVID-19 within aged care homes. Increasing demand for aged care services and the associated concerns of the costs and budgetary pressures that this will place on the Commonwealth is perhaps the more pressing concern of the next few decades. In Australia, the number of people aged over 65 years is projected to increase from 15.8 per cent in 2019 to approximately 19 per cent by 2031. Concurrently, the population of people aged 85 years and older will double. These individuals are the principal consumers of residential aged care homes and will place a greater strain on available resources. Irrespective of this, our aged care system is currently in crisis and it should come as no surprise.

The Commonwealth Government has commissioned inquiry after inquiry into the treatment of the most vulnerable and marginalised. The most recent inquiry into this sector, being conducted by the Royal Commission has revealed that poor regulation, an absence of minimum staffing ratios, widespread over-prescribing of drugs, a high incidence of abuse, and inadequate palliative care, are just some of the entrenched issues. We know the problems and have done for years – yet the Government has failed to implement, let alone propose, any policies to address these concerns.

The question of how we reached this point can be answered by assessing deliberate and heartless policy decisions made over a number of years. These decisions have focused on the marketisation of this sector to reduce the financial burden of our ageing population. Simultaneously this has also seen a removal of regulation and an opaque screen being cast over a sector in desperate need of more not less transparency.

Successive Liberal Governments have had ample time and warning to enact meaningful change. Instead, they have continuously cut funding from this system. There has been no investment in the aged care workforce and no additional support for residents with dementia, despite both expected to experience huge increases. The Abbott-Turnbull-Morrison Governments have a history of neglecting to appoint Ministers for ageing and aged care, instead merging the portfolio under a larger umbrella. When they have appointed them, they are rarely in cabinet and do not possess adequate knowledge in this area. The portfolio is seen as – and thus treated as – a second rate policy area for underperformers. As the consequences of its inaction are currently unfolding amidst the COVID-19 pandemic, the Morrison Government has yet to implement a plan to overhaul the aged care sector. Labor has recommended an eight-point plan, which addresses the recommendations of the Royal Commission Interim Report into Aged Care and seeks to improve the problems, which are currently entrenched within this sector.

The former Federal Labor Government's credentials in the aged care space are well documented. The *Living Longer Living Better* reforms, which passed into law on 26 June 2013 by the Gillard Government introduced a $3.7 billion program over five years. This program included $1.9 billion to deliver better access to aged care services, $1.2 billion to address critical shortages in the aged care workforce and improve working conditions, $268 million to fund more support services for dementia in aged care and capping home care and residential care costs at $60,000 over a person's lifetime. These policies would have driven reform in the aged care sector and cater to the changing needs of our older population.

With the change to the Liberal Government in 2013, the

workforce supplement was subsequently cut, and no plan has been made to further develop this vital workforce since. Funding for dementia treatment and innovation ceased, with no replacements being proposed by the current Liberal Government. The dementia supplement, meant to help with the costs of caring for those with severe behaviour and psychological problems associated with the dementia disease, was cut. The Abbott-Turnbull-Morrison Governments failed to drive the *Living Longer Living Better* reforms appropriately and now we have an aged care system in crisis. With all these cuts and inaction, it is little wonder that the sector is in crisis and our elderly are suffering.

In the wake of the current crisis in aged care, the Labor Party has proposed an eight-point plan. We need a long-term strategy, not only to tackle the current COVID-19 pandemic, but to ensure that older Australians can live out their final years in dignity and comfort. Labor will ensure:

- Minimum staffing levels in residential aged care.
- Reduce the home care package waiting lists so more people can stay in their homes for longer.
- Ensure transparency and accountability of funding.
- Independent measurement and public reporting as recommended by the Royal Commission.
- Ensure adequate PPE in every residential aged care facility.
- Better staff training, including for infection control.
- A better surge workforce strategy.
- Provide additional resources so the Royal Commission can inquire into COVID-19 without delaying its final report.

A bold new plan for Aged Care

The fiscal contribution that the Australian Government makes to the operational funding of residential aged care is determined by the Aged Care Funding Instrument (ACFI). ACFI is a tool which assesses the care needs of residents and is the largest source of revenue for residential aged care providers. ACFI is based on dependency, so there is limited incentive for aged care providers to actively encourage reablement and rehabilitation methods. This mechanism is broken and needs a complete overhaul if we are going to overcome our self-imposed aged care crisis. Concurrently, many aged care providers are not commercially viable. These corporations usually employ complicated business structures, which, while being legal, cast a veil on their financial performance and transactions. Transparency must accompany this sector by increasing reporting requirements. This will allow for more informed policy and investment decisions.

The growing incidence of dementia is one of the biggest health challenges of the twenty-first century with the number of people living with dementia predicted to rise from 436,000 to 900,000 by 2050. We need a stable supply of well-trained and empowered doctors, nurses, and personal care workers to deliver quality care for older people. People living with dementia deserve to be an integral part of our communities and therefore reform should be instigated from the local level. The introduction of dementia-friendly communities and active ageing agendas, that have been adopted in other countries, must be supported at all levels of government. Local government is uniquely placed to have a positive impact on our ageing population and associated increase in aged care. They have a greater insight into the needs of their communities and know how to better target action. This could include such initiatives as dementia education for key retail and service staff, particularly in banks, supermarkets, and other essential retailers. Such programs could be executed by an age-friendly community development officer. We have youth development officers, why don't we have an age-friendly community development officer in local governments?

Creating dementia and age–friendly communities, centred around a high level of public awareness and understanding, being inclusive and facilitating people having control over their own lives, will empower this marginalised segment of the population and cause a shift in public attitudes towards our older Australians. Local Government is ideally placed to drive this plan to create a community that embraces its elders instead of disregarding them.

It is essential that there is an introduction of a national training scheme for aged care. Currently, training for aged care is patchy and lacks any real career path. We have proposed that the Commonwealth facilitate and fund a workforce development strategy in a co-design approach with unions, aged care providers and consumers. This strategy needs to look at remuneration, precarious employment, skills development, attraction and retention and opportunities for job redesign for older aged care workers. Currently, there are over 366,000 workers in the aged care sector, and this will need to increase to approximately one million workers by 2050 to accommodate our ageing population. However, this predominantly female workforce is plagued by low wages, a high rate of casual workers, minimal career prospects and no adequate training for residents with high needs. This has culminated in a relatively high turnover of staff who are overworked and undervalued. An appropriately skilled and professionally qualified workforce is fundamental to the delivery of quality aged care across both the residential and homecare sectors.

Despite the best efforts of staff working in aged care, there are no mandated staffing levels and skills-mix to ensure a standard level of care across the sector. This policy shift resulted in more generalised requirements regarding staffing levels and skills mix. Subsequently, greater than half of Australia's aged care homes experience unacceptable levels of staffing. We need nursing ratios now to provide better care. Higher levels of staffing and better skills-mix, with greater numbers of registered and enrolled nurses would provide better infection control and health care as well as greater support to nurses, care workers, and other staff. Workloads in aged care are often unmanageable and have been intensified by the COVID-19 pandemic across the sector.

There is no obligation for aged care providers to publish the number and type of staff employed or on shifts at any time. Aged care providers should be compelled to publish minimum and maximum staff/client ratios to create a more transparent system. In an open marketplace, this information is essential for consumers making an informed choice about who will provide their care and support. There could be a website, or a section of My Aged Care, that allowed consumers to review performance indicators of aged care facilities. These indicators could include accommodation standards, staffing numbers and types of staff, activities for residents, food quality and personal and clinical care. Provision could be made to include a transparent feedback and complaints section. Essentially it needs to be driven by the consumers who need to be well-informed when making these choices. Let's face it, choosing aged care services, particularly residential aged care, can be distressing. These decisions can be made at times of crisis or at short notice.

Arguments that the free market delivers improved choice, efficiency and quality are commonly not realised in aged care – and are often the cause of the problem. Individualisation of care should empower consumers, but in aged care there is significant risk of abuse as many of the older residents lack the cognition and awareness of their options when they make decisions in these frameworks. If they are not properly informed, they cannot make the best decisions in their interests. Families and older Australians place an incredible level of trust in this system to provide quality care and it is up to our system to deliver on that trust. It is imperative that the Federal Government has enforceable regulation around the standard of care that is provided.

In order to prevent elder abuse and enhance transparency, there should be an introduction of an accreditation and licensing system for direct care workers. This includes mandatory minimum qualifications and ongoing continuing professional development. Many aged care workers are unregistered. The Council of Australian Governments (COAG) Health Council has noted that this may present risks to persons receiving care. In 2016 the Australian Law Reform

Commission (ALRC) recommended in 2016 that aged care workers should be subject to a national code of conduct, in order to provide a further safeguard relating to the suitability of people working in aged care. There is already a National Registration and Accreditation Scheme for registered health and allied health practitioners, such as nurses and midwives, physiotherapists, psychologists and others. In addition, these professions are regulated by a corresponding National Board. The ALRC proposed that aged care workers providing direct care should be included in the existing National Code of Conduct. This would ensure aged care workers were held to a national standard where disciplinary actions could be taken. Additionally, employees should be subject to a screening and clearance process to determine if a person is suitable to work in aged care. This would assess such issues as criminal history, reportable incidents, disciplinary proceedings, complaints, and the like. As in other professions, there could be a national database to record the outcome and status of employment clearances. This would ensure that all aged care workers were appropriately qualified and do not pose an unreasonable risk. Importantly, it would give confidence to families.

Another important component of aged care is the provision of home care. As the 2011 Productivity Commission report, along with subsequent reports, have illuminated, there is a preference for older Australian's to remain in their own homes for as long as possible. Labor's Living Longer Living Better reforms combined three previous programs to form Home Care Packages. Consistent with the changing nature of people's preferences, there has been a greater demand for Home Care Packages. Regardless, the Liberals have underfunded these programs. Despite this, there are currently around 103,000 older Australians waiting up to 18 months for home care. This means that many were forced into aged care prematurely during this pandemic, where over half the number of new infections occurred. The Department of Health reports that 30,000 Australians have died in the past three years while on the waiting list for a home care package. The Aged Care Royal Commission's interim report labelled the home care system as unfair, cruel and discriminatory. Labor has repeatedly called on the Government to reduce the waiting lists for Homecare Packages. In November 2019, as a response to the interim report in to aged care, the Morrison Government pledged an additional 10,000 extra home care packages, with a further 6,000 promised as a part of the COVID-19 supplements. However, the Department of Health data revels only 7,000 extra packages have been delivered, less than half what was promised. There are concerns around the lack of regulation of this provision of care, with no mechanism to follow-up with people on waiting lists to inform them of how long they will need to continue waiting. The funding from the Federal Government should be enough so that older people receive homecare packages in a timely manner.

How are we going to fund services to address dementia and our ageing population in the future? The legacy of the Labor Government of compulsory superannuation has facilitated a means by which the age pension and aged care could be a more sustainable form of government expenditure. In addition, it alleviates some of the pressure of the decreasing dependency ratios in our tax system – the ratio of Australians aged over 65 years of age against the working population, or those aged 20-64 years. Not only has the dependency ratio decreased, but younger people are also more disadvantaged, experiencing higher rates of unemployment, low wage growth and squeezed out of the housing market, meaning they're less able to cope with the load placed upon them. Superannuation provides structural integrity to sustain our current population trajectory. To further facilitate this, the Superannuation Guarantee must be lifted to 15 per cent over the coming decades. The additional three per cent on the legislated 12 per cent would be designated for longevity. By scrapping the increase in the Superannuation Guarantee from 9.5 per cent to 12 per cent, the Morrison Government would place even more strain on an already overworked system.

People are living longer. Anyone born in the 1970s is likely to live past 105 years of age. So, if they retire at the age of 65, they have 40 or more years in retirement – something we did no contemplate when we first set up the pension. In this instance, our system would be struggling to cover costs at the current rate of superannuation.

Labor has acknowledged that there cannot be any advantaged position of income in retirement without some extent of self-provision. Increasingly, older Australians are having to contribute to their aged care costs. Irrespective of this, the Federal Government remains the predominant funder of aged care and its regulator. But, as the unacceptable waiting lists for home care demonstrate, the funding mechanism is not adequate. A solution would be to shift the dynamics of aged care from a product to a universal entitlement. The Federal Government could extend loans to older Australians to pay for aged care and then, upon death, a credit provided to the loan account from the estate of the deceased person. If the deceased person does not have any assets, the Federal Government would pick up that balance. This would take pressure off the reducing dependency ratios and ensure those with the ability to pay will and those who don't still have access to adequate aged care.

Australians are being forced to fight for an aged care system that will give them dignity at the end of their life. It should not be this way and it does not need to be.

Labor understands the sector needs major reform now. The sector needs leadership and a bold plan implemented with courage and a commitment to a generation of Australians who built our country. We need funding for aged care as a priority, not a second thought. If we do not get the policy settings right now future older Australians will not receive the better care we all deserve as we age – and what is a crisis today will become a national pandemic of neglect. That is not an Australia in which any of us want to live in.

* * *

Helen Polley is a Labor Senator for Tasmania and has been a strong Labor supporter her entire life. Senator Polley is extremely passionate about her community and ensuring Tasmanians have access to well paid jobs, education, and healthcare. Helen is extremely passionate about ageing and dementia and has become a familiar name in the aged care and services sector during her time as the Shadow Assistant Minister for Ageing. Senator Polley spends much of her time creating opportunities for Tasmanians and ensuring Tasmania has a strong agriculture, tourism, I.T and aquaculture industry for future generations. Helen takes great pride in the work she does, and is passionate about her community, women's issues, worker's rights and is a big believer in equality of opportunity.

17. Economic justice

Josh Peak

The Australian Labor Party was not just built for working people, but by working people. Built to secure a just, dignified and meaningful life. Now, in search of the Labor Party's future, we must look to our past, and reflect on why our party came to be. By looking to our DNA and history we will find our path back to success at a national level.

It is a simple yet regularly forgotten fact by some that the Australian Labor Party was fundamentally borne out of a desire for ordinary working people to live a dignified, meaningful life and to give their children hope for a better future. The struggles of the nineteenth century – from the eight-hour day movement and early closing associations of retail workers to the great strikes and the Eureka Stockade – make this abundantly clear. Through this period, workers and their families tied their hopes for a secure and prosperous future to the labour movement. The Australian labour historian Brian Fitzpatrick credits early Labor figures with:

> Representing the determination of common men to obtain from this community… citizenship, with its commitments to a fair wage, decent working conditions, "a vote in the laws they make, a home on the land I till."

These struggles tell us much about the labour movement's founding purpose and enduring mission, the inherent aspiration of working people to a better life. In a piece titled, 'The Plea For Eight Hours', by American Labor leader, Terence Powderly, wrote:

> Previous to 1825 men worked from sun-up to sun-down, and they saw but little of their homes… He knew but little of the wants of the household except those that pertained to food… Fewer hours of toil mean more time to read, and

after the adoption of the ten-hour system the workman took more of interest in the press of the land; he had more time to read.

In South Australia, the labour movement first contested elections in the 1890s. Within two years, the United Labor Party won 10 of 54 seats in the House of Assembly and would hold power in coalition with Premier Charles Kingston for five years. Kingston was also the founding trustee of the South Australian Retail Assistants Union (one of the first branches of what would become the SDA) and a staunch supporter of the Early Closing Movement. With the support of the ULP, Kingston passed the Adult Suffrage Act, the Village Settlements Act, a Conciliation Act, the Factories Act, and the Workers' Liens Act. From the very beginning, the labour movement, in government, were delivering democratic rights, improved housing and fairer working conditions. Within twenty years, the ULP would win government in its own right.

A fledgling group of trade unionists went from a handful of candidates in a newly formed party to winning government in only twenty years. This is an incredible achievement, and something perhaps not truly appreciated for its significance. Our predecessors did those with a sharp focus on fighting for economic justice: better wages, improved housing, stronger workplace protections and a voice for ordinary people in workplaces and in government. Time and again, this has proven to be the winning formula for Labor when it has been most successful.

In recent times the connection with the aspiration of voters by the Australian Labor Party has been overrun by a new form of paternalism. Where we once empowered, we now preach. Rather than listening to voters, we preach a 'we know best' attitude to the working men and women on which our party was formed and once based. How is a Labor version of paternalism any better than the Liberal Party's version? This attitude and approach can and must be overcome. Giving a voice to working people is of course, the reason for our existence.

Refocusing on the basics

Our shifting focus away from the core issues affecting working people has coincided with a period of increasing electoral irrelevance. Federal Labor has won one federal election in its own right since 1993. Throughout this period, working people in the suburbs and regions have left us. These are the very people who founded our party. This erosion of our working-class base should shock us to our core. As working people turn their back on Labor it not only challenges our reason for being, but it also fundamentally alters the character of the party, making us even more distant from working people in ever reinforcing cycle of disenfranchisement.

And yet our mission is more urgent than ever. The COVID-19 pandemic has highlighted the fragility of our economic system. But whilst appetite to act during this period is high, Labor's founding mission of economic justice is and must be enduring. The challenges working people are facing, are not confined to this political moment. Record casualisation, attacks on penalty rates, stagnant wages, labour hire abuses, enterprise bargaining in crisis and the reality of a 'gig economy' that fleeces workers are all challenges that pre-date the pandemic and will be exacerbated in the fallout.

The blueprint for a political offer which can command widespread public support and deliver for working people can be found by returning to the principles that guided our Party to success during equally precarious times. We must remain determined on delivering not only jobs and opportunities, but *good* jobs and *good* opportunities. This needs to be the number one focus for Labor in presenting itself as the party of economic justice. Taking a broad view of economic justice has been central to our Party's success by recognising that workers' rights should be broadly defined, universally enjoyed and enshrined in our legal system. This is what makes our country great and truly unique throughout the world. When praising our robust safety net, the ALP's version of "what did the Roman's ever do for us?" is well-known: Medicare, universal superannuation, the minimum wage, equal pay, four weeks annual leave and the list goes on. These achievements represent the best of Labor in government.

One often overlooked addition to this list is the ability for service economy workers such as retail workers to live dignified lives. The abundance and quality of this work makes Australia special – we are a nation where if you work you are rewarded with a life worth living. In the United States, the median annual wage for a retail assistant in 2020 is just over $22,000. Add to this, no guaranteed healthcare or pension, zero annual leave or sick leave as well as no protection from unfair dismissal and the picture gets even starker – if you work in retail in the US you're like to be in the precariat or what we would know as a 'working poor'. Comparably, the base full-time adult wage for an Australian retail worker is over $42,000 – the second highest in the world. Contrary to what those in the lunar IR right might say, this is a statistic worth celebrating and defending.

But it's not just the dollars and cents that deliver economic justice for these workers – there's more to the good life than your pay packet. It's rostering protections, job security, four weeks annual leave, safety laws, workers compensation regular pay rises and a union voice that gives them a good job and for many, a lifelong career. This gives dignity in work and in life. This must be Labor's enduring mission – protecting a society and system where we can work to live not live to work. As I visit shops and warehouses to talk with union members, one thing is clear – they enjoy an Australian way of life and are able to provide opportunities for their children and grandchildren because of these conditions. The same cannot be said for most workers in the retail and service sectors around the world. Again, this matters.

That is not to say that working people in Australia have succeeded in their aspirations. The desire to defend what we have won and to improve on this baseline must be our mission. The continued pursuit of economic justice for labour is where Labor's future lies. Attacks on penalty rates, denial of public holidays, flattening of wages and curbs on enterprise bargaining are all threats to the dignity of work and a dignified life. Coupled with the demise of companies and industries with secure and unionised workforces that are being replaced with precarious and insecure jobs, Labor has something to fight for – but we must be able to paint this picture in convincing terms.

The Labor Party must fight for these workers to ensure that no worker – whether they're driving an Uber or stocking shelves in a supermarket – is left behind during this crisis and the upheaval it creates. Fighting to maintain and secure economic justice for these workers must be the top priority for our Party not just in its policies and platforms but in its daily communications to the community. In order to be trusted, we must show *and* tell. And we must mean it. Too often, the economic security of these workers is overlooked by some in our party for other periphery issues that receive a greater share of attention. Labor is a party of government, so it should have a broad agenda and policies across a range of issues. But when working people look at Labor, they must see that Labor's absolute priority in government will be economic security for them and their families. It is not a question of ignoring other issues – but one of emphasis and priority.

Don't say we weren't warned

The retail, warehousing and fast-food workers I talk to every day make clear that if the Labor Party continues to project the wrong priorities, we will do so at our electoral peril. If we need reminding of this fact we should look to our record over the last quarter of a century. These people are the descendants of the workers who created our party. The shop assistants, factory workers, miners, cleaners, transport workers, nurses, and everyone in between, they are our genuine, yet often forgotten, backbone. We stand on their shoulders and we exist for them – not the other way around.

The Labor Party has expanded its support base throughout its history and all for the better; we must do so to remain electorally strong. But all too often the voices of those who our party was created by, and for, are diluted in a Party that champions too many of the wrong priorities. Labor gave workers a voice to champion their concerns and aspirations – "a vote in the laws they make, a home on the land I till". This idea was and always will be the source of the Labor Party's success. No issue is greater than the ability of working people to have access to decent and secure employment.

The results from the 2019 federal election and trends in the United States and Europe show the growing divide between university-educated voters living in cities and those without a university education living in the suburbs and regions. Labor cannot hope to win if it fails to bridge this divide or retreats to the cities. The Australian union movement has always provided the best link to these voters and represents the best avenue for rebuilding and strengthening the Labor Party's support amongst working people in the suburbs and regions where they live. The union movement must ensure the Party has a disciplined and strategic focus on the issues that matter most to these voters.

Undertaking this reorientation must begin with recognition of why the Australian Labor Party has been successful in the past. In 1913, Queensland premier T.J. Ryan told the Labor Party convention that, "there is no other party that has a policy which is formed on the initiation and at the instance of the people themselves."

When our Party fails to continue this tradition, our enduring success ends and failure follows. Losing sight of the need to deliver economic justice for working people will, in the end, be terminal for our Party. Failure can only last for so long. When these voters ask, 'Why Labor?', Labor must clearly respond that ALP is an economic party fighting for social and economic justice. We must loudly say we are party that believes every man and woman who wants a job should get a good job, and that that job must come with wages and conditions that provide a dignified life for workers and their families for now and for the future.

The idea that working people can get ahead in life and that their children are able to live better lives than they did is the core of what the Australian Labor Party is all about. Labor wins back working people, not by telling them what they want, or promising handouts, but by speaking to their hopes and aspirations – that working hard will give them the good life. Because, Australians are aspirational, and aspiration is fundamentally a Labor idea. The workers who created our Party in the 1890s – "working from sun-up to sun-down, and they saw but little of their homes…" – understood this. Published by *The Bulletin* in September 1890, one worker wrote,

> We do not ask our masters to do other than is right. …
>
> We do not want to take from them the wealth which they have earned;
>
> We do not want to take from the knowledge which they have learned;
>
> We do not want their ships or mines or sheep or cattle runs;
>
> But we want a fairly good time for ourselves and our little ones.

At its best, Labor lives up to these two ideals: creating good jobs and opportunities for workers who aspire to more for themselves and their families. What else could possibly matter more?

* * *

Josh Peak is Secretary of the SDA the union for workers in retail, fast food and warehousing with over 28,000 members in South Australia and the Northern Territory. Josh has been proud to work in the Labour Movement for over 12 years. From union Organiser to union Secretary working people have been the heart of everything he does. Secretary of the union since early 2019 Josh previously served on the ACTU Executive from 2009 to 2015. Josh has been a member of ALP State Executive in South Australia since 2014 and is the current Junior Vice-President of the Branch.

18. Defence Industry: Strategic, Nation-Building Business

Matt Keogh

"World Peace". It's not just the obvious answer to a Miss Universe question – it is what we all would like to see but we can't take such a thing for granted. Indeed, as the 1930s, also a period of economic upheaval, came to a close and concerns heightened about the apparent failings of appeasement, Australians did not expect to be entering another all-out global war – the first to see bombing raids on our own soil. In fact, it was the establishment view in the UK that war should be avoided at all costs and "peace in our time" had been secured.

So, while we must always strive for peace and diplomatic solutions, it is prudent – and indeed incumbent on any national government or any serious alternative government – to be prepared for the potential of armed conflict. Clearly, the existence of a standing defence force, such as our Australian Defence Force (ADF), is an embodiment of such preparation. Many, many pages are devoted to the doctrines, strategies, equipment, kit and capabilities, as well as the overall force structure of the ADF. However, instead of getting bogged down in what type of submarines we need and how many, it is first necessary to have a rationale behind the importance of a local defence industry and with it, our sovereign Australian industry capability to support our ADF.

Contesting defence policy from opposition

For too long the desire for bipartisanship has meant there has been little more than a cigarette paper between the major parties on defence matters. That in turn has meant that while the mishandling of specific projects is seen as fair game, actual commentary or debate about how Defence goes about its business has been largely off limits. There are a number of reasons that Defence and Foreign Affairs have been traditionally less combative in a partisan sense than more domestic focused areas of policy, as outlined by Dr Andrew Carr in his 2017 Australia Institute discussion paper; *I'm here for an argument: why bi-partisanship on security makes Australia less safe*. In part, as much as possible, it is seen as more constructive to delivering on Australia's national interests if its major parties are aligned in their public protestations, as the main audience can be as much international players as domestic. Further, recognising the importance of an apolitical military, it is beneficial to keep Defence policy a 'politics free zone' altogether.

While nobody wants partisan point scoring to take precedence over good defence policy, the effect of this approach has been that Opposition attacks on a Government (otherwise known as accountability) in the realm of Defence have almost exclusively been limited to delays and cost over runs in equipment purchase or maintenance on the basis these result in a lack of support for our serving men and women.

With hundreds of billions to be spent over the coming decades, more scrutiny – not less – is absolutely demanded. We need to be getting bang for our buck when it comes to defence spending. But such a confined approach cannot be maintained, because to leave some matters for when an Opposition may be fortunate enough to be in government will likely be too late, with decisions not only made but locked in. Such a cycle of policy making is not in the national interest.

Not just industry policy

Defence industry policy is one such area where the current approach is putting our nation at future risk. The problem stems from the approach of trying to use defence industry policy as a fig leaf for a complete lack of industry policy, an approach that has not only seen Australian manufacturing decline rapidly, but resulted in the car industry being literally chased out of Australia by an incumbent government. Defence industry policy cannot merely be a proxy for industry policy – something sorely needed in our country – nor just a way to make up for the loss of jobs in the car industry, as important as that is.

Two clear issues arise from the current approach: a lack of genuine commitment to defence industry policy, rather the apparent use of it to resolve short term political problems; and a complete lack of any strategic rationale, imperative of philosophical underpinning for defence industry policy in Australia.

It is Labor that has a legacy of investing properly in the defence of Australia. The tireless work of Curtin as Labor Prime Minister during the Secord World War is legendary but the commitment and investment of the Hawke Government in deciding to build the Collins class submarines here in Australia should not be forgotten either.

While Labor has built industry, the Coalition oversaw the closure of our car industry. Labor has sought to build industry policy, while the Coalition removed it. The current Coalition Government has rightly embarked on a national naval shipbuilding program, however it is more committed to the photo-op than the follow through in obtaining the benefits that a truly national sovereign defence industry endeavour should deliver. The problems being created for the long-term sustainability of not just our defence industry, but for the integrity of Australia's capacity to service and sustain its defence are not just limited to our ships and submarines but exist across our defence capabilities. If our approach to defence procurement and sustainment does not fundamentally change to incorporate the strategic imperative of developing sovereign defence industry capability, Australia can leave itself not just at the mercy of overseas primes but vulnerable to the sort of shocks that are inherent in international disputes.

Australia needs a rational Australian Industry Capability building approach to defence industry policy based not merely on employing more Australians – as important as that end is – but on a strategic rationale that recognises that as an island nation located closer to areas of conflict than to our allies, we need to maximise our own capacity to build, sustain, upgrade and indigenise our defence materiel.

Culture change

For too long we have allowed a defence bureaucracy limited in major project management experience to take hold of our procurement and sustainment of defence capability. The civilian equivalent of this would be to allow doctors and long standing health officials to be in charge of the construction of hospitals – large and complex facilities where capability upon opening is as important as their need to meet future requirements, as well as be maintained over the long-term. Unsurprisingly, that won't work: it's the wrong expertise.

Rightly, Defence and Government focus on delivering the capabilities (equipment) Defence need to fulfil their objectives, when they need them. Though in practice, this is more about what Defence says it wants, rather than what would be the best fit capability for it, and all procurement, whether local or imported, is inevitably delayed. Either way, this results in the locations of manufacture, the overall costs and development of sovereign capability, being significantly pushed down the hierarchy of decision-making priorities.

When it comes to this overall cost, what seems to be front of mind for Defence and Government is the upfront sticker price, rather than the total cost of ownership that many procurers of large and long use equipment in the private sector are used to. Indeed, nearly every car magazine refers to this concept, being not just the cost of buying the car but also the on-road, servicing, and operating costs. Similarly, the cost of a frigate is not just the cost of building it and integrating all the systems, weapons and equipment that go with it – there are also the costs of maintenance, sustainment, and the necessary overhauls and upgrades that will be required to ensure necessary capability over time as the frigate progresses through its lifecycle. Some of these costs are very hard to determine, such as upgrade costs when you don't know what the upgrade will be, but others, such as operating, crewing and regular maintenance costs can be predicted and factored in. Further, steps can be taken to mitigate these costs, even the less easily determined, by ensuring access to necessary capability here in Australia to perform such works (i.e. using local supply chains), further developing a local skilled workforce, requiring the transfer of designs and technology to Australia and a proper investment in Australian sovereign defence industry capability to protect against foreign vendor lock-in.

Currently these sorts of decisions are de-prioritised as they are perceived to increase upfront cost – even if reducing ongoing and overall cost, let alone reducing other strategic risks. This results in, as well as being because of, a lack of capacity within defence to properly deal with the management of risk, to ensure that such an approach does not risk provision of needed capabilities in a timely manner but also protect against over reliance on the views of primes. These problems all stem from a lack of strategic rationale underpinning defence industry policy and highlight the need for culture change within Defence from its Ministers down.

A strategic approach to defence industry

The objective of any policy concerning the supply of defence materiel to our ADF must always be to provide the world's best appropriate capability to best achieve objectives in the safest way possible. The strategic starting point to meet this objective must be a belief – based on past performance – that Australian industry is as capable as any other nation, and as such capable of delivering the best for our ADF. Conversely, to accept a view of Australian industry capability as being inferior or bringing greater risk, creates an obligation to improve the state of Australian industry. Not doing so not only brings with it even greater risk and undermines us as a nation, it demonstrates a lack of faith and belief in Australian capacity and capability.

Beyond building things, our approach to defence industry must be about ensuring that we have sovereign capability to maintain and sustain the equipment in use by our ADF. Without this, as highlighted through the supply chain constraints we saw during the COVID pandemic, not to mention our geography relative to our friends and allies, we put our own national security at risk. If we cannot service and sustain our kit, we are adopting a strategic weakness to be exploited by an aggressor. Therefore, it is essential to our national security that government policy ensures we retain our sovereign industrial capacity to maintain and sustain our defence equipment.

It is also in our strategic national security interests to develop a local defence industry that not only sustains our own requirements but also provides export opportunities as well – military equipment is big business and brings big opportunities economically and more importantly, strategically. Such an imperative is not about maximising foreign revenues to Australia but rather assisting Australia in projecting its strategic weight with other nations. This can occur through providing regional maintenance for joint strike fighters and land transportation equipment through businesses and facilities down our East coast, supporting the maintenance and sustainment of friendly navies operating in and around the Indian Ocean through the Australian Marine Complex in WA, as well as the production of equipment such as remote operated weaponry and naval ships for use by other nations.

Finally, when we zoom out from the defence and traditional national security view, defence industry policy that supports development of local technologies and skilled workforces for defence purposes adds opportunity and capability to our civilian industrial capability, particularly our advanced manufacturing and technology sectors. High tech defence industry provides a broad national interest benefit from defence industry policy and virtuously reinforces a properly designed national industry policy – which is incidentally, a requirement for a properly functioning defence industry policy itself.

Meeting the strategic objectives

Meeting this challenge requires defence industry policy that delivers on these strategic imperatives. This means that as far as possible, Australian defence businesses that can take the lead on projects (Australian primes), not just subcontracting to foreign lead contractors, being contracted directly by Defence to provide new capabilities to our ADF, requiring Australian shipbuilders to be engaged in all future shipbuilding programs – not just providing shipbuilding labour but also in the design, engineering, drafting and integration work.

It also means requiring as much as possible, Australian industry capability (AIC) be used when procuring new equipment for our ADF but also, that it be continually developed and enhanced to develop and sustain a sovereign defence industry capability here in Australia. This means we need to have measurable, enforceable, transparent, and audited AIC requirements in the contracts that Defence signs with the prime contractors providing such equipment. An Australian government truly committed to defence industry in the long term needs to look at how it can assist the development of Australian mid-tier defence industry businesses, from which we can grow indigenous prime defence contractors.

While some may be scornful of this proposal for a greater Australian defence industrial complex, and Government should never let that tail wag the dog, without it we will only be failing ourselves. Not only in a defence sense, but also in the opportunity to grow industry and advanced manufacturing more broadly – when we are spending this money, we have an obligation to maximise not just the defence capabilities for the Australian people but also the economic and strategic opportunities it can leverage.

The Government has budgeted $270 billion for defence capability acquisition over the next decade. If just 10 per cent more of that was required to be spent with Australian industry, we would see an additional $2.7 billion spent in the Australian economy every year, which would go a long way to developing local, high skilled workforces and technical capability right when we need it most. This would provide important spill overs into other parts of the economy, the likes of which are enjoyed by those who we currently send our defence dollars to.

When industry isn't in a factory

Finally, it must be recognised that there is much more to a proper functioning sovereign defence industry capability and defence industry ecosystem than just the physical building of equipment. There is the design, drafting, engineering and technological integrations, as well as the software, systems integrations and high-end technology development that goes into modern warfare equipment. All areas requiring skilled workforces in highly capable design houses, not in factories.

Less obviously, yet possibly more important now and into the future, are our cyber capabilities, including cyberwarfare, cyber defence, cyber security, and all aspects connected to the cyber domain of defence (as well as non-defence areas). Not only does this area represent a whole industry in and of itself, it is fundamentally one about developing skilled capability by developing a non-traditional defence workforce vital for both defence and civilian businesses and industry.

While there are many areas of defence that can be discussed as requiring the next big steps in technology, doctrine and strategy, the main battle ground now sits in cyber. It is an area that provides advantage to mid-sized nations such as Australia, but only if we get it right. The development of autonomous weapons, remotely operated equipment, the use of artificial intelligence and friend or foe technologies, and the use of swarm technology highlight how cyber is an area that Australia needs to get right now, and we could do it rapidly with the right policy settings.

Alas, relying on the Government that brought us the 2016

Census, RoboDebt and the myGov crash of 2020 to get anything right in the area of cyber provides the clear case for why we must have contestability of ideas in the defence policy space.

Once the reasoning is made clear, the imperative for action is inescapable and the consequences of Oppositions saying nothing is also clearer.

A clearly articulated rationale underpinning Australia's defence industry policy can be a game changer for our nation. Working together with a national industry policy, we can ensure we provide the best technological and state of the art equipment to our ADF, maintain and sustain it into the future and obtain the strategic and economic benefits for the Australian nation. But only if we grasp the opportunity.

* * *

Matt Keogh is the Labor Shadow Minister for Defence Industry, Western Australian Resources, and Assisting on Small & Family Business, and Federal Member for Burt, in Perth's south-eastern suburbs. Before Federal politics Matt worked with a leading international law firm in Perth specialising in corporate and financial services regulatory work, as well as anti-bribery and corruption. Prior to this Matt worked as a Federal Prosecutor, prosecuting corporate crime. Throughout his legal career Matt worked alongside various organisations to benefit the community including family and domestic violence service, Starick Services, serving as the President of the Law Society of Western Australia and as a director of the Law Council of Australia. Matt is passionate about securing better access to justice for all Australians and a more equitable approach to providing social infrastructure and services to our outer suburbs.

19. GENERATION NEXT

Ros Kelly

It's a bit presumptuous to give advice to young activists in 2020. Especially women. I wonder what I would have thought in 1970, if a Labor elder, say Andrew Fisher (or Billy Hughes!) from 1920 had given me advice on how to change the world. Fifty years is a long time in Australia's story and the world of 1970 is as different from 2020 as 1920 is from 1970. But there are familiar issues across the hundred years: pandemics, wars, the environment, social policy, the economy, women in politics.

The best I can do is offer some of my experiences. Finding your passion. Having a go. Doing the job. Being resilient. Moving On. I first joined the Australian Labor Party in 1968 and was elected as the Federal Member for Canberra in 1980. There were just three Labor women in the House of Representatives then. I joined Joan Child and Elaine Darling. The late Susan Ryan (her memorable slogan 'A Woman's Place is in the Senate') was there too. Susan and I had been among three women elected to the ACT House of Assembly in 1974. Susan was the first Labor woman into Cabinet from the Senate, and I was the first from the House of Reps. I was the first woman to answer questions on the floor of the House of Representatives, as a Minister, the first to have children while serving as a member of parliament.

I was in the first cohort of women smashing barriers. I wasn't a card-carrying member of the women's movement, but I wanted women to have an equal role to men in society – and in parliament. Back in the 1980s it was hard to live down the stereotyped perceptions in my own colleagues and the media. I tried to avoid being labelled a super housewife in an apron but then found the media wanted to treat me as just a stylish blonde clotheshorse. There were no precedents. I think the lesson for women from my experience is to try to understand the culture you are working and living in. Do not let it change the person you are, try to change the culture.

I had to experience the culture of the parliamentary Labor Party and learn from it if I was going to succeed and to make a difference. Susan wrote in her book *Catching the Waves*, 'as far as the Labor Party is concerned, factional power play has stymied more women than uproar in the chambers or stoushes in Caucus.' I was not aligned to any faction early in my career but ideologically I was socially progressive and economically conservative, so more at ease with the Right, especially in the deregulatory programs that hallmarked Australia's economic policy in the 1980s.

Have a go – a step at a time

It's hard work, whatever your passion is. In 1973, thinking of standing for secretary of the Woden Valley branch of the Labor Party I asked my friend Peter Wilenski, then Whitlam's Principal Private Secretary what he thought of the idea. He said, "Well Ros, the philosophy I have is that I look around and I say, ' Am I the best person to do this? Do I think I am the best person, or can I do this job as well as anyone else?' If you believe you can, I think you should go for the job." And that's what I did.

I had found my passion, and that is my best advice: find your life's passion. It was making a difference as a woman in the Parliament in the ALP. I think it is critical to identify and remain focused upon your personal passion and purpose and use it test against each new significant decision in your life. Ask yourself will this option or decision take me in a direction consistent with pursuing my passion and purpose.

My passion is reflected in my genuine interest in other people and my love of change. Combined with my energy and enthusiasm and can-do approach in all situations, it drives me and has done from the moment I threw my energies into politics. It did not abate as I got older. Back then the Whitlam government was pushing a very exciting agenda at a hectic pace and we really did feel that Australia was entering a brave new world. The troops were home from Vietnam, conscription had been abolished, 18-year-olds could vote, and more change was in the air.

When the call came for candidates for the 1974 ACT House of Assembly elections, I remember thinking that I was secretary of the biggest branch which had given me the chance to get to know some of the members. I thought I was the only woman motivated enough to who would have a chance of winning preselection. I took advantage of all the knowledge and expertise of my friends in the branches to help me bone up on areas such as the economy and immigration and I personally visited the 300 people who would be voting in the preselection. I was thrilled when Gough Whitlam came up to me at a Canberra branch meeting and said, "You've got my vote".

Eventually I was voted into the top spot on the ticket and became one of four ALP members of the Assembly – including three women. I became chair of the ACT Schools Authority in 1977 but only after surviving the Teachers Federation vote against me in the election. Naturally enough they had wanted one of their members as chair. A taste of things to come. This was a turning point in my career. It made me known in the electorate. The whole school system in the ACT was being overhauled and there was a lot of media coverage for the Schools Authority and for me. It was an excellent training ground for a young politician. I found myself at the age of 30, with my most recent job being an assistant teacher, chairing forums with headmasters about how best to run schools. It was a good way to learn a bit of gravitas and humility. I learned about meaningful consensus after the Federal Government attempted to close Narrabundah High School because of declining student numbers. After negotiation, the school was reborn as Narrabundah Senior College, now recognised as one of the best schools in Canberra.

That result demonstrated to me that I could have an impact and that achieving meaningful outcomes not always requires an 'all or nothing' attitude. It made me better known in the electorate and reinforced my decision stand. I realised there would be big personal and family sacrifices involved but didn't want to get to 40, which seemed such a long way off at the time and regret not having a go.

Getting elected

The key to winning the marginal seat of Canberra was getting a larger profile and winning over swinging voters. It was the fastest growing seat in Australia and profiling the electorate was a vital part of our planning. Our work on profiling the swinging voter was very advanced for its time. I had *Ros Kelly Cares for Canberra* T-shirts printed, published *Ros Kelly's Cookbook,* hosted regular morning teas to meet as many women in the electorate as possible and roped my friends into hosting gatherings.

My team and I letter-boxed most of the seat. Then, as the survey had revealed that Weston Creek had a large concentration of swinging voters, I decided that pamphlets were not enough so we door-knocked the area, which covered some 10,000 households. The door-knocking team would ask people if they would like to meet Ros Kelly the candidate and I would then visit them later. We would go out as a team and work from 6 pm to 8.30 pm, Monday to Friday. It was an exhausting business but proved its value on election day. I was helped by leading Labor figures including Bob Hawke and Neville Wran. I used the business community for raising money because there was no union base in Canberra with access to campaign funding and party funding for advertising was only available as the election came closer. It worked. On 18 October 1980 I became the new member for the seat of Canberra. I achieved a 5.7 per cent swing and was one of thirteen seats Labor gained. Bob Hawke and Kim Beazley were among the other winners.

You're not here to keep the seat warm

This was a new beginning, and I was full of hope and fear. Would I do well? Could I make a difference? Could I make the world a better place by my efforts? We were the first three Labor women ever elected in into the House of Representatives: Joan Child the trailblazer and Elaine Darling and me coming next. It was a small beginning on the long road to gender balance in the Australian Parliament.

Our parliamentary welcome was not entirely effusive, on both sides of the House. The simple fact is that you need the numbers to change a culture. Three women were not enough: the only way for us to change the culture in parliament was to build the numbers. You cannot get on with your job and singlehandedly try to change the culture at the same time. Life is sometimes too hard on women in this respect: the unreal expectation is laid on them to be perfect in every way: as wife, as mother, as politician. It just cannot be done. I had arrived in parliament aligned with the Right but not a rigid member of any faction. But before long I became a member of the NSW Right. The NSW Right were a conservative bunch compared with ALP branches in the ACT; I would never have been preselected for a NSW seat, but the Right was a good fit for me ideologically – I agreed with its policy gurus such as Paul Keating and his view that we needed to deregulate the economy and I lived with an economist who had taught me a lot about the workings of the economy and the proper way forward with economic policy: it all matched with the Right position.

In June 1981, an opening appeared in the Public Accounts Committee (PAC), and with the support of Kim Beazley and Michael Duffy I successfully nominated for the vacancy. The PAC reviewed government expenditure and it was the most powerful committee in parliament in those days, especially under the chairmanship of David Connolly. I found that it was in these committees that friendships could develop, rather than in the parliament, and they were friendships that crossed party political lines. When parliament was not sitting, committee members travelled together, investigating aspects of their brief and had time to get to know each other away from the formality of parliamentary procedure. It was also suggested that I run for the job of Secretary of Caucus. I asked Paul Keating what he thought of the idea. His response was simple: "Look kid, you aren't here just to keep the seat warm. You should take any opportunity to get yourself ahead of everyone else." I was elected unopposed and set about making the job my own. I used the position to coordinate policy committees, develop new networks and learn how the party operated. It was a perfect way to initiate me into the inner workings of the party machine.

In my first term in parliament, from 1980 to 1983, I worked extremely hard to secure my still-marginal seat and I became a very good local member but at the same time I needed to earn the respect of my colleagues if I wanted to become a Minister. All backbenchers need to do an apprenticeship to learn how the parliament works, by serving on parliamentary committees or within the structure of the Labor Party, such as my job as Secretary to the Caucus. I wanted to do more than become a good MP: as Paul Keating reminded me, I was there to "make a difference". For myself and on behalf of my electorate I felt I had a responsibility to go to the next level. Why? Because I could do more for my constituents if I was at the table making the really big national decisions. It's the way I always have lived my life: it seems the logical thing to do. In every new job I have ever undertaken, I look to see how I can progress, get promoted, and use my talents to get the job done better. In parliament, I knew I had the enthusiasm and energy and determination to help make Australia a better place, but this was not enough to win me a seat at the Cabinet table.

Resilience

In parliament or outside it, there will be ups and downs, criticism from friends and enemies, factional colleagues and ideological opponents. But if your beliefs and passion are strong, and you are resilient, then you will make progress by achieving pragmatic outcomes. I was a fan of the Rolling Stones in 1969, and still am:

> You can't always get what you want
> But if you try sometimes, well, you might find
> You get what you need

In August 1983, I gave birth to the first baby born to a serving Australian federal politician. There was some criticism (and a lot of praise) about me returning to work. In an interview with Anne Maria Nicholson in *The Australian* on 2 September 1983, (which had the subtitle, 'Amazement and Outrage'), I remarked: "I don't want to make myself a martyr to the cause of the working woman. I'm just doing what I have to do as my responsibility to my electorate and my family. I am in the middle of my career and I just can't afford the time to opt out. If I hadn't been at work in Budget week I would have been criticised and told I was neglecting my job."

So, although my life was busy, I was in a remarkably fortunate position. I had family support, financial security and I could even dash home to breast-feed because we lived just minutes away from both my electorate office and Parliament House. Not every mother is so fortunate. Although I would not recommend to anyone to go back to work after six days. But for me there didn't seem any other options as in those days there wasn't any maternity leave. Now it's different of course.

And to make life even more difficult Ben was born fourteen months later and went to the opening of the election campaign on 1 December when he was three weeks old. I was completely exhausted from the campaign, and two children, with no break and David working seven days a week on tax reform. We invited the Keatings to Christmas lunch. It was a disaster, as my body just gave in that day and I could not get out of bed. The turkey was destroyed despite Paul and David's best efforts. I had pushed myself physically to the brink which is something I would not recommend! Paul was a good family friend but as I frequently said to my colleagues he didn't see me as a woman but just a number, like everyone else. I valued that!

Despite all this I still had ambitions for a ministry of course, but in 1984 I still had to learn what to do if a door slams in your face – I believed a spot had been organised, but 'numbers' intervened. I needed to work my way through this, and I had to do the thinking for myself. Perhaps, I was considered to be manipulative and ambitious, but I was no more so than any man. Because I was a woman it was thought that I should be gentle and nice but if I had been gentle and nice they would have walked all over me. Politics is a tough business.

After some internal politicking I was eventually made Minister for Defence Science and Personnel in September 1987 – the first time a woman had handled any aspect of the Defence portfolio. I introduced useful reforming legislation, and I think, earned respect in the mostly man's world of Defence. After more hard work, good collegial relationships and savvy politicking I was, at last promoted to Cabinet on 4 April 1990, as Minister for Arts, Sport, the Environment, Tourism, and Territories. There wasn't much support in Cabinet for the ambitious promises the pre-election Minister Graham Richardson had made, but we made a lot of progress bringing climate change and the environment generally to the fore, and against the all-or nothing Greens, and some skeptical Cabinet colleagues we passed the Endangered Species Act, established the Environment Protection Authority, brought in the CFC reductions strategy, signed Australia up for the UN conventions on biodiversity and climate change at the 1992 Rio Summit, made major advances on world heritage listing of Shark Bay, Kakadu and Fraser island, and banned mining at Coronation Hill.

Every achievement was a battle, not only in the community but in cabinet and in caucus. But they were substantial achievements, getting the issue beyond saving trees, important though that was and is, to considering climate change. I took a climate change position to the Rio Summit in 1992 which we haven't yet reached.

The white board affair

Sport had mostly been a good news part of my portfolio. Major policies were implemented, including the establishment of the Australian Sports Drug Agency, and banning cigarette advertising in sport. Australia was one of the first national jurisdictions to achieve this lasting health reform. It invoked an extraordinarily vindictive response from male shock jocks and their tabloid brethren. It was in this atmosphere that sports grants came under scrutiny in 1992.

The Auditor-General's report into the sports grants program was finally presented to parliament in November 1993, nearly a year after that first question in Senate Estimates. The report noted that there were anomalies in the approval process of grants and that the reasons for decisions were not adequately documented, so that claims of party-political bias could not be put to rest. The Auditor-General criticised my department, finding that insufficient information was sent to me to allow me to make informed decisions, but he made the point that that was the way it had always been administered by every Minister, including most recently, Graham Richardson. I just happened to be the one standing without a chair when the music stopped.

The issue was that there was not sufficient paperwork to justify the decision-making. Because these were grants of public money, there were regulatory and business requirements to keep records, and certainly a high community expectation that the decisions and decision-making process would be documented and available for scrutiny. This was ultimately my responsibility, and this is where I failed.

I was never accused of breaking the law or mishandling funds. The sports grants were spent well and went to facilities that needed to be built, with priority given to indigenous communities, areas with high unemployment and areas with large migrant populations. It wasn't about fraud: it was about politics and directing money into Labor seats. It just happens that the greatest need for those grants were Labor seats.

My greatest sin in retrospect was that I tried to defend the indefensible. I thought, 'What's the point of me doing this?' I thought I was doing it for Labor, but they aren't supporting it. If the party machine wasn't supporting me, it really was time to go. Paul Keating tried to convince me to stay and fight, but I had had enough. I resigned from the Ministry.

Would I have handled all that the intense pressure for all those months differently if I had been a man? Probably. Was I strong enough defending myself? Probably not. Robert Ray told me I should have said that the decisions were political. Richo certainly would have done this, if the issue had been raised during his time in the portfolio. I had got it wrong. I resigned from Cabinet in March 1994 and returned to the backbench until I announced my resignation from parliament eleven months later.

At first, I was too battered to be able to know what the future held but I knew in my heart that I wasn't going to stay in parliament. I really should have left at the time of the 1993 election. I was never going to get another Cabinet position: I had reached my use-by date. Women get a higher profile in Australian politics, get it faster and use it up more quickly. Any woman in public life was a tall poppy and I was the only one in Cabinet at that time. That's one of life's lessons. Often you stay on a course even though you know it's wrong, but you do it for external reasons like loyalty, and justify it in all sorts of ways, but it's not the right outcome for you or your family.

Moving on

We moved to Sydney and I spent some time working on my skill base and how I could apply it to the private sector, because there is an enormous gap between what the public and private sectors know about each other. I didn't know exactly what I wanted to do but I did know that I didn't want to be a lobbyist as many of my previous colleagues had become. I wanted to work in the environment because my passion had been ignited when I was minister and I knew that if there were to be real environmental solutions the private sector had to become a willing partner in the solutions. I realised that I had skills which were important to the private sector and one of these was my ability to resolve complex issues, because this is what a Cabinet minister must do all the time. I wanted to be involved in environmental solutions to ensure environmental sustainability, not just to be an adviser and that meant I had to get involved in a company that had technology expertise. My research led me to Dames and Moore, an American company working in Australia.

The way I approach new challenges is that whatever needs to be done I get down and learn and work hard to understand the whole situation, rather than imposing decisions from the top down. In the mining industry I was constantly in the position where I had to prove myself, as most women of my generation had to prove themselves, every step of the way, in a male-dominated working situation. It is still true today that women succeed not just because they are clever or talented but because they are willing to work hard, and it helps to have a bit of luck as well.

One essential area that often gets neglected in women is their own health. I had a rude awakening with this when I was diagnosed with breast cancer in 2001. Being confronted with your mortality does help to reset the priorities. What a shame it is that we need a shock like that to put emphasis on ourselves. If women aren't fit and healthy how can we do all the roles we set ourselves? Our health is something we should be constantly monitoring. Breast cancer lead me to Chair the National Breast Cancer Foundation for six years. It showed me passion is limitless. Once you have found it, your passion can take many forms. It doesn't have to involve public life; it can be for your family or for your garden. It doesn't have to lead to power or money as its rewards are deeper and more personal. My passion has now turned to the Commonwealth War Graves Commission, education and supporting young women.

And after the children had grown, studied and married we moved to London in 2010, where my experience in Defence became a factor in being appointed by the Queen to the Commonwealth War Graves Commissioner, a new passion for a former History teacher, helping conserve Australia's stories of service and sacrifice.

While in London for the 2020 Olympic Games, then Governor-General, Dame Quentin Bryce, asked to meet some Australian young women living and working in London. This was the beginning of a program I created called Inspiring Women Reflect that has continued in both London and Australia since then. A highlight for me were my interviews with former Australian Prime Minister, the Hon. Julia Gillard AC at Kings College London. In all my interviews with leading women in the public and private sectors, I draw upon their experiences to crystalise key lessons for younger women on their journey to future leadership roles. In this way, I am continuing to help forge the path for our future women leaders.

My passion is now focussed on education and supporting young women. Those are my experiences. Find your passion. Have a go. Do the job. Be resilient. Move On.

* * *

The Hon. Ros Kelly AO has worked across the political, private, and not for profit sectors. Ros was a member of the Australian Government for 16 years serving as a Minister in a number of portfolios. She was the first woman ALP cabinet minister in the House of Representatives. After leaving politics, Ros worked at the interface between mining and the environment. Ros was Chair of the National Breast Cancer Foundation from 2005 to 2010 and a Director of Thiess from 1998 to 2012. Ros has recently retired as a Commissioner of the Commonwealth War Graves Commission and Chair of the Commonwealth War Graves Foundation, having joined the Commission in 2012. Ros currently serves as an advisor to Women On Boards UK. Ros was made an Officer (AO) of the Order of Australia in 2004 for services to the environment, mining, women's health and the Australian Parliament.

20. COVID-19 AND AUSTRALIA'S AGED CARE SECTOR

Diana Asmar

'Heroes on the frontline'. It's a term coined by the Health Workers Union (HWU) at the very start of this COVID pandemic in reference to our aged care workforce. Within days, politicians, journalists, and social media across the community begun labelling humble aged care employees as saviours. Heroes, I would argue, are worth far more than $23 an hour.

The HWU represents thousands of Victoria's aged care workers. Our aged care members have been at the coalface of Victoria's second wave over the Autumn and Winter months of 2020. Our hardworking personal care workers, cleaners, leisure and lifestyle workers, kitchen staff, administrative workers, laundry workers – anyone who works in an aged care facility – do not view themselves as heroes. They do this line of work because they fundamentally care for their fellow human beings. They love their elderly residents. They certainly deserve the Australian community's heartfelt thanks. But they deserve so much more than kind praise.

The crisis in Australia's aged care system has been brewing for well over a decade. Legislative change has not kept up with the exponential growth in the industry. We've known for some time that the baby boomer generation was ageing. Whilst the Hawke/Keating government's big vision of what impact this burgeoning population would have on our nation's finances, (enacting superannuation), no such foresight was provided by the Howard Government with respect to how Australia will care humanely for our elderly. The fate of our elderly was left, by and large, to the free market. Thus far, it hasn't worked out well.

Profits before people

The growth of the aged care industry has been phenomenal, particularly in the last ten years. The latest data indicates over half a million Victorians are now employed in the health sector, with an estimated 120,000 employed in the aged care sector. This figure grows daily. In 2005, aged care workers constituted 10 per cent of the HWU's membership. Today, it is approaching 50 per cent. There are now thousands of registered aged care providers in Victoria. For nearly two decades, the industry has been a license to print money. Like the pioneering days of the Ballarat gold rush in the 1850's, everyone wants a piece of the action. The industry has attracted the same cowboys – with the same dollar signs in their eyes. Profit is the name of the game, not care.

Take, for instance, mavericks like Peter and Areti Arvenitis, owners of the embattled Epping Gardens, where only two carers earning $23 an hour were on shift for over 150 residents at the height of the second wave. The Arvenitis' glitzy $12.95 million dollar Toorak mansion, recently downgraded for a $10.5 million mansion in not-so-salubrious Canterbury, boasted "Gucci in almost every room". Maserati's, Lamborghini's and a Rolls Royce fill their heated garages.

Do the maths. Over 150 residents that have had to fork out at least $550,000 to get their foot in the door at Epping Gardens. Two staff earning a pittance of an hourly rate. Now multiply their profit margins by their other facilities they own. It's a tale of greed and utter bastardry. Conditions at Epping Gardens ultimately got so bad at the height of the second Victorian wave that health authorities were forced to take control of the facility. Residents and their families have since launched a class action in the Supreme Court.

The sheer greed of Australia's aged care industry bosses is replicated across the sector. Regis Healthcare founder Bryan Dorman is estimated to be worth $459 million and ranked 233rd on *The Australian's* 250 Rich List of the year. (Mr Dorman is up $49 million on the previous year). The owners of Arcare (with over 40 aged care facilities), the Knowles family, are reportedly worth over $562 million, ranking them as the 24th richest family in Australia. The owners of Estia, with 69 homes, are worth more than $725 million. If Kerry Packer were still alive, he would have sold his media and casino empire and started his own aged care empire. The industry is well on its way to becoming Australia's billionaire factory.

That factory relies on the blood, sweat and tears of low paid workers – often migrants, and predominantly women. The average aged care worker is paid, on average, approximately $23 to $24 an hour. The HWU had to fight tooth and nail, for instance, to extract a 1.5 per cent per annum pay rise from BUPA Aged Care during its last protracted EBA negotiations. Put simply, our aged care workers are overworked and underpaid. Facilities are chronically understaffed. Workers regularly do unpaid overtime; such is their bond and level of care for their elderly residents. Their compassion is ruthlessly exploited by their employers. There is simply too much to do in a one day.

Take this excerpt from 'A Day In The Life of A Personal Carer', published recently by HWU activist members who gave formal submissions to the Aged Care Royal Commission:

7.00am – 8.15am

"I start work at 0700hr. My first responsibility is to sign on and pick up a phone. I then place the number of my phone on the board in the office, so that I can be contacted at any time. I have started to do this at 0650hr, so I am on the floor at 0700hr. After picking up my phone, I stop by the kitchenette and organise my wing's breakfast trays. I have 16 residents today in my wing, and I have to ensure that the fruit, water, Milo, and jugs are all in place. While I'm doing this the cook is doing the toast for the trays. Once all this is completed, I then proceed to wheel the trolley to my allocated area for distribution. Before I get to start them, I hear a buzzer. I check my phone, and see that it's a resident from my wing, so I leave the trolley and go to the resident. The resident has requested the toilet, and I oblige by raising the low/low *bed to a height that she can safely stand from. I then raise the head of the bed so I can assist the resident to actually sit up, as she finds this task difficult. It takes some strength from me to assist her. When she is sitting on the side of the bed, I retrieve the w/walker and commode chair for her to use to stand. I place the commode under her and then remove her underwear so she can sit on the chair. I wheel her to the bathroom, where I place the chair she is on over the toilet. I place a towel over her thighs to keep her warm and feeling dignified. Whilst helping the resident in the toilet, I'm becoming anxious about getting behind with delivering the breakys. I can't let on to the resident that I'm feeling the pressure as it will only increase her stress levels. I try to continue being relaxed and calm, and offer her a face cloth so she can freshen up. I then gather her clothes so I can dress her while on the toilet. I also ask her for her teeth and give them a brush. At this point I am grateful she is only a 'dress' because if she was a 'shower' I would have to double handle her (which means having to come back and shower her.) Once all this is done, I move her from the toilet and give her bottom a wash with a warm cloth and ensure it is dry. I then push her to her room, help her to stand with her w/walker, then pull her pants up, and straighten her clothes. I then encourage her to ambulate backwards to be able to sit in her recliner for breakfast. She is very grateful for the assistance I have given. I inform her with a smile that it's all OK.*

She then apologises about holding me up, and I once again respond with a smile, and say, "It's OK, we'll get there don't you worry." I then return to the alcove of my wing and start to prepare the trays one at a time with hot water and milk. I also grab a jug of water to take with me. As I walk around the corner with the first tray I note a few residents popping their heads out of their doors wondering where their breaky is. I announce that I have started and I will have their breakys to them asap. Some of them settle back into their rooms, and others grumble under their breath, as they retreat back into their rooms. (I stay calm, realising the majority are just curious that they haven't been forgotten).

I keep my smile on and continue to deliver the breakys. I have done two, when another resident comes out of her room. She is heading down to the dining area for her breakfast. When I realise she has dressed herself without putting on a pad (she has dementia), I stop her, ask gently if she has one on. She replies, "No I don't think so, why? Do I need one?"

I tell her it would be a good idea, and she should come with me and I will help her put it on. She is clearly annoyed but nevertheless comes with me. I then assist with her pad and encourage her to have a wash. I do her teeth, and then do her hair. She is now ready.

Once I have done that, I send her on her way to the dining area again. I wash my hands and proceed to fix her tray up, follow her down. I set her up with her breaky and return to my wing. (Every time I pass a particular room with a very high risk resident I look in to make sure he is on the bed and ok.) I'm starting to feel the pressure now, as I need to get these breakys out. I then hear moans from another resident coming from the dining area. She is in a 'princess chair' and is totally dependent on carers. She is stating she needs to go to the toilet. Realising the current pressure I'm under, I return to the dining area and place her in front of the TV, in the hope that this will distract her for a little longer."

All this by 8.15am. It paints a clear picture of the stress our aged care workers are under.

These are our people

Chronic understaffing in our facilities in the name of maximizing profits has been bubbling under the surface for many years. In 2014, the Health Workers Union launched a campaign for mandated carer/resident ratios in our aged care system. This campaign has been gaining traction, with other trade unions also jumping on board. Why is it that we have mandated carer/children ratios in our childcare centres, mandated nursing/patient ratios in Victorian public hospitals, yet no ratios exist in aged care. It defies logic. It is unacceptable. The closest we have come to resolving this issue was a private members' Bill from then-Senator Derryn Hinch, from Victoria, who took up our cause in 2018. His Bill was defeated. We never expected support from the Morrison Government. What was most disappointing was the lack of resolve (and awareness of community sentiment) from the Federal Labor Opposition at the time. Labor's Aged Care Spokesperson, Julie Collins (who remains in this role), understanding there would no doubt be a tricky cost component to this Bill, led the charge and opposed ratios. The Federal Labor Opposition voted against the Bill. They instead chose to go the last election spending $6 billion subsiding the wages of private sector childcare workers. (Clearly, that was a winner).

The issue of carer/resident ratios remains unresolved. To date, Federal Labor under Anthony Albanese has not formally committed to ratios. We've seen instead weasel words used like "minimum staffing levels". It's politico speak, yes, but some form of progress.

Change must come

Yet nothing has changed. Aged care providers continue to exploit their workforce and rip-off their residents in the name of profit. Costs are cut wherever possible. On average, residents are fed on $6 a day. One major provider, Mecwacare, was outed by the HWU in the Fair Work Commission last year for using instant mash instead of potatoes to feed their residents. Elderly Aussies are stumping up half a million to be fed prison slop.

It is little wonder the Morrison government was forced to call a Royal Commission into the industry. The Commission has unearthed systematic failures across the sector. The HWU's submission to the Commission documented shocking tales of neglect of residents caused by chronic understaffing, mistreatment of aged care workers, and grotesque conduct by employers that bordered on criminal negligence.

COVID19, however, has exposed the industry in a way that the Royal Commission could never do. It's neglect of residents, even when lives were at stake, could no longer be concealed thanks to daily media scrutiny. It's the only good thing to come from this dreaded disease.

Take for instance the issue of PPE (Protective Personal Equipment) for aged care workers. PPE – gloves, hair caps, gowns, eye wear, masks, and face shields – saves lives. It stops the transmission from aged care workers to vulnerable elderly residents.

Having adequate and sufficient PPE for aged care workers would have saved hundreds of lives during Victoria's second COVID wave. Since March 2020, the HWU had called on the Commonwealth and Victorian Government's to work together to ensure strict protocols in place for PPE (and provide sufficient quantities), particularly in our aged care sector. We knew from mortality data in New York that the virus would have its deadliest impact in aged care facilities.

We also know, from bitter experience, that the aged care sector would have to be dragged kicking and screaming to provide PPE for their workforce, especially if they had to purchase it. PPE costs employer's money. The industry simply could not be trusted to do the right thing, even if it meant saving elderly lives.

The ineptitude of Federal Aged Care Minister Richard Colebeck and then Victorian Health Minister Jenny Mikakos (both emblematic but not the sole cause of this problem), by not planning for adequate PPE across the aged care sector, and by not coordinating an effective response, have cost hundreds of lives and damaged the livelihoods of hundreds of thousands of Victorians. Instead or taking responsibility for this shambolic mess, we saw politicians opting to play the blame game instead. The real culprits, however, are the unscrupulous owners of our aged care facilities.

Throughout Victoria's second wave, it was HWU protocol to call all members at a worksite if there was a COVID outbreak. Our members are best placed to tell the world what was really going on. Time and again, be it at St Basil's Aged Care in Fawkner, Epping Gardens Heritage Care, or Baptcare Wyndham Lodge, we heard the same old story. Employers refused to provide their workforce with adequate PPE. Employers rationed out twenty cent masks. Employers only gave their workers PPE after there was a COVID diagnosis within the facility. All too little, too late. The one recurring theme – money. Employers were more concerned about the cost of PPE than the safety of their staff and residents. The safety of the broader community was the last thing on their minds.

Tales like this suggest the aged care industry is doomed. But there are solutions to fix this industry. There is hope for aged care workers. The Aged Care Royal Commission has made a series or preliminary recommendations to the Federal Government. Central to reform of this industry is the treatment of its workforce. Adequately staffed facilities and better trained and better remunerated workers comes at a cost. In November, the Federal Branch of the Health Services Union advocated a substantial increase to the Medicare levy to pay for industry reform. Some leftists would even like to see the nationalisation of the industry all-together. It remains to be seen whether the broader Australian community would stomach such measures, and whether putting the cost back on to Australian taxpayers is politically viable. History shows that simply throwing government money at the sector always seems to be syphoned at the top end, not ending up on frontline care.

The Gillard Government's subsidisation of childcare workers with government money, much like Federal Labor's attitude to the setting of paid maternity leave using the minimum wage and paying it as welfare, exposes the vacuum that Labor's Right has left. The childcare and maternity approaches utilise government funding and welfare, through 'churn', as the answer – taxes paying for government spending. However, this is not the answer. Rather the free market vagaries of the aged care system should be reduced through union action and the increase of wages as a share of profits, with regulation and legislation both enabling this and requiring better ratios of patient care; in other words, more workers on the job and better pay for those workers.

For now, let's hope to see a legislative framework around staffing levels, stricter rules for accreditation to help weed out dodgy industry cowboys, and the adoption of key recommendations from the Aged Care Royal Commission. Real, lasting reform, however, won't come from governments. It won't come from changing community sentiment. And it certainly won't come from aged care industry providers. It will *only* come from aged care workers themselves. *Only* when aged care workers have had enough of being used and abused, *only* when they finally unite, *en masse*, by joining their trade union, will we see real and lasting reform. The HWU won't stop fighting for these frontline heroes.

* * *

Diana Asmar has been Secretary of the Health Workers Union (HWU) since 2012. The HWU is the biggest branch of the Health Services Union in Victoria. With over 16,000 members, the HWU represents aged care workers, hospital workers, pathology workers, and disability workers. Diana Asmar is a former pathology collector and laboratory assistant, having worked at Royal Melbourne Hospital, Northern Hospital, Sunshine Hospital and Melbourne Rehabilitation Centre. Since 2012, Diana has worked tirelessly to rebuild the union in conjunction with grassroots members and delegates. With HWU coverage of over 400 enterprise agreements, Diana's focus for the union has been to negotiate better pay and conditions for Victoria's low paid health workers, as well as providing growth, financial stability and respect for the union. Diana is a mother of two.

21. Small Business and Labor: Finding Common Ground

Deborah O'Neill

Personal encounter

My Irish-born parents were already economic emigrants before they chose to head to Australia. They met in Manchester. They couldn't see an opportunity filled future there in England for them, so in 1960 they set sail for Australia as '10 Pound Poms', a bit of an identity problem really seeing as they were Irish Nationalists. Nonetheless, they had bought the messaging of the land of opportunity at Australia House in Manchester and the images of washing drying in the sun in your own back yard were the ones that sealed the deal for my Mum who prayed for love and babies, in that order, all through her adolescence. Jim and Mary arrived in Australia with barely any money in hand but a lot of hope in their hearts. Well-founded hope it turned out, as they got jobs within their first week in Sydney: Dad as a brickie's labourer for six weeks before moving into his role as a plant operator for G.H. Thomas, then Arthur Baxter (later ABAX) and later Abignano (the forerunner of today's Abigroup); Mum in a factory in Rydalmere until I came along when she stopped working to stay home and look after me. They scrimped and they saved, including a stint in a caravan in the backyard of the lovely Iris and Neville Wootton of Toongabbie. Mum and Dad bought their first home, a three-bedroom fibro place, in Curran St, Blacktown. Within five years they had done it – achieved the great Australian dream of buying your own home. Life was settled; at the edge of civilisation according to their many Irish friends in Sydney but settled. They had three kids, the washing flapped on the line just like the promo they'd seen in Manchester – and then they did something extraordinary, they decided to sell the house to buy a backhoe front end loader and start their own business.

It was a gutsy move – it turned out to be a great move. But why did they do it? Indeed, why do so many Australians born here or those who settle here from overseas do it? And why is knowing the answer to that question vital for Labor?

Why does anyone start their own business?

Bill Shorten in his 2016 book *For the Common Good* captures the employment context of the day: "Since I started work, factories that employed thousands of people have been flattened or converted into apartments. Manufacturing jobs that gave people straight out of high school predictable, stable and reasonable incomes have been erased from the landscape. Our steel industry is at a dangerous tipping point. Service industry jobs have been undermined by increasing casualisation, automation and contracting".

It's a pretty confronting description of the reality driven by what Bill called 'seismic economic and technological changes." The harsh reality of the vulnerability of all workers, despite the extraordinary and successful advocacy of our unions, has only become more apparent in recent times. Workplace mental ill-health claims are reaching unprecedented levels from injury suffered in workplaces that have become dangerously toxic. What will Australian workers do? Maybe in this context starting your own micro business is a form of self-care, an act of resistance to the feeling of vulnerability. Are business starters simply creatively responding to the threats of the workplaces of our times and choosing to make their own worlds of work?

Reid Hoffman, founder of LinkedIn is reported as saying: "All humans are entrepreneurs not because they should start companies but because the will to create is encoded in human DNA." It's an interesting idea, that business is about creativity. Maybe it might help Labor to look at it that way – that business makers are creatively responding to the challenges of their current working lives and rejecting old notions of working, of workplaces, of the roles and rights of bosses and workers, rejecting the combative nature of workplace relations and opting out of workplace power relations in search of agency and security in a world awash with change and uncertainty. In short "I might succeed, I might fail – but at least I'll be in control, and I can creatively respond in my own way and my own time the challenges that arise". In my view, that is particularly the case with the owner of micro-businesses. If they keep it small enough, they can indeed control the workplace culture to align with their own values and the life they want to live. But what do we, as Labor people really know about the motivations and daily realities of small business owners? How many of small business owners 'live' amongst us?

In a time of declining unionism, with increasing job insecurity, ongoing reports of workplace bullying, harassment and performativity pressures it really isn't so surprising that the possibility of being a sole trader or owner of a micro business or even the boss of an SME where you get control of your workplace becomes increasingly alluring. There is the sacrifice of no regular pay-cheque but if it means there is no regular bullying, that might be a trade-off working making. The world is changing at a rapid pace – it's no surprise really that people would seek the sense of control over their work habits, movements and interactions each day that owning your own business can bring. Further, there is the increasing perception of a wealth gap developing between many employed workers with PAYG obligations and business owners of similar age and education status who have the capacity to offset costs of running a home office and business vehicle when tax time comes around.

In 2017 Suncorp released a report of the top 10 reasons cited by Australians who took the plunge and started their own business. The number one reported reason by just over half the sample was the desire to be their own boss. Other high rating factors were the opportunity to do what you're passionate about, the find a better work-life balance, to take greater control of your life, to be in control of who you work with, spend more time with family and to take on a personal challenge. Money was not the primary driver, neither was the arrival of a great idea for a product or service with only 14 per cent of respondents declaring innovation as their motivator.

Slightly different, but similar results, emerged in a survey of 1000 Australians asked about their job satisfaction and plans for their career in 2020, by GoDaddy between 19-28 December, 2019 and reported in *My Business* 20 January 2020. The demographic found most likely to follow their entrepreneurial dreams were the 18-29-year-old cohort of whom 48 per cent were looking for a more flexible career offered in their own business. 35 per cent were motivated by the possibility of making more money, 30 per cent by the possibility of improved work/life balance and 17 per cent declared they wanted to pursue their passions in their own business. The survey also revealed some gender differences with men more likely to feel dissatisfied with their job (41 per cent) than women (36 per cent).

The rise and rise of ABN's

The surveys cited here reflect the reality that Labor has always known that the work you do is about so much more than the money you earn. So, if we know that work is about personal satisfaction, about who you are and how you want to live – why do we have such difficulty in being seen as the natural party of choice for the entrepreneur. It is clear to anyone who takes the time to talk to the local owner operator of your favourite new café, your self-employed painter, your accountant or your lawn mowing provider, the local computer repair business or even your financial advisor, that much of the journey of these business owners is about meaningful work, personal identity and their sense of their own capacity to control their world of work in the community they know. Not so the Deliveroo rider or cleaner – but that is a whole other discussion. But whether disgruntled or delighted in their small business experience, one pressing question lingers for me: how have we so completely allowed the Liberal Party to colonise an entire section of the Australian populace, who upon acquiring and ABN think they are somehow obliged then to vote Liberal? The same preference for Liberal governments dominates most of the peak bodies that claim to represent millions of Australians who self-employ.

There are now almost 8 million active ABNs in Australia today. I wonder how many of those ABN holders will still have a business or the same business when this is Covid-19 crisis is over. And only time will tell if there will there be more ABN holders in the future as people respond to newly found unemployment by trying to create their own job. Perhaps there will there be fewer ABN's as businesses close? Time will tell but one thing is certain, there will still be millions of them and currently far too many of them think that Labor has nothing of value to say to them while we speak to ourselves in our own dialect and wonder (too often quite arrogantly and judgementally) at how they vote against their own self-interest?

Perhaps some insight into why we have such a problem with our engagement with small business Australia can be gleaned from the insights of Melinda Gates.

Along with her extraordinary life partner Bill, this power couple has transformed health outcomes across the world and engaged communities to act in self interest in ways previously never attempted, let alone achieved. In her 2019 book *The Moment of Lift*, she writes, "If you don't understand the meaning and beliefs behind a community's practices, you won't present your idea in the context of their values and concerns, and people won't hear you." Is that our problem? Are we adrift in a policy making frenzy totally untethered from the beliefs and actual practices of all those ABN holders? Or put another way, are we as Labor so culturally disconnected from their world that we are speaking a language unintelligible to them?

What are the beliefs and practices of the small business community?

In Kincumber, on the NSW Central Coast in the once Labor seat of Robertson, during the 2019 federal election, I saw the sons and daughters of the Labor voting parents who had brought their kids up on the Central Coast turn out to vote against us. Some silently, but many stridently making it clear in a myriad of ways, that we were not worthy of their vote. I've never felt that level of disdain for our party.

They rolled up in their late model sign written Hilux utes, men in high vis, tradies alone on the way home from a job, and others like them with wives in hospital scrubs and kids rollicking around their feet. They walked on by our loyal Labor booth workers and we got smashed.

Our policy offerings, by our own reckoning, supported small business. We are the ones who established the instant asset tax write off, the loss carry back policy, the support for R& D. Yet, they voted against us. We know we are the champions of Medicare and we are perhaps a little arrogant in our presumption that health professionals will vote for us. Yet, they voted against us. And for those kids who trotted past us swinging off their Mum's and Dad's arms and legs we had $14 billion to invest in schools. Still, they voted against us. Something has got to change. We have got to change. We have got to actually understand and engage with interest and humility with those ABN holders whose beliefs and practices we clearly didn't register or understand. Perhaps our presumptions and hubris overrode their concerns, as was detected post-election with other notable constituencies... We need to learn to better comprehend and talk 'tradie', to talk SME, to talk microbusiness and mum and dad partnership. We have first, before we talk, before we pontificate to, listen to what they have to say, to tap into the cultural and identity elements of what makes small business owners and their staff actually tick and slowly build relationships of mutual respect and trust in context specific ways in every seat across the country.

Melinda Gates, offers another important insight, the concept of 'empathy barriers' which might help explain what it is that has kept us from the necessary levels of trust to support engagement in the first instance and to engender support further down the line. She argues that well intentioned outsiders approach some communities insufficiently aware of the inculturation practices of that community. No amount of good intent will make up the ground when there is insufficient empathy with the community being approached, hence the empathy barrier.

I think we might have more than a barrier, I think it more like a large brick wall. Not quite like the one of Berlin fame – but something akin to it. We want and need small business owners to change their voting behaviour, to rethink the option of Labor because we think, no, we 'know' what we have to offer them in government will be good for them in business and also good for their family, their employees, for national sovereignty, for our environment and good for our economy. We come to them with good intention, but our intention is not enough. Changing minds and votes of an entire constituency is only possible if we actually show real and deep understanding of why the people in small business do things the way they do. Have we, in all honesty, prioritised small business in our language, our level of ongoing engagement, in our research, in our recruitment into our branches and onto our policy making committees, and have we proudly and deliberately brought small businesses into our parliamentary ranks. I have no doubt that our foes have done exactly that, and they've just about totally convinced the whole sector that we are anti-small business. It's not true – but it's a myth with currency and favour.

What I know from my own immersion in small business

Somewhere between the age of 11 and 12 it came to my attention that my mother was sending out invoices for the family business in handwriting. She was putting forward quotations for work in the plant hire, drainage and road construction business she administered and partnered in with my father, in handwriting. With all the experience and outrage of an 11-year-old, I told her that it was an unsatisfactory practice and didn't meet the professional standards of the time. Like the good business-owner she was, she took note of what I said, and for Christmas that year I received a portable typewriter and an instruction book on how to touch type. There began my close encounter with 'our' family business. I did all the typing of course, but I also got to see and share in the tidal movements of the business over the next 11 years until I left home. Today, young people across the nation are honing their skills and capacities in their own parents' businesses, solving problems, helping out and even those not doing anything are watching and learning. Some will take on those family businesses, but all will take the good and the bad experiences of being part of a small business with them into their futures. Such knowledge is a remarkable asset to those bizkids who face a profoundly changing world.

Being a part of the family business was a formative experience. I saw my Irish immigrant parent's endeavour, their sacrifice, the risk, the pride, the achievement, the pressure, the care for their workforce, the flexibility, the debt, the late payments, the community contribution and the hours they invested in keeping the business afloat, innovating, adjusting to the market conditions, seeking out new work and in the midst of all that raising six kids, building a community BMX track, washing, cooking, shopping, cleaning, looking after sick kids and in the middle of all that taking us all on a trip to the 'auld' country. That tumultuous mix is life in a family business, so much of it blended, the life bits and the business bits intertwined. That was part of its appeal and part of its cost. There was flexibility built in, to work around the rhythms of family life and balancing that out there were the ill-timed and unpredictable demands placed on family time necessary to deal with the impact of wet weather, equipment failure or job completion timing necessities.

Like so many immersive experiences, those who've lived it know it but don't necessarily voice it to 'others'. Small businesspeople speak small business to one another but seem to have decided we don't speak their language. Valiant efforts by senior shadow ministers to bridge the gap must be applauded – but they cannot do the work of an entire movement that seeks to govern for all but is not talking with some. It will take a far more pragmatic, sociologically informed, culturally aware, long term, language rich, empathic and ongoing engagement with small business by Labor before we understand what it is that they need from us to overcome the empathy barriers we have built up over the last three decades. Until we do that and move to heal our relationship with the diversity of small business, until we build and grow our connections based on trust and ongoing mutual respect, we won't be in the business of winning elections.

* * *

Senator Deborah O'Neill is a Labor Senator for NSW, a position she has held since 2013. Before then she held the nation's bellwether seat of Robertson on the Central Coast in the Gillard and Second Rudd Governments. She is the current Chair of the Senate Privileges Committee, Junior Vice-President of NSW Labor and Deputy Co-Chair of the ALP's National Policy Forum. She is active in the policy areas of small business, finance and corporations, women's rights, education, and industrial relations. Prior to entering Federal Parliament, Senator O'Neill was a high school teacher on the Central Coast for the best part of two decades. She lectured in the School of Education at the University of Newcastle, where she co-ordinated courses in teacher education. She lives on the Central Coast with her husband Paul, three wonderful children and a dog, Einstein.

22. Faithful and Labor: What Labor Ignores at its Peril

Michael Easson

The history of the ALP at the national level is one long lesson in humility. More often defeated than victorious, glorious in government but only in retrospect. This is our party. The thirteen-year golden era of Hawke and Keating between 1983 and 1996 created Medicare and universal, compulsory superannuation; broke the back of inflation; set the economy up for a quarter century of continuous economic growth; changed Australia for the better. At the same time as those governments fought to earn credibility and support, enthusiasm waxed and waned within the wider labour movement.

The battles of the 1980s onwards are different from what we face today, but several constant threads remain. The margin of electoral victory in Australia is usually close; landslides are few, especially for us. Labor only ever wins by creating a coalition of voters, not just believers, *voters* – people who decide at an election to give Labor a majority in the House of Representatives.

Maximising Labor support means building the widest coalition of voters possible. That requires garnering a majority from an electorate of conservative disposition. In every winning combination are voters who are traditional, conservative in some things, interested in Labor reforms, but far from rusted-on radicals. To see in a publication on the future of the labour movement insistence on a conservative tinge to the Labor constituency might be surprising. But bear with me. Labor ignores this reality at its peril.

The Burkean tradition

Separately, in an essay on '[Edmund] Burke and Australian Labor' in a book *The Market's Morals* (2020), I argue that Australian Labor is non-revolutionary, reformist; a party that historically respects its history and traditions, and sees progress in an evolutionary sense. In referencing the Burkean character of Labor, this is not a call for Labor to abandon its best radical instincts. In part, it is a plea to understand our history, electoral politics, and what needs to be done to win.

From the historical record, Labor's appeal has long extended to faith communities. Indeed, any account of the pioneers in the movement, and of many thousands since, shows the inspiration of faith. As Bolton observes in *Protestantism and Social Reform in New South Wales 1890-1910*:

> A Protestant radicalism went into the making of the Labor Party. It was not just that some radicals were Protestants – they had a Protestant sensitivity to conscience and to brotherhood. Bible reading had been part of their political education, and a people healed of divisions and true to the moral law was what they hoped for from reform.

Gary Dorrien in his comprehensive study *Social Democracy in the Making. Political & Religious Roots of European Socialism* (2019) notes that in the UK: "Christian socialism and socialism were ethical, pragmatic, liberal, non-Marxist, culturally British, not very ideological, and thus exceptional." Similar observations can be made about Australia. The Bible and Ruskin's *Unto This Last* (1860) on labour's place in the political economy, as Stiles argues in his 2010 PhD thesis 'Reading Ruskin', were more influential than Marx in the early formation of Australian Labor. Lay preacher and co-founder of the Australian Workers' Union, William Spence, saw unity in the temporal and spiritual worlds: "The New Unionism is simply the teachings of that greatest of all social reformers, Him of Nazareth, whom all must revere." In one of his columns in *The Worker* newspaper in July 1896, he wrote: "Labor has a most sacred mission and should rise above all petty things. It seeks to secure justice for all who dwell in the land. It seeks to govern and has for the first time brought into politics aims and aspirations which are worth fighting for." Fisher and Scullin were steeped in Presbyterianism and Catholicism respectively and drew inspiration from heaven and about what to do on earth. Curtin, an agnostic, frequently deployed religious language. Most prominently, Chifley's "Light on the Hill" was an allusion to a new Jerusalem. In contemporary decades, several of Labor's most prominent agnostics, Whitlam and Hawke, knew their Bible and often couched their rhetoric in Christian-inspired terms.

A constant tension

There is a constant tension between the party as a generator of ideas, and radical reforms, and keeping the flame alight in the hearts of those who (once were and) should be sympathetic to Labor. Nearly sixty years ago the British Labour politician and intellectual Anthony Crosland in *The Conservative Enemy* regretted that the traditional Labor Right "still lacks a truly radical appeal and often seems insular, class-oriented, conservative and middle aged." He saw that the traditional 'Left' were more conservative in a pernicious way: "clinging to outdated semi-Marxist analysis of society in terms of ownership." He was reflecting on the UK, but his points applied here too.

No Labor thinker cherishes a movement which is slack in the development of policy, lazy and complacent. Whitlam, speaking in 1997 at the launch of the Trade Union Education Foundation, remarked just how tough it was to get the party to think and act creatively on policy before the late 1960s. He said:

> The rewriting of the Platform at the 1969 Conference was the culmination of a process which had taken place against the background of the electoral debacle of 1966. It brought to an end the stultification of policy-making engendered by the 1949 defeat and worsened by the Split. The Party appeared to become obsessed with the idea that rather than bring about renewal for the future, its purpose was to revisit past successes – not renovation but mere restoration. Exhausting its energies in epic but sterile factional battles, the Party stagnated, and the platform was stultified.

He went on to say:

> The important thing … is to recognise that those post-1949
> failures were not inevitable, any more than, I believe, the
> Split itself was inevitable. In particular, the High Court's
> invalidation of bank nationalisation in 1946, instead of being
> a challenge to new thinking became an excuse for avoiding
> it. Health and education policies were notable casualties.
> The platform called for the nationalisation of health; the
> High Court had ruled against nationalisation; the party
> spokesmen relieved themselves of the obligation to develop
> a Labor alternative.

Many of the Whitlam government reforms, including Medibank
(the precursor of Medicare, introduced by Hawke, after the Fraser
government emasculated the Whitlam/Hayden health reforms) were
inspired by work done in opposition. Canada presented a national
model of health insurance in the early 1970s, but what eventually
emerged was a scheme with Australian characteristics. Similarly, as
Hayden proved, policy development and innovation in the opposition
years during the Fraser government was vital and the basis for many
of the successes of the Hawke/Keating period. It is interesting that
in cultivating policy overhaul and practical action, there is a long
history within the ALP of seeing the state as the *facilitator* of change,
of betterment, rather than championing a powerful state in and of
itself.

There needs to be the distinction drawn between conservatism
in policy formulation, and the pitch to traditional voters who have
always formed an important part of Labor's base. But even here too
much can be made of the contrast. There is sense in policy renovation
and ingenuity and contemporaneously understanding and respecting
history; regeneration with a perspective of the best of a tradition is
the art of good Labor politics.

As for potential elements of a broad Labor coalition, noticeably
many Christians believe they are 'forgotten' by our political class,
sense that they lack political agency, providing fertile ground for

conservatives to appeal, so that they feel heard and empowered. But Labor also can see such people as part of a potential coalition. This core idea undergirds this essay's argument.

George F. Will suggests in *The Conservative Sensibility*: "A sensibility is more than an attitude but less than an agenda, less than a pragmatic response to the challenge of comprehensively reforming society in general." And goes on to ascribe some vague ideas as to what this might mean:

> The conservative sensibility... is a perpetually unfolding response to real situations that require statesmanship – the application of general principles to untidy realities... The conservative sensibility is relevant to all times and places, but it is lived and revealed locally, in the conversation of a specific polity... revealed in practices.

The idea of a sensibility that is cautious, careful, considerate, cooperative, is reminiscent of what it means to be Labor in Australia. For over a century, the conservative temperament, much to the chagrin of socialists, has mostly dominated Labor's behaviour and actions, of what *being* Labor entails.

In the UK, there is the recent debate about "Blue Labour v. New Labour", a respectful nod to George Orwell's *Road to Wigan Pier* critique of out-of-touch, doctrinaire socialists, repulsive to many workers. This is an interesting debate in the UK, but there are too many qualifications to make in saying how applicable this would be to Australia. Besides, in Australia, hardly anyone wants to stay working class. Interestingly, one of the Australian polity's greatest successes is in forming and sustaining what is arguably the largest, most stable middle class in any western liberal democratic society.

In the Labor coalition, there needs to be space for conservatives on economic, political, and social issues. All parties are coalitions; every person is a mix of thinking, feelings, outlooks, with cultural, religious, and tribal affiliations. Few people are one-dimensional; most of us are multitudes. Many of us are liberal on social matters, conservatives on fiscal issues, and mixed economy social democrats on others – and combinations betwixt and between. The temper of mind, recognition of the complex mix of ideas and feelings, their connexions with each other, their distinct operation side-by-side, the need to understand practice in terms of such relations, and to conduct politics with attention to habitual linkages amongst people's ideas and activities, suggest the required sort of thinking.

People of faith, particularly Christians, believe that life is sacred (for many, from conception), that no man is an island (we belong to and are sustained by a community), and live by the golden rule: In the language of the Jerusalem Bible's Matthew 25:40. "...in so far as you did this to one of the least of these brothers of mine, you did it to me." How we treat others is indicative of our moral worth. How a people treat disadvantage is indicative of any moral assessment of society and its agents, including government. In any such appraisal, there are of course many overlaps between contending positions and nuances to be considered with economics, particular measures, and administration, as well as that powerful motivation: moral indignation.

The main point to make here is that this religious outlook is completely compatible with Labor and social democratic ideals. Showing people of faith that the ALP is not a hostile, anti-religious secular, disdainful force means recovering an understanding of where we came from, our history, the best of our tradition, and to win. In 1962 at a Socialist International Conference in Oslo a resolution was adopted that championed principles that Christians, social democrats, labourists and democratic socialists could all live with:

> We democratic Socialists proclaim our conviction that the ultimate aim of political activity is the fullest development of every human personality, that liberty and democratic self-government are precious rights which must not be surrendered; that every individual is entitled to equal status, consideration and opportunity; that discrimination

on grounds of race, colour, nationality, creed or sex must be opposed; that the community must ensure that material resources are used for the common good rather than the enrichment of the few; above all, that freedom and equality and prosperity are not alternatives between which the people must choose but ideals which can be achieved and enjoyed together.

Everything here is compatible with the pithy summary, offered earlier, on how most Christians see themselves.

Major challenges

But any serious observer of the party admits a series of issues and real problems with this summary. The party faces ideological, attitudinal, and stylistic challenges in winning over support, and calming suspicion. Admittedly, Australian Labor is now overwhelmingly secular; but so too is Australia. Sometimes leaders of deep religious faith emerge – more frequently in politics than in the wider society. Think of the evangelical Anglicanism and schooling in Catholic social teaching of Rudd; the muscular Catholicism of Abbott; the quiet, subdued religious outlook of Catholic convert Turnbull; the Pentecostal sympathies of Scott Morrison. Of Opposition Labor Leaders, in recent memory there was the Anglo-Catholic Beazley and the Presbyterian Crean, and the atheism of Latham and Gillard. The latter said that Methodism was an important, continuing influence. Gillard respected difference and faith, which is why she wrestled so long with various moral issues and the appropriate Labor stance. Latham was less constrained, unsubtle, sometimes contemptuous of the religious, but he never argued for abolishing the conscience vote. (Interestingly, in his current manifestation as a Pauline Hanson NSW state MP, he is championing religious freedom protections. Latham has an eye to appealing to voters, particularly in western Sydney.)

Bill Shorten's Jesuit education was important to his political evolution (even as he migrated to Anglicanism.) Yet under this right-wing Labor Leader, the conscience vote (for MPs and members on life, faith, and morals) was in jeopardy. At the 2015 National ALP Conference, in the rush to conform to constantly changing social attitudes and the mood of "give me identity politics or give me death", Labor adopted a hard-line position on same-sex marriage, intolerant of the 20 per cent of traditional supporters with more conservative views. The resolution foreshadowed that the right to a conscience vote would be "rescinded upon the commencement of the 46th parliament." What once might have been considered mainstream among Labor supporters was excised. The party resolved that there would be a sunset clause on conscience on this issue. There was resentment at then Prime Minister Abbott's refusal to offer a conscience vote and parliamentary debate to his MPs. I am glad, following the plebiscite in 2016, that this debate is over, never to be revisited.

In 2019, under Albanese, a liberal, non-practising Catholic, Labor swung back to emphasising the importance of the conscience vote. This is very important to evangelicals, Church-going Catholics, and other faiths who suspect Labor is hostile to their beliefs. Perhaps "Albo" realised that the way things were going, there would be no place in the party for his beloved mother, who brought him up to believe in the Church, Labor, and the Rabbitohs. Andrew West, the host of the Religion & Ethics Report on the ABC's Radio National, perceptively writes on the fractured relationship between Labor and religious voters, not just Christians. In a piece on 'How Religious Voters Lost Faith in Labor: Lessons from the 2019 Federal Election', he asks: "How, then, should Labor begin its dialogue with faith communities?" and answers:

> At very least, with sincerity, accepting the right of religious Australians to maintain their values, no matter how unfashionable they may seem to the cultural left that influences modern Labor. They must not present conservative Christians with false moral choices. They mustn't confuse conservative Christians with political conservatives. Above all, they must not make faith communities choose between Labor and the God they worship.

One example to ponder is that of Dr Dick Klugman (1924-2011), Federal Labor MP for Prospect, 1969-90, founder of the NSW Council for Civil Liberties, a member of the Humanist Society, who supported a morally liberal agenda, but saw the other side. In a parliamentary debate in March 1979 on the funding of terminations of pregnancies, he said:

> ... the general attitude on termination of pregnancy depends completely on one's assumption or otherwise that a foetus becomes a human being at the time of conception; that is an important point ... That is why I state my belief. I do not believe that this happens but, at the same time, I do believe that there is a continuum from the time of conception to the time of birth and that the foetus is closer to a human being than, say, the whales about which people are becoming very excited at the present time. I do believe that there is something more to a human foetus, even at one month or two months' gestation, than there is to whales about which we are supposed to get very excited because they have brains approaching those of intelligent dogs, or something like that.

Knowing that someone understands your position, disagrees, but strongly appreciates where you are coming from, and respects the moral coherence of your viewpoint, is one response. The attitudinal problem is this: the higher the level of education, the lower religious observance and, usually, the greater the intellectual snobbishness towards and about those who practice. This is reflected in the put downs too often heard: that people who seek spiritual understanding and meaning through faith are stupid and/or otherwise contemptible. An article by former WA Labor MLC Bill Leadbetter in *The Toscin* directly addresses this topic.

Throughout its history, the NSW party was leavened with believers and others respectful of belief, people of faith and Labor traditions, both in the leadership, as well as the membership. The ennui of 'anything goes' and 'whatever it takes' amorality of more recent years coarsened and devalued a rich legacy. In addressing the issues considered in this essay, Labor needs to appreciate and re-engage with its 'lost' supporters. The problem with modern identity politics is its impoverishment of imagination. Sometimes, choices need to be made, whether to be broadly inclusive or narrow and exclusive in focus.

In the formulation of progressive, 'Labor' positions, an overly militant position can be struck. For example, with the hugely commendable push to get more women elected to parliament, representing Labor, Emily's List Australia, an offshoot of an American initiative, has won support across the factions. Most Labor women MPs are members. Its website prescribes a pro-choice agenda noting: "Women are a diverse group and considering the needs of all kinds of women is essential." Commendably an effort is made to suggest that being pro-choice does not necessarily mean a pro-abortion position. A 1999 quote from Hillary Clinton is featured:

> I have met thousands and thousands of pro-choice men and women. I have never met anyone who is pro-abortion. Being pro-choice is not being pro-abortion. Being pro-choice is trusting the individual to make the right decision for herself and her family, and not entrusting that decision to anyone wearing the authority of government in any regard.

But this is only a half-hearted effort at inclusion. The 'SDA women', the female Labor parliamentarians who mostly hold to more critical positions on, say, late term abortions, and the utility of counselling for women considering abortions, who are members of or loosely aligned with the Shop Distributive and Allied Employees' Union (the SDA), are not members of Emily's List and are opposed in pre-selections by it. The more liberal position has won in parliaments across Australia on this issue. In Queensland in 2018 on an abortion Bill, the entire parliamentary Labor caucus was "whipped" to vote for "reform". If Labor wants to appeal to a broader constituency, however, a little tolerance could go a long way. Unless, in the alternative, exclusion of the seriously faithful is part and parcel of a wider agenda.

The argument here brings to mind the debate in US Democrat

circles, where there is almost no space left in the party for pro-life Democrats. Why make it so difficult for some people of sincere faith, uncomfortable with the hard-nosed capitalism and mean-spirited individualism of the right, to support the party with the more generous vision of mutual social obligation? More broadly, in allowing the issues of the cultural (rather than economic) left to define membership of the party, this does not allow those who would like to be supporters on other grounds to do so; in fact they are actively rejected as fellow travellers. The Democrats have much to answer for. So many people of faith and the "deplorables" felt shunned and were herded into the arms of someone as odious as Trump.

Generally, it would help if all Labor MPs and candidates were curious about and respected their fellow Australians. The best are. In visiting and getting to know the interesting, historic, Assyrian Christian communities in Australia, for example, it is not just a matter of enjoying dolma, grape leaves, Assyrian maza, burek, and their popular garnishes. What they believe in is also fascinating. You cannot appreciate multiculturalism fully unless you respect religious diversity. Religion is central to most cultures, particularly interestingly with the 'enduring nations', the Greeks and Jewish people. It is interesting, in this context, that the drafter of multicultural policies in the Australian Department of Immigration in the early 1970s during the Whitlam administration, James "Jim" Houston, was religiously inspired. (He later became an Anglican minister in the Melbourne Archdiocese.) Of related interest, Stuart Piggin and Robert D. Linder in their impressively researched book, *Attending to the National Soul. Evangelical Christians in Australian History 1914-2014* (2020), argue that existing and new churches in the evangelical and Pentecostal traditions have obligations to not only worship Our Lord, but to take social justice seriously: "To survive and thrive in a secular context, local churches must be Jesus-centred, Bible-based, and imaginatively led. For denominations as a whole, two more ingredients must be added: social concern and ministries to people of non-English speaking backgrounds in this most multicultural of nations." If Labor cannot grasp opportunity in those words on "social concern", then heaven help us.

Respect, please

If anti-Catholicism is the anti-Semitism of the intellectuals, as Peter Viereck once remarked, evangelical, and Pentecostal dispositions are even more hostilely regarded. If we define certain religious temperaments as weird or wacko, it is unlikely that truly, deep, warm bonds of affection can be established. Those Australians of Islamic faith enrich our culture and do much good. If Muslim voters, however, are unscrupulously regarded merely as recruitment opportunities for whipping up anti-Israel sentiment in the ALP, their valuable place in our society is disrespected. There is only one thing worse than intolerance – condescension. Give me respect please. Alleluia.

Labor not only has its problems with evangelicals. There has been a long 70-year seepage of the Labor vote among Catholics. As O'Farrell says in his *The Catholic Church and Community in Australia. A History* (1977), during the Church divisions during and after the ALP Split in the mid-1950s:

> The Sydney opinion was that the DLP with its strong Catholic complexion verged on being a church party, representing a stupid and deleterious isolation of the Catholic body from the rest of the Australian community. The Melbourne view was that the ALP was past redemption ... The ALP must be opposed from outside, until it came to its senses.

A consequence, however, of the Split was rising anti-Catholic sectarianism in sections of the party. Before the NSW government fell in 1965, under pain of expulsion and further Federal intervention, the NSW Labor administration was ordered by the Left-dominated ALP national executive to cease matching Commonwealth government funding for 'science blocks' at non-government schools and any other form of state aid. Though small in numbers, the DLP waged an effective campaign in the NSW Catholic community to narrowly tip the balance; the Askin Liberal government was elected with a majority of one seat. Only under Whitlam's leadership of the ALP, post Calwell's retirement in 1967, did the party support state aid to needy schools. One consequence of the 1965 NSW state election defeat was that 'fortress NSW' was no longer an option. The NSW Right saw that the party nationally had to change. Whitlam was the person to lead reforms of the party's policies and its constitution. Labor had to appeal beyond its working-class base to the middle class.

In NSW, in the late '50s and '60s, the Left campaigned against the Paulian Society, a Catholic lay organisation in NSW, as they correctly saw them as a potential recruitment and formation organisation of Catholics in the ALP. The Left falsely claimed that the grouping was inspired by Santamaria. Evidently, for reasons I have not researched, the matter having been decided before my time, the Paulian Society was wound up. The Society of the Legion of Mary, the St Vincent de Paul Society, and others, were once rich recruitment fields. As Paul Keating can attest, his family and supporters actively mined this source of membership for the party, for winning pre-selection for Blaxland in 1969. This was not sinister. People with a practical interest in social justice can see that the Australian Labor Party is compatible with their beliefs.

Susan Ryan (1942-2020), responsible for one of Labor's great reforms, the *Sex Discrimination Act* 1984, a fighter for justice and women's rights if ever there was one, deeply appreciated working on the same Labor team as Deputy Prime Minister Lionel Bowen (1922-2012), a Catholic conservative on many moral issues, who thought being a Christian required making society profoundly face up to addressing need, respect, and the dignity of all. They knew they fought for the good, the same side, even if on certain matters they furiously, if respectfully disagreed. When Pope John Paul II met the Australian Cabinet in 1986, Kim Beazley remembers: "All agreed to shake his hand. But the nuns still had a grip on Sue who dropped to her knees and kissed his hand. She was always grateful to many of the nuns who taught her." In any Australian Labor caucus, we need more Ryans and more Bowens.

In a tribute to the former shoppies' union official and Labor state MP, Johno Johnson (1930-2017), Rodney Cavalier wrote that there would never be another Johno because those types no longer belong. He did not say that out of any malice. He liked him. It was just that in his assessment, traditional, Church-going Catholics were an anachronism in modern Labor. He wrote: "Conservative Catholics no longer have cause to join the ALP... Conservative Catholics join the Libs and the Nats. Catholics with a radical bent join the Left in its many guises. The ALP Right will not ever have another Johno." In mid-2020, the Johno Johnson Forum was formed to encourage debate and discussion of ideas among people of all faiths who are members of or sympathetic to Labor. Another initiative, Labor for Christians, is in formation. It remains to be seen how successful these moves might be. Faith will never (and should never) pre-determine political stance. Yet Christian principles (and the Jewish idea of *tikkun olam* – repair of the world) prove the capacity of faith to light the fire for radical social change.

Why this matters

Perhaps religious ideals and sympathy never subdued the land, but it held a place in Australia. Without Christian idealism, life would have been different, more brutal, savage, and uncaring. Some of Australia's greatest reforms and institutions were inspired by the Gospel teachings. One of those was the Labor Party itself. Chris Wallace's recent book (*How to Win an Election*, 2020) on Labor's campaigning problems argues: "successful leaders need to be able to do both [theatre and substance], ideally in a way that enables voters to say yes when asking themselves the question: 'Do I like this person and, more importantly, would they like me?'" This is Politics 101. Faithful and Labor should not be an oxymoron. Understanding this is important because welcoming people of faith reconnects us with a swathe of the population that we risk losing if Labor is seen as dominated by a metropolitan elite. Also true is that accepting people of faith avoids alienating those who are broadly centre-left, but politically homeless because of cultural/faith issues.

Embracing people of faith returns Labor to a position of respectful tolerance in accepting that reasonable minds and generous hearts may differ on major questions. Diversity of viewpoint is not always well countenanced on either side of politics, but that hypocrisy is more damning on our side because of our insistence of 'diversity' as a core value. Is it? Previous generations took the party and the country into better days socially, culturally, and economically. There are many reasons to regret the transformation of the party by identity politics and exclusionary diversity. Our traditions make us Labor, however, even in these days of cultural amnesia and secular snobbery. The present danger is that secular dogmatism is recapitulated in dogmatic identity politics, where the nuances and coalitions mentioned here are intolerable.

Refusing to tent our presence in vast territories of the Australian population, including faith communities, makes it harder to win. If winning is merely nice-to-have rather than essential, then such attitudes ensure that the Australian Labor Party merely deserves to be a party of occasional success. And in the purity of a liberal and intolerant agenda, we shall reap our reward.

* * *

Dr Michael Easson AM joined the ALP in late 1973, served on the NSW and National Foreign Policy and Defence and the Education Committees, and over the years was an alternate and full delegate to ALP National Conference. He was Secretary of the Labor Council of NSW, 1989-1994; Senior Vice President of the ALP, NSW Branch, 1994-95; Vice President, ACTU, 1993-94. Subsequently, his career traversed real assets funds management, technology, and superannuation. He is chair and co-founder of EG Funds Management and the independent chair of the Association of Superannuation Funds of Australia, and former chair now director of Willow Technology Corporation which he co-founded. The author, inspired by remarks by Andrew West at the Johno Johnson Forum in August 2020, is grateful for comments on an earlier version of this paper by the editors, Rev Frank Brennan SJ AO, Michael Dwyer, Dr Damian Grace, Catherine Harding, and Elizabeth Stone.

23. REGIONAL QUEENSLAND – LOOKING FORWARD, LOOKING BACK

Anthony Chisholm

During the last week of the recent State election campaign, I found myself at a campaign rally with the Premier in a hall opposite Townsville State High School. Looking at the school it had me reminiscing back to 2007 when I found myself working for the Leader of the Opposition, Kevin Rudd, as he aimed to end the Prime ministership of John Howard. I was travelling with Kevin around Queensland during the election campaign and was with him in Townsville for a policy announcement.

On 30 October 2007 at Townville State High in the seat of Herbert, Kevin announced our commitment to a 20 per cent renewable energy target. It seems politically mad now that we announced this policy in Townsville, but I can't recall anyone raising an eyebrow, let alone their voice within the campaign team to suggest this was a political mistake. To give this some further context, it's about a five-minute drive from Townsville State High to Adani's new HQ in Townsville – the mine that has been such a political football in recent elections at the State and Federal level.

How is it possible that the political mood has changed that dramatically over the last thirteen years? Why in 2007 was taking action on climate change a net-positive through regional QLD, including in the mining and industrial seats of Flynn, Capricornia and Dawson, whilst in 2019 our vote was decimated in those exact same seats, with climate change and a perceived hostility to coal mines and workers identified as a significant factor in the decline?

What is going on?

I understand that Labor people from down south scratch their heads about Queensland and, as the saying going, I am here to help. In Australian politics, federal elections tend to be decided in Queensland. In 1996, 2007 and indeed 2019 – Labor's performance in Queensland tends to tell the story for Labor federally. Labor required a big swing to win the 2007 election and Kevin's home state of Queensland was identified as a prime target to win a swathe of seats in the South-East and up the coast. Outside of the South-East corner, Labor was chasing Hinkler, the newly created seat of Flynn, Dawson, Herbert, and Leichhardt. The only seat Labor had held outside of the South-East since Keating lost in 1996 was Capricornia, which we regained in 1998. We campaigned strongly on climate change in Queensland both in free media and paid advertising. Looking back, I can't recall one campaign conversation where we were wary of an electoral back-lash because of a focus on climate change.

What's changed in regional Queensland since 2007? Plenty. The resource towns were enjoying prosperous times in 2007, so much so the Moranbah KFC – inland from Mackay – had to reduce its operating hours because they couldn't find staff to open at full capacity! Given the boom times it would have been almost impossible to paint a negative outlook on the future of coal mining in regional Queensland. Times were good, people were happy. But times change. And so, has the mood of the electorate.

The long and the short of it

In my role as State Senator for Queensland, I travel up north quite a bit. I've also run many state and federal campaigns over many years in my home state; I like to think I have some sense of how people are thinking, acting and voting – even if it means I'm sometimes wrong on election day! Talking to the people of regional Queensland, the most significant shift since the 2007 election in terms of the outlook for this part of Australia is long term versus short term expectations. In 2007 voters were thinking long term, over the horizon about what a better Australia could be. It's easy to do that when times are good; it seems like they will never end, and the future is full of rose petals.

At every election since then, short term thinking has been the dominant mindset. It's unsurprising then that Labor, with its bold vision for emissions reduction out to 2050, has a hard time selling that vision. What has led regional Queensland to change their thinking and what are the policy implications for the Federal Labor Party desperate to avoid a decade of opposition? Surely the state home to the Great Barrier Reef and reliant on its natural beauty could be persuaded to act in defence of the environment?

There is no doubt that Tony Abbott's period of time as Opposition Leader where he ended any prospect of bipartisanship climate policy and through his destructive and divisive political style set out to turn any action on climate change into a hip pocket issue started to turn the tide, but it is worth asking why this message was so easily received and why is it that the growing evidence of the urgency required to tackle climate change hasn't impacted politics in regional Queensland.

The economic fortunes of Australians have taken different tracks over the last thirteen years since Kevin Rudd won that 2007 election. Many of us in capital cities have enjoyed prosperous times compared to people in regional Queensland. And this plays out in our politics. Take housing for example. Median house prices in Boyne Island, a suburb of Gladstone in the Federal seat of Flynn peaked at $490,000 in 2012 and have now decreased by 36 per cent to around $315,000 in 2020. In North Mackay in the federal seat of Dawson, median house prices peaked at $400,000 in 2013 and have declined by 30 per cent to be worth $280,000 in 2020, whilst Railway Estate in Townsville has seen median house price decline by 14 per cent over the last ten years. This compares to median house prices in Greater Brisbane up 79 per cent, Greater Sydney up 92 per cent and Greater Melbourne up 144 per cent over the last fifteen years. For most Australians the most significant asset they own is their house and as you can see, the asset value has taken a different trajectory depending on which part of Australia you live in.

People in regional Queensland feel – and are – poorer. This shifts your mindset when you vote. Population is, as they say, destiny. It has had its role to play in this story. With the exception of Townsville, which has enjoyed modest population growth, most regional town populations have been steady or declined over the last decade. Gladstone and Mackay have tread water over the last five years, whilst the capital cities of Brisbane, Melbourne and Sydney have seen significant population growth over the last decade fuelling demand and creating jobs.

People go where the jobs are, and while this has an obvious reinforcing economic impact, it also impacts on the confidence of people in regional towns reliant on the eb and flow of mining. People can sense whether the tide is coming in or out for them. While the capital cities have seen growth in the number of people employed, towns like Mackay and Townsville have seen the number of people employed go backwards since the peaks in 2011-2013. The number of people employed in the Mackay region has decreased by 6.4 per cent since 2013 and Townsville is down nearly 10 per cent since 2011. This, coupled with the rise of insecure and labour hire work, is contributing to the gap between the cities and regional Queensland. For example, Townsville in the last 15 years has seen a 43 per cent increase in people working part time while over the same time only a 3.5 per cent increase in the number of people working full time. The Mackay region now has fewer people working in full-time jobs, down 10 per cent from a peak in 2013. The rise of insecure work means that workers no longer have good, dependable jobs. This sense of economic insecurity means they are forced to focus on the short term – when the next shift is, whether they have enough hours to pay the bills and many are unable to secure mortgages or car loans to give them the stability of thinking long. All of these factors influence voting patterns and intention. If you're focus is putting your feet on safe terrain, you're hardly going to be interested in talking about the horizon.

Mining country

For many years the mining sector has played a crucial role in growth in regional Queensland economies, both from direct investment and indirect investment. Wages grew quite significantly during the mining boom peaking at 6.7 per cent in mid-2008. This additional income flowed back through into the communities where these workers lived in, thereby sharing the prosperity. Everyone, as they say, got a drink.

Since 2013 it has been a different story. Wages growth has dropped significantly, increasing only 1.6 per cent from 2013 to 2018 – barely tracking inflation – compared to other sectors which a saw 2.2 per cent rise. All of this happened while the mining sector itself decreased in size by 1 per cent. The Queensland Government estimates around 30,000 people work in the coal sector across Queensland and 63,000 across the mining sector. In the Rockhampton/Gladstone CQ region around 10,000 people work in mining. In the Mackay Region its 15,700 and Townsville 4,100 are employed in mining. Importantly it largely peaked in 2012 – about five years after Kevin was elected and 1 year after he lost office in his second go at the top job.

It really is important to get your head around the sheer scale and size of the mining sector up north and its relative importance to Queensland. Mining is important to Australia, but its critical to Queensland. In 2017-2018 (the latest available data from the QLD Government) mining activity made up 11.8 per cent of Queensland's economy, worth $38.8 billion. Overseas exports of Coal, LNG and Minerals accounted for 83 per cent of the nominal value of Queensland's overseas merchandise exports. It's not just the mining itself – it's also the supply chain and flow on work. In 2019-2020 the output of Coking Coal was 152 Million tonnes to 86 Million of Thermal coal, a majority of which was exported through Queensland Ports, including Gladstone Port, Dalrymple Coal Terminal and Hay Point south of Mackay the majority heading to Asia. It is important to note that Queensland Coal production has remained largely stable in the last five years with 2019 year being one of the largest export years.

Looking forward

When you consider these economic factors, you can understand how regional Queensland would view a policy proposition that could have a negative impact on their livelihood. Voters in regional Queensland are not living in clover. It is understandable why many in regional Queensland would be thinking short term, they are consumed by worrying about tomorrow and don't have the luxury to think beyond that. If you bought your house in Mackay in 2013 and have watched the price drop over the last five years, the thought of their being less people employed in coal mining would likely scare you. You might be more worried about the impact of negative gearing changes on housing prices too. If you lost your full-time job and are now working part-time, you could be more concerned and persuaded about any claim that Labor is going to 'crash the economy' and less worried about forward projections about coral bleaching.

So how should this impact the policies we take to an election? Labor's long-term prognosis on climate change is correct – the science is irrefutable. We are the only party of government that has consistently advocated for action on climate change, yet our vote in regional Queensland – a state that will be deeply impacted by climate change – goes backwards at each election. We need to look at our policy proposition in that same short-term versus long-term way that voters do. For the purposes of my argument, let's say short term is in the next ten years and long term continues from there into the future.

We need to continue to advocate that urgent action is required, but we need a policy setting that reassures regional Queensland they have nothing to fear from an incoming Labor Government. We will protect your job and livelihood, but we *also* want to ensure your grandchildren have the same opportunity to live and work in regional

Queensland which is why we need to take action to create a better future for them. We must not let these factors come into competition – because when they are, we lose. In the short term, the biggest threat to good, well paid resources jobs in regional Queensland is not Labor's wild plans. It is automation and insecure work, evidenced by the increasing use of labour hire in the industry. The truth is that mining is probably not going anywhere for some time – but the good jobs may very well be, at least to the level which we currently enjoy.

Automation is happening now

BMA (BHP-Mitsubishi Alliance) in November 2019 announced that it would automate 300 Jobs at Goonyella Riverside Mine converting 86 trucks to become autonomous in 2020. The claim that no employees would lose their jobs, doesn't include the vast swarths of labour hire workers that are forced to do the same job without the same pay or conditions. These people don't count, apparently. This program is part of BHP's $1.2bn program to introduce 500 autonomous vehicles across WA and QLD. Rio Tinto started trial of the technology in WA in 2008 and now has 300 autonomous trucks. A study by McKinsey and Co has suggested that up to 27 per cent of Jobs in Central Queensland could be lost through automation by 2030, with mining jobs some of the most at risk.

The World Energy Outlook projects total world demand for energy sourced from coal to be marginally lower (down 1.1 per cent) in 2040 compared with 2018, with demand for power generation down 3.0 per cent and demand for industrial use to be 13.3 per cent higher. People will want and need coal and it's important that Queensland, and Queenslanders, supply it. Queensland's coal industry continues to enjoy key advantages, including its geographic location and the quality of its coal, compared with most of its global competitors. Therefore, under the main scenario outlined in the International Energy Associations projections, it is likely that international demand will support Queensland's coal exports over the coming two decades, with the long-term prospects for the State's metallurgical coal likely to be more robust than for thermal coal. For this debate it is worth noting that in 2019-20, Australia exported a total of 175.6 Mt of metallurgical coal – used in the making of steel – of which 120.6 Mt was hard coking coal. Significantly, almost 90 per cent of Australia's metallurgical coal exports originated from Queensland.

Capturing value

Earlier, I discussed the fact that Queenslanders were happier when times were good, and the wealth was shared around. If a boom in jobs and population is not returning in the near term, and automation and insecurity undermine what remains – we need to find ways to arrest this problem. Tackling insecurity through labour hire reform is one way, but it can't be the only way. We need to use the royalties and wealth being created by mining in regional Queensland to set up that long-term future for generations of Queenslanders to come. That means thinking about new industries in the long run. But it does *not* mean thinking about them at the expense of or exclusion of coal in the shorter term. Hydrogen, rare earth minerals, defence industry, hydro and renewable energy, agriculture and manufacturing all present significant new opportunities, but this will not and cannot come at the short-term expense of our current strengths. People won't cop it, and nor should they.

Industry policy needs to be in addition and is achievable because we are leveraging off our current strengths. It requires Governments to take risks and invest money in regional Queensland. That is how regional Queensland works – it needs leadership. This process worked in the past with coal mining, with the State Government playing an active role in that expansion, and it can work for new job creating industries as well. Over the last 170 years, ports, railways and other infrastructure has been built by Government in regional Queensland to help develop new industries, create jobs and economic wealth for Queensland families. Let's use our current strengths and government resources to ensure we build the modern opportunities that are going to provide the future jobs for the grandkids of our current day miners. Policy such as this will mean future generations can continue to enjoy living in regional Queensland, earn a good wage and contribute to the economic wealth of the nation. It's a future only Labor can deliver and it's one regional Queenslanders would embrace. But to do it, we need to win elections – and that means taking the people with us.

* * *

Anthony Chisholm was elected to the Senate in 2016. Prior to being elected, Anthony has had an active role in Queensland politics serving as Queensland Labor State Secretary between 2008 and 2014, before taking on the role of Campaign Director for the 2015 Queensland State Election, which saw the Palaszczuk Government sweep to power. In a big decentralised State like Queensland, Anthony is passionate about ensuring that affordable healthcare and a quality education is available to all people in Queensland, no matter where they live. Anthony is also focused on fighting for regional Queensland, as he believes that the conservatives have taken them for granted for far too long.

24. Shaking Off History, Re-Imagining Our Future

Ed Husic

As a Labor MP in the 2020s I often feel that if I need to look ahead someone nearby will turn my head 180 degrees to look four decades back. This is especially so in the aftermath of the 2019 Federal Election. We are often urged to remember the past as we seek to sketch out a path to future electoral success. And we are often reminded of the need to recall the legacy of the Hawke-Keating era. There's a rich vein of this supposedly free advice offered up by conservative politicians and their media backers. They keep telling us that we're nowhere near as good as the Hawke-Keating generation and if we would only be more like them we'd do better, conveniently ignoring that Bob Hawke and Paul Keating were resisted by some of the same people and similar voices.

So I'm taking a hammer to that free advice in this chapter. Not because of my lack of respect for the herculean efforts of our forebears. The Labor family rightly respects the achievements that endured from Hawke and Keating's reform agenda. But the biggest impression I want to leave with readers of this chapter is this: the trajectory of the Hawke-Keating Government wasn't defined by the guard rails laid down by their predecessors, or those laid by their opponents. They tore up those rails and refashioned them. We must think the same. Be prepared to challenge orthodoxy that sits outside of our party and within it. Our future success will be defined by evolving with the times we're in, crafting a compelling agenda that earns wide support and being courageous enough to reform where circumstance dictates.

Breaking the handcuffs

History is something to learn from, not to be handcuffed by. Applying learned lessons – without the strictures of a pre-shaped mold – will be important. But equally critical will be the lateral problem solving that will be demanded of us as we face up to varied challenges: responding to climate change in a timely and meaningful way, adjusting to accelerating and dislocating rates of automation and technological change, a recast of fiscal policy, shifting relations among global neighbours and a profound reshaping of how our country trades and makes its wealth on the world stage. Generations that didn't need to contend with war or recession will be tested in their own way, in a new way. So the questions for those of us in social democratic movements – how will we manage change? How do we look after people feeling the pain of that change? How do we ensure forward movement propelled by trust, confidence and hope as opposed to anxiety or dread?

Rethinking Hawke-Keating

Which brings me back to the weight of past success: the Hawke-Keating mantra. It's worth starting by noting that there wasn't a Hawke-Keating Opposition, there was no time to establish the name – and let's face it, the bitter reality is that few remember the legacies of oppositions other than the scale (or improbability) of their defeat. Hawke's election as Labor Leader occurred within breaths of the Coalition announcing the 1983 Federal Election. The dynamic between them emerged only after their success at the polls. It developed when it mattered most and where their weight was truly felt: in government.

At that point, on the cusp of the 1983 Federal Election, Hawke and Keating had to quickly make their relationship work effectively, projecting economic reliability in an attempt to shake off the lingering misgivings about the Whitlam experiment. As Craig McGregor details in his 1983 work 'Time Of Testing', Labor had its work cut out for it: "The Labor Party... seemed to represent the politics of the old… The old Labor tradition was one of communality, the welfare state, social reform and promoting the interests of ordinary working people, overlaid with a socialist philosophy which was taken seriously on the left of the part and opposed by those one the right."

The prime recollection of the short-lived 'Hawke Opposition' was the focus on a theme: "Bringing Australia Together", recovery through consensus. People remember Hawke and Keating dragging the nation out of a debilitating recession by getting capital and labour working as one in the national interest, spearheaded from the outset by a prices and incomes accord. That was step one. The steps that followed over a period of time. The broad, powerful, and lasting economic reform instantaneously associated with Hawke and Keating. The floating of the Australian dollar. Financial deregulation. Major budgetary, tariff and industrial reform. Privatisation. Along with social reform that saw a lift in the income of the lowest-income households, the introduction of Medicare, taxation reform that helped go some way to rein in – albeit not entirely – the growth in inequality.

Lessons learned

Step one: get the country and its economy moving again. Step two onward: to avoid repeated long term pain, reforming the economy, breaking a few orthodoxies along the way, looking after people while you're doing it. For me, that's the distilled essence of Hawke-Keating. It is a philosophical approach to problem solving through government, not a handbook. It doesn't involve picking up the template they worked with and pressing it awkwardly over our current economic situation. Rather, reshape the template to suit the times, while remembering that it will be a challenge in itself. Because at the time, there was a strong belief – from party members and voters – that the upstart Hawke-Keating Government was trashing Labor tradition. In echoes of today, the Hawke-Keating Governments were being asked why they had to be different to the Labor generation before them. Not surprisingly, as the nation evolved rapidly from the late 60s and 70s, Labor's makeup began to change. Gone were Prime Ministers who drove trains, replaced by eventual household names: Wran, Cain, Bannon, Hawke. Many emerged from households Labor members weren't familiar with – Australia's growing middle class.

When I think back to the Hawke-Keating years, I inevitably think about my own family's experience. I grew up in a single income family, Dad the sole breadwinner. He was a blue-collar worker, making his wages from welding and often travelling to find work where he could. I recall three things vividly. First, I remember how tough that job was for him: how often Mum would have to patch Dad's burn-pocked work uniform or how often Dad would come home sporting gauze over eyes injured by flash burn. Second, I remember how often he would be out of work and then back into a job as booms and busts messed with his employment. Finally, I remember how often he complained that "this Hawke Government was nothing like Whitlam's". He wasn't alone: ripping back layers of tariff protection along with a move to reform industrial relations disrupted the order of things in the world of work. Australian blue-collar workers would complain there was no way their wages would let their firms compete against low cost overseas competitors. And could this even be happening under the watch of a Labor Government, they'd ask. As much as we celebrate the record of economic growth, behind glory is a painful reality that dogs major debates about change today: who benefits from change and who pays?

Trusting politics

While we rightly laud the reforms ushered in by the Hawke-Keating Governments who opened up and reinvigorated our economy, we must acknowledge the impact of these changes on our blue-collar base. Sure, we tried steel plans and rolled out one structural adjustment program after another. But did we make sure they actually delivered anything other than a headline? Those reforms were carried out when trust in government was significantly higher. And now we're trying to convince the children of those blue collar workers – who lived it and are adults in a modern labour market – that we have another series of reforms to undertake, from tackling climate change to technological change. And that they should trust us to get it right.

It's not a country specific challenge either. Australia isn't alone in vowing to help communities affected by change and job dislocation or failing to ensure that promises match lived experience. In her work *Janesville*, veteran *Washington Post* reporter Amy Goldstein focuses on one particular area in Wisconsin affected by the shutdown of the auto industry. Goldstein claims many journalists will cover the shock of an announcement about major job losses, but few hang around to see what happens next. She goes on to cover in detail what happened to workers in Janesville, Rock County. While unemployment in the county fell after the GFC (or Great Recession, as it's referred to in the US), Goldstein notes: "But not everyone who now has a job is earning enough for the comfortable life they expected. Real wages in the country have fallen since the assembly plant shutdown... The county had 9,500 manufacturing jobs in 2015 – almost one fourth fewer than in 2008 and nearly 45 per cent fewer than in 1990." She also takes the time to document the lacklustre performance of specific Obama administration initiatives citing a Government Accountability Office critique of the outcomes of the White House's Auto Communities Council and Labor Department recovery office, Goldstein observed both were "...useful as listening posts – but ...no one kept track of whether any hurting auto communities got extra federal assistance as a result".

It might be boring, or perhaps uncomfortable, for a government to account for the performance of its announcements. But it means something in the longer term if you're pushing reform. Vulnerable communities with fewer options relative to those living in the inner circle of our major CBDs can't build serious futures off the empty promises contained in a media release. It's something to bear in mind when debating 'where to next' on climate change and energy policy. And as much as conservatives champion coal, they're never there to support the workers extracting it: turning a blind eye to industrial conditions, contracting out, exploitation of labour hire workers, watering down of workplace safety protections or redundancy rights.

The regular refrain we hear is 'RE-TRAIN!' because 'jobs in the services sector are booming everywhere'. Will displaced workers have faith in government job programs getting them into work, employment providers with patchy success in getting them into jobs or conservative governments unwilling to clamp down on age discrimination that cruels opportunity for the older unemployed? Why do we then struggle to understand why our former supporters are attracted to fringe parties offering false promise to stop change in its tracks? We need to not only face up to the frustrations and concerns felt by our supporters – and those who left us – we need to prove we listened. If we think we have to undertake change for the good of the country, we really need to work for it beyond the declaration. Because things are going to get tougher, economically, and politically. Polarisation is an easier choice these days. Picking a side and fighting the other mercilessly – throwing whatever claim you can, regardless of mis-truth – that's the zeitgeist.

Technology – it's not an either or choice

As much as I'm a fan of technology, it hasn't helped. Gone are the days when we thought the internet would bring the world closer together, helping to build understanding by better access to facts. Now it's a platform for – and I never thought I'd ever hear this term – 'alternative facts'. Mind you, I don't veer to either end of the spectrum, from dystopia to utopia and back again. But I'm a realist: before we can reap the reward, we must recognise risk. Aside from tackling climate change, accelerating technological development will be a major issue for our nation. Not just because of its impact, but because we don't take it seriously until we absolutely have to – by which point responding to and managing change is so much harder.

It's already been established that Australian firms invest in technology at a lower rate relative to their overseas rivals. We are starved of skills, conservatives more comfortable in importing talent as opposed to investing the skills and long-term prosperity of locals. Worse still, when it comes to innovation their attention span lurches between enthusiasm and resignation. As a result – while other countries recognise the economic and strategic benefit of investing in the development of areas such as artificial intelligence capability – our government tinkers or, at worst, says it can just adopt someone else's technology instead of levering off our own smarts. Terrific: a Cronulla Sharks scarf draped over Menzies-like inertia.

Since humans fashioned their first wheel, they've continued to make tools that make life easier and work more efficient. There's no way we can stop the march of this change. But we can think ahead and make sure people are looked after, and we can make sure the benefits don't simply accrue to capital. The problem in our nation at the moment is that the reward distribution from productivity gains are completely out of whack. Labour productivity is up 9.8 per cent since 2013 yet wages growth is mired in quicksand. That's the story of our economy and politics. The power of workers and their representatives to change this is hampered by wave after wave of conservative driven industrial relations reform and a timidity by our own side to even up the game.

Other productivity gains through technological investment see pain felt by workers, gain made by investors. Dividend growth since 2013, fuelled in part by capital investment in technology, continues an upward march. And in a post-pandemic world, there's already speculation that automation will accelerate (in the absence of an effective vaccine) to ensure the wheels of business keep turning in situations where lockdowns or a reluctance to return to work disrupts the operation of business.

How do we get business and labour coordinating more effectively to ensure we avoid this? A prices and incomes accord worked back in an era of centralised wage control. A dysfunctional enterprise bargaining system, eaten away by an equally dysfunctional approach to assigning reward and profit growth, leaves little hope about forging a new accord. While Labor can and should argue for Australian firms to grow into big, profitable businesses it's only going to be our side that will care to – or can push for – a better share of that profit. Importantly, the answer to lifting the wealth of working Australians is not a continued reliance upon transfer payments and tax cuts by conservatives compensating for the refusal by business to deliver concrete growth in wages.

It can either be achieved through active engagement with business or will require a serious reform of workplace law to improve the bargaining power of labour. Neither option is easy, both fraught with challenge. But a failure to address this remains a surefire way to retain distrust about the merits of change and boost the attractiveness of extreme politics to bust through stalemate.

Belief in government

Obviously, I'm a believer that government has a role to play. Ronald Reagan famously invoked the phrase "I'm from government and I'm here to help" as the supposedly the scariest thing one could hear. Labor people don't believe that – but to get others to, we need government to succeed. Conservatives have taken as an article of faith their need to sap confidence in the ability of governments or the public sector to effect meaningful change. We will need to rebuild and defend the institution and concept of government itself. For decades Australia has privatised government business enterprises or outsourced public sector functions. Fiscal policy has driven this: to relentlessly steer towards near term surplus even if it's detrimental to the broader health of the economy. Only now, as a pandemic threatened crushing long term economic damage, have we seen conservatives forced to drop their caricature of the demons of "debt and deficit". But I'd put that down to short term circumstances as opposed to the emergence of enduring philosophical revision and re-direction.

Importantly, how has the conservative approach to public service created a self-fulfilling prophecy about the capability of government?

A key function of government – public servants providing advice and acting on it – has been steadily and surgically removed, transplanted by consultants and external labour hire. All of which has slowly run down something else that is vital: that residual quality valued by organisations, 'corporate memory'. This is not a precursor to the conservative's bogeyman of 'big government and high taxes'. What I'm really championing is effective – not bigger – government. Conservative governments pay through the nose for consultants and external labour hire, using definitional chicanery to camouflage the reality that the work that would have been done in-house has just been shifted externally to help declare the arrival of "smaller government". It's a mirage designed to create a world in which their narrative prevails – government can't do anything; so don't bother hoping it will. And certainly, don't vote for the party that promises it can.

If governments are going to undertake the reforms Australia so desperately needs and have the capacity to genuinely follow through on the promise of a better and fairer future, we will need to fire up a belief in the role of our public service to help play a part in the process. This won't involve supplanting private sector effort with public servants but recognising that *both* need each other to be successful. While talking about 'delivery' is hardly the stuff of political inspiration, it speaks to a value that does inspire: the character of a political movement and the ability to trust in it. Labor, after all, is not a debating society – it aims to be a party of government. Effective Government. Labor believes in not just protecting communities from the harshest, sharpest edges of change but that managed change can deliver a dividend that enriches or lifts up those communities most impacted. But to get people to believe, governments must have a record of proven delivery, as opposed to the conservative version of this: that making the announcement is delivery in and of itself.

Winning government is our mission. But effective government is our duty. It's an ambition we must always return to and be accountable for, to ensure Labor voters – our people – tangibly share in the gains, not just the pains, of change. Our ambition resides in gaining the trust of the Australian people – to govern and deliver for them.

* * *

Elected to Parliament in 2010 as the Member for Chifley, Ed Husic has served in a number of portfolios including Shadow Minister for Human Services, Employment Services and Workforce Participation, the Digital Economy and now as Opposition Agriculture and Resources spokesperson. He was also Parliamentary Secretary to the Prime Minister and for Broadband. Much of his policy focus has been on the role of technology and its impact on workplaces and communities, an interest sparked via his previous role as National President of the Communications, Electrical and Plumbing Union. He has also held roles in the energy sector. Ed was among the first wave of graduates to secure a degree at the now Western Sydney University.

25. The Good Life: Permanency, settlement and migration in regional Australia

Raff Ciccone

Half a century ago my parents emigrated to Melbourne from struggling post-war Italy. Australia offered them hope for a better future, one simply not available to them had they stayed in their respective homes of Bari and Conza della Campania.

As my parents discovered, working people could come and put down roots and find opportunity in this wide, brown land. They arrived with little more than the contents of their respective suitcases, but they worked hard, eventually bought a modest home in the suburbs, raised their children, and lived a fulfilling, happy life together.

This is our cherished old migration story and vividly reflected in the lives of the hundreds of thousands who came to Australia post World War Two; people in search of a better future for themselves and their children, the chance to live a good life. In turn, migrants played a significant role in building Australia's prosperity. It is very much the story of modern Australia. Sadly, things are very different in 2020.

For more than two decades our migration program has shifted from being mostly premised on permanence to a system based on transience. Today, our migration program focusses heavily on temporary migrants; international students, skilled workers who fill short-term gaps, seasonal workers who labour in semi-skilled jobs or backpackers working short stints to extend their visas.

There lies great opportunity for Australia in broadening the scope of our policy settings and focussing on permanent migration, particularly as we recover from the COVID-19 pandemic. There would be enormous benefits for regional communities which, when scaffolded by renewed investment in infrastructure and services, could better rely on permanent migration for growth.

All this would put the good life in Australia more easily within the reach of people who come here hoping for that chance. For Labor, investing to make a good life more achievable in regional Australia is fair, equitable, smart and good politics.

The Howard years

There were two significant shifts in migration policy in Australia under Prime Minister John Howard between 1996 and 2007; the move from permanent forms of migration to temporary, and the efforts to encourage migrants to settle in regional Australia.

Undoubtedly, one of the key legacies of the Howard Government was and will be the increase in temporary migration it encouraged and implemented.

There are three relevant moments to this; 1) the late 1990s policy shift to open up Australia's borders to temporary migrants; 2) the 2001 federal election and the focus on 'Tampa'; and 3) subsequent changes to citizenship requirements that began in September 2005.

These three factors have turned Australia from a nation of permanent migrants into one with a growing exploited and excluded temporary migrant worker class.

In the late 1990s, it was factors including a rapidly ageing population and severe skills shortages that led to several initiatives to broaden Australia's intake of temporary migrants, including the introduction of the Migrant Occupations in Demand List (MODL) as well as international marketing campaigns designed to promote Australia's education and training services industry. Importantly, policies of the day included clear pathways improve qualifications and build the skills of temporary migrants to allow them to eventually meet requirements for permanent residency and then citizenship.

However, during the 2001 federal election, former Prime Minister Howard exploited the politics of the MV Tampa to conflate migration with congestion on Australia's roads and linked refugees to a welfare system under pressure.

By September 2005, the Australian Government had made citizenship harder to obtain. As Australian Bureau of Statistics (ABS) data shows, Australia's temporary migration intake outstripped its permanent intake, but fewer people were being offered the opportunity to remain here.

Up until COVID-19 hit, this remained the case. Overall migration continues to be high despite the political trickery of the Howard and now Morrison Government.

The number of permanent visas granted in 2019/2020 year was just over 140,000, 2018/19 was just over 160,000, all down from 183,000 two years previously. But this number masks the true nature of Australia's migration number. On 31 March 2020, there were 2.17 million temporary visa holders in Australia. International students and skilled migrants report growing difficulties in applying for permanent residency while the waiting list for family reunification and partner visas is frustratingly long.

While the Liberal and National parties may believe they have satisfied their political concerns over congestion, ABS data shows the actual migration numbers, through the net overseas migration figures, have increased in order to (artificially, some might argue) prop up continued economic growth.

As former immigration department official Mr Abul Rizvi told the Senate Select Committee on Temporary Migration during a 2020 public hearing, our pathways to permanency have become opaque, punitive and impossible to access.

In the meantime, over several decades and through a combination of specific visa classes, designated migration zones and sponsorship arrangements, Australia has sought to build the regions through migration. Unfortunately, evidence reveals that while these efforts can be effective in the short term, most new migrants move out of regional Australia when their visa conditions or residency status allows them to.

A failing system

It is hard to gauge whether or not Prime Minister Howard understood the long-term effects of his 2001 election campaign at the time. But, as Senator Kristina Keneally argued in her 2020 John Curtin Lecture, the legacy of that election lives with us today. Despite being well into their third term of Government, the Liberals and Nationals are still failing to invest in infrastructure, affordable housing, and public transport among others.

These failures significantly contribute to the difficulties related to retaining new migrants in regional Australia. The evidence reveals that most new migrants will leave regional Australia once the visa conditions that require them to stay are lifted. This is unsurprising. If there are no accompanying policies to make these areas more economically attractive, then new migrants will leave the area just as locals currently do – compulsion doesn't work in the long run. In a 2019 paper for *Australian Population Studies*, Charles Darwin University scholars show that in 2015 37 per cent of migrants in the South Australian designated regional area intended to leave or had already left South Australia, while a further 37 per cent were undecided on their future movements.

This research underscores an Australian National University review of 1981-2016 ABS Census data by Raymer and Baffour for *Population Research and Policy Review*. It found that migrants in regional and remote areas have a very low chance of staying in the area. Up to 70 per cent will leave, and if they stay in Australia they go to Sydney or Melbourne. The data also shows the chances of migrants leaving regional areas is growing amongst newer migrant groups from China and India.

Migrants leave because they face the same challenges faced by all communities in regional and remote Australia; social isolation, limited essential service provision including health, education and employment, poor infrastructure, a lack of housing and a lack of adequate support and settlement services, as the Federation of Ethnic Communities Councils of Australia (FECCA) outlined in a 2015 paper titled *Migration: An Opportunity for Rural and Regional Australia.*

FECCA's paper reflects an earlier 2014 Department of Immigration review of the critical factors for successful regional retention of migrants. Those factors are related to employment, family connections and settlement, social connections and welcoming communities, the availability of services and infrastructure including appropriate and affordable housing, health care, education and settlement support.

Transience and permanence

A failure to invest in the regions hurts the ability of local communities to live good lives and presents a significant barrier to growing and strengthening regional Australia through migration. Indeed, it is creating communities of transience.

The evidence is out on the short-term impact of transient populations in regional Australia. However, some stakeholders have commented on the impacts of transience on communities over the long term, particularly around issues of social cohesion, as Settlement Services International pointed out in a 2020 submission to the Senate Select Committee on Temporary Migration.

Temporary migrant workers are also vulnerable to worker exploitation in part due to their temporary status and the linking of their visa to their employer. For example, prior to entering the Senate, as a union official for the Shop, Distributive and Allied Employees Association (SDA) I represented workers at 7-Eleven when it was revealed that many of their temporary migrant workers were subject to a systematic pattern of exploitation. These workers were paid between $8 and $10 an hour, and in one instance I met a young foreign student, who was making as little as $5 an hour. They came to Australia to get an education and improve their future, but were instead too scared to speak up, or simply not aware of their workplace rights. I can't fathom the fear these workers would have felt, studying, struggling to make ends meet and feeling powerless in the face of employers determined to rip them off – because their bosses had all the power and they had little or none.

A number of media reports over the course of 2020 have revealed repeated incidences of sexual harassment, wage theft and other forms of exploitation temporary migrant workers have endured.

Anecdotally, regional Australians have told me they worry about the impact of transience on their communities. They want to welcome new Australians to their towns and see them establish themselves as valued members of their community – they want neighbours not strangers sent to work only to be sent home or who will leave the first chance they get.

Permanency, on the other hand, comes with significant benefits for both communities and migrants. Migration is demonstrably part of the Australian success story. As a nation, migrants have helped drive our economic growth and strengthened our egalitarian identity. For migrants, the opportunity to prosper, to develop a sense of belonging and live out more stable lives is key. For regional Australia and for the nation, migrants who have permanency are predisposed to make positive contributions to their communities, as the Committee for Economic Development of Australia (CEDA) highlighted in a 2020 submission to the Temporary Migration Committee. This makes sense – if you feel secure in your settings, you're likely to take the time to invest extrinsically in your community and surroundings.

Backing the regions

Strong arguments exist for refocusing on permanent migration to Australia. But in order to ensure effective long-lasting migration for regional Australia we must address the factors already outlined as critical for successful regional settlement.

Regional Australia is overflowing with creativity and energy, as Federal Labor Leader Anthony Albanese highlighted in his regional vision statement of September 2020. Indeed, regional Australia is full of talented and ambitious Australians. They work hard, contribute to our economy, and enrich the fabric of our national life.

However, Regional Australia needs to be backed in.

Regional and remote communities need governments to invest in new pathways for economic growth, training and skills, efficient and affordable telecommunications, roads, and public transport – not as afterthoughts or ill-conceived pork barrels but as genuine economic growth plans. As FECCA highlights, to encourage more migrants to regional Australia, we must ensure that adequate support and settlement services are available. Regional communities need infrastructure, schools and health services, and economic opportunities through safe, secure work. In other words, we must make sure a good life in regional Australia is within reach of all. If we make the areas attractive for locals and others, then attracting migrants will be a breeze.

This is absolutely possible. Indeed, the Regional Australia Institute points to regional centres like Orange, Bendigo, Mt Gambier and Toowoomba as examples of success stories. We've done it before. In her Curtin Lecture, Senator Keneally described meeting growers in Shepparton who told her of Albanian migrants brought to our shores during the years of the Fraser Government. As Keneally recounted their words: "They came here. They built homes. They sent their kids to local schools. They put down roots. They brought others here. They were great workers and they built up our community. They became Australians. Can't we just do that again."

COVID-19 has seen a new interest in regional Australia. Seeking to get away from the frustrations and dangers of congestion, Australians have flocked to regional communities in ways not seen for decades. This could be a much-needed shot in the arm of human and financial capital – but only if we back this in with investment.

What do you need to live a good life?

Throughout our 130-year history Labor has focussed on answering the question, what do you need to live a good life? The shearers on strike in Barcaldine in 1891 were seeking proper pay and safe working conditions.

John Curtin, who found himself his family's primary breadwinner at the age of 18, expanded the nation's pension schemes and maternity allowances. The Light on the Hill speech of his great contemporary, Ben Chifley, reminds us that Labor seeks to bring "something better to the people, better standards of living, greater happiness to the mass of the people". Gough Whitlam abolished conscription and established the basis for equal pay. Bob Hawke was the Prime Minister of Medicare, and his minister Susan Ryan the architect of the Sex Discrimination Act. As Treasurer and then Prime Minister, Paul Keating's stewardship of our superannuation program will leave an indelible mark on the lives of Australians for at least a century, if not more. More recently, Kevin Rudd introduced a universal paid parental leave scheme, Julia Gillard reformed education funding, and in the period of 2007 to 2013 they were responsible for the National Disability Insurance Scheme, and the National Broadband Network.

Importantly, for decades Labor governments have had a strong focus on the economic and social livelihoods of regional Australia. Often, regional communities are poorer communities. They reflect the populations that have historically been integral to Labor's working-class heritage and our electoral success – Ben Chifley after all was a train driver from Bathurst. These communities have been abandoned by successive Liberal and National Coalition governments, who seem focussed on cutting taxes for the wealthy, making it harder to find a safe and secure job and slashing support for the struggling – all problems that are worse when overlaid on regional areas.

As the Australian Labor Party looks for opportunities to grow its support, some in our movement display a narrow focus on the issues of the left and in organising in inner cities. But I believe there is a better way forward; a way that keeps the question of what we need to live a good life at the heart of all matters, that ensures we can continue to be a multicultural success and that brings a renewed focus to regional Australia.

We should invest in regional Australia. We should help permanent migrants move to the regions and make those regions a more viable option for permanent settlement. We should reopen pathways to permanent migration. We should make sure regional communities are cohesive and inclusive. We should ask ourselves the question, 'what do you need to live a good life?' over and over again, and continue to answer that question with a focus on affordable homes, secure jobs, social support and infrastructure, and the opportunity to build a future in regional Australia. We must seek new answers to this enduring question and never stop striving.

Migration is a force for good. Not just for migrants like my parents, but for our regional communities and for our nation. Making it easier for migrants to secure a pathway to permanency, to settle in the regions and to build a good life will serve our nation well for generations.

* * *

Raff Ciccone is a Federal Labor Senator for Victoria. Before being appointed to the Senate, Raff was a senior union official for the SDA representing retail, fast food and warehouse workers. He previously worked in financial planning and served as a board member and Chair of his local community health organisation. Raff is the proud son of Italian migrants. He grew up in Melbourne's south-east suburbs, attended local Catholic schools and graduated from Deakin University and the University of Melbourne. Raff is committed to shining a light on the issues that affect working Australians, to put social justice front and centre of the national conversation and to work towards a fairer Australia.

26. Community Safety and Social Justice

Michelle Roberts

At most state, and some federal, elections in Australia over the past fifty years, safety and security has been a major issue. Almost without fail, in government or seeking it, the conservatives (the Liberals, the Nationals, or One Nation) make claims about crime escalating out of control, lenient magistrates, criminal gangs and the availability of illicit drugs. They do so for a largely cynical reason: that it is the single issue with which they think they are most likely to get cut through with people who otherwise have no reason to be sympathetic to their policies or views. It's the straw man they use to try and scare people away from voting labor.

All of us place a high value the our safety and the safety of our loved ones and if people can be frightened into thinking that they or their loved ones are at risk of violent crimes and that those who perpetrate such crimes will go unpunished it can be a potent wedge.

The response, for the past half-century, from people on the progressive side of politics has been to despair at this base opportunism. Less energy, however, has been directed at understanding why this is such a visceral issue and has been used over decades to the advantage of political conservatives.

The 'Southern Strategy'

The answer does not belong in the deep convict history of Australia. Rather, it more likely begins with the protest movements of the sixties, both here and in the United States. For the most part, the traditions of political protest and civil disobedience belong to the Left. It was against these in particular that Richard Nixon and Ronald Reagan in the United States constructed a 'law and order' message that successfully turned white, socially disadvantaged males against the Democrats – the Republicans so-called 'southern strategy'. Likewise, in Australia, the moratorium movement during the Vietnam War led to mass protests against conscription and against the war itself. This enabled Liberal Premiers like Sir Henry Bolte in Victoria and Sir Robert Askin in New South Wales to turn law enforcement into a partisan issue. Yet this was only the start of the law and order electoral wedge. Bolte's refusal of clemency to Ronald Ryan, and his subsequent execution, has been interpreted as a deliberate ploy to bolster public support in an election year. Askin, less lethally, but equally potently, aided developers in suppressing demonstrations by Jack Mundey's Builders Labourers' Federation against property developments in inner city Sydney. For many years, motorists exiting the Cahill Expressway at Woolomooloo would be greeted by a huge graffito reading "Bob Askin loves Laura Norder".

To many of their opponents, the police who enforced the restrictions on public demonstrations became an easier target for resentment than the conservative politicians who created the circumstances.

This is a luxury that people who are genuinely concerned about equity and social justice cannot afford. It plays into the misleading characterisation of Labor as 'soft on crime', which in turn has served to enable the conservatives to engage in increasingly hysterical fearmongering both at a state and federal level.

Few elections pass by without some fanning of the flames of community fears. At the beginning of 2018 in the context of an impending state election in Victoria, for example, the Federal Home Affairs Minister, Peter Dutton, deliberately raised the issue of "Sudanese criminal gangs" operating in Melbourne. In July of that year, former Prime Minister, Malcolm Turnbull joined the chorus, and then Scott Morrison, added his own contribution to this public discussion. These remarks were timed and calculated to affect the Victorian State election. Subsequent analysis revealed both the inaccuracy of these comments, but also just how much they play to fears within the community. The deliberately crafted sub-text of all of this was to reinforce the traditional view that the conservative parties are 'tough on crime' and more particularly, tougher than Labor. In reality though it served more to exacerbate the issue than quell it, adding to more resentment on each side of the divide.

The scare campaign however did not shift overall voting intentions and the Andrews Labor Government was convincingly re-elected. It is critical to note, however, that whenever their backs are against the wall, whenever they have nothing else to say, almost without fail the conservatives play the 'law and order' card. Interestingly though I expect any movement of voting intentions these days isn't necessarily just in the one intended direction, as many as many educated and compassionate traditional Liberal voters see though this base politics and are repelled by it.

Tough on crime; tough on the causes of crime

For conservatives, a punitive approach to law and order is a logical and natural approach, consistent with a philosophy that identifies individual choice as our society's principal economic and moral driver. It's a lazy approach that doesn't work and doesn't get results.

Labor's approach has, by contrast, been more nuanced, and has sought to develop policies that recognise the origins of most crime in disadvantage and alienation. Labor's view is that these are the underlying issues that need to be addressed so that the community can reduce crime and promote positive life and community outcomes. These kinds of policies are smart, research-driven, long term and vastly more effective. Yet because they are not the "quick fix" they are much more difficult to communicate to voters. They don't fit into a simple sound bite for the evening news.

All too often the loudest voices, and those which find themselves media soapboxes, are those that call for increasingly severe punishment as the most effective way of deterring crime. This is despite the fact that many who break the law have no idea what the punishment is when they do so, or alternatively are so confident that they won't get caught that the punishment is the furthest thing from their minds when they commit the crime.

The voices of those calling for tougher penalties, though, cannot be dismissed. Indeed, they need to be taken seriously by Labor and progressives. These views are borne out of a very real frustration. Many people have been victims of crime themselves or have had family members victimised. When they see perpetrators getting off scot free or with minor consequence, they are rightfully outraged. Consequences for our actions are important. Crime that is not punished is not justice, especially for its victims. Yet what we can all agree is that the best possible outcome would have been for the crime not to have occurred in the first place. That's the "win/win"; that's why crime prevention is not the soft option but the better option.

In 1990's Britain, Tony Blair as Shadow Home Secretary and then as Labour leader and Prime Minister, developed and implemented a policy approach which sought to give victims a voice and which understood that, while criminal acts may have deep social drivers, the acts were criminal and the perpetrators needed to take responsibility for them. The policy approach came to be known by the catch phrase – "tough on crime; tough on the causes of crime".

It is tempting, and perhaps fashionable for some, to reject this as a Blairite flourish. But the truth is that, in 1990's Britain, Tony Blair hit a nerve, and it is the same nerve that Australian conservatives have been picking at for decades. The principal victims of crime are not the wealthy and careless. They are those on low or middle incomes, generally living in inland suburbs. By contrast those who are least likely to be the victims of crime are those who live in wealthier areas, protected domestically by elaborate security systems and socially by ready access to good legal advice.

It's a little published fact that the group of people most likely to fall victim to a non-family serious assault are not the frail, elderly or children but young fit men. They are both the perpetrators and the victims. So if we want to reduce violence and serious assaults in the community dealing with the underlying issues that lead to young men assaulting others has to be key. Alcohol and drugs are one significant element as are the underlying drivers that impel them toward those social crutches.

While people may be venture into criminality as a consequence of social and economic circumstance, their victims are often those who can least afford to be preyed upon: who can least afford home security systems or even domestic insurance. They are the people who have the most muted voice in seeking to clean up their streets. Their local governments are often not rate rich and able to put more rangers on their streets and in their parks or more CCTV in community spaces.

As Tony Blair argued, such victims of crime deserve social justice and legal empowerment. They deserve it because they deserve to live in safe communities. Community safety ought not be dependent upon capacity to pay, but upon a social network of mutual trust supported by effective laws and rigorous policing. Penalties need to be appropriate, both as a deterrent and as a tangible and meaningful consequence for actions.

In punishing we also need to an emphasis on rehabilitation. Not because it's a softer option but because with the exception of those who've committed the most heinous crimes, sooner or later people are released from prison. The best outcome for us all is if none of those people reoffend. It's good for them but it's great for us; none of us want to be their next victim no matter what the crime is. So we aim to prevent, but if crime isn't prevented then it must be punished – there have to be consequences. We must also aim to rehabilitate those who've justifiably been punished because it's only through rehabilitation that we can protect the community from falling victim to further offences.

Prevention and rehabilitation

Prevention, rehabilitation and diversionary strategies in which Labor governments have traditionally invested have ongoing long term benefits, as too is dealing with the even earlier community building strategies such as investing in early childhood education and family supports that can change life outcomes completely.

In Government, we need to both protect the community in the here and now, but also invest in the longer term preventative strategies for the future. When the McGowan Government came to power in Western Australia at the beginning of 2017, we were confronted with a major methamphetamine epidemic, which had become a serious driver of property and violent crime. We developed an integrated plan across government bringing together both the preventative and the punitive. One of the first pieces of legislation we passed increased the penalty for meth trafficking from 25 years to life imprisonment. We recruited an additional 100 sworn police officers and an additional 20 specialist public servants to a Meth Border Force, and provided it with the best technology available to enable it to detect consignments of meth being smuggled into WA. Equipping our Police to be able to detect crime and reduce the distribution of drugs are part of a broader integrated policy across government that also focuses on prevention and rehabilitation.

Indeed, our meth rehabilitation prison, Wandoo, which we set up on coming to Government, has had significant success. Opened just over two years ago, it has a return to prison rate of less than one percent (that national average is 46 per cent), with over a hundred women successfully completing the program. It has remained drug-free throughout its operation, and provided a positive model that is being explored by other jurisdictions. An equivalent facility for male inmates, the Mallee Rehabilitation Centre has recently been opened. The alcohol and other drug recovery programs are being run by experienced service providers the Palmerston Centre and the Wungening Aboriginal Corporation. It's a volunteer program and the number of participants demonstrates that prisoners are keen, given the opportunity, to break the cycle of addiction and drug-related offending.

We've also set about implementing a series of measures to support the community's efforts at prevention. We've provided crisis funding for families and individuals; made a significant financial commitment to the development of localised personal support services; increased funding to the training of health professionals and provided funds for public and school education programs.

While this is one policy response, it is not isolated. In Western Australia, Labor Governments have invested significantly in diversionary and preventative programs designed to provide active interventions in the lives of vulnerable young people to provide positive life alternatives. One example is our Police and Community Youth Centres but there are many others. Since World War II, our PCYC's have exercised a vital diversionary function, engaging vulnerable young people in healthy and positive activities. Likewise young aboriginal women and men are given positive role models and serious life choices through organisations like the Clontarf Academy. At Clontarf, it's sport that engages young people. At Challis Primary School in Armadale, there is an outstanding music program that gives children from disadvantaged backgrounds, a sense of connection, community and achievement. Other schools offer similar opportunities. Organisations such as Parkerville Children and Youth Care provides safe spaces and advocacy for at-risk young people. It does not matter here that not all the initiatives come from Government. What does matter is that governments support these endeavours through both real and in-kind funding. It also gives real community buy in. This is the most effective way to reduce crime, to build and strengthen our communities. To provide fantastic options for young people for positive engagement and in supporting one generation we build for the next. Today's teenagers are tomorrow's parents, if we can't help them, we condemn another generation to the same outcomes.

These policies are not bids in some crass law and order auction. They are tailored responses to a major community safety challenge. They reflect that, as makers and implementers of public policy, we have a duty both to respect and protect victims of crime, and also to do what we can to prevent or limit the occurrence of that crime. It's about balancing the desire for prevention with the requirement for legal consequences.

Fair cop

Our police also need to be respected for the job that they do. Some police give their lives to protect their community; some give their physical health; some give their mental health. For many years, our Police in WA were denied Occupational Health and Safety protection, something that Labor remedied in the years of the Gallop Government. Only now with the election of the McGowan Government have medically retired police been able to leave with honour, and those who suffered ongoing medical and psychological issues have had access to a Redress Scheme. A Labor Government has a particular and especial duty to support and honour these workers who have given and continue to give so much to protect the community and respond in their time of need.

2020 has been a challenging one for Police. They've been at the frontline of the Covid 19 response. They've locked down state and intrastate borders, they've run our WA G2G app monitoring and recording every entry into our state. They've staffed our ports, airports, public venues and any places where people gather. Their necessary role in enforcing quarantine, social restrictions and border closures has led to groups of people on the right of politics confronting them at so called 'Freedom Rallies'. At the same time, the Black Lives Matter movement in the US has sparked similar demonstrations here, highlighting Aboriginal deaths in custody. These rallies and campaigns have been associated, by some of those on the left side of politics, with calls to 'defund the police'.

These are absurd and naïve demands that will only punish the decent working people that our police protect and reward the criminals who prey upon them. Our Police are agents neither of authoritarian threat to personal liberty nor of a narrow and racist ruling class. They are who we are. They are drawn from our community, come from a range of ethnic backgrounds, have significant professional experience in civilian life and have a greater gender diversity than in past eras. They are our mothers, fathers, brothers, sisters and spouses. Their interests are our interests. Their powers are governed by law; their practices by codes of conduct, their operations by a strict and accountable chain of command.

The cost of failures in providing community safety are disproportionately borne by those who are least able to pay. It is this fact that political conservatives grasped two generations ago. Labor hasn't necessarily helped our own cause over the years by developing a public rhetoric that, in seeking to nuance our response to crime in our community, appears sometimes to be excusing it. If Labor is to continue properly to advance the interests of working people in this critical public policy arena, then we need to develop policies that balance punishment, prevention and rehabilitation. We also need to ensure that we resist the absurd calls to 'defund the police' and, instead, give our police forces the support they need to keep our communities safe.

* * *

Hon. Michelle Roberts MLA has served in the WA State Parliament since 1994. Between 2001 and 2008, she served in the Gallop and Carpenter Governments in a range of portfolios. She was Minister for Police from 2001 to 2005, and was the first woman in Australia to hold the Police and Emergency services portfolios. In 2017 she returned to the Police and Road Safety portfolio and continues in that role. She was the first woman to serve as President of the WA ALP, and has served for many years on the Party's national executive. Michelle is currently the longest-serving parliamentarian in the State Parliament and, as such, WA's first "Mother of the House". She is also the longest-serving woman parliamentarian in the history of the state.

27. True Believers

Sam Crosby

It was two days before the May 2019 federal election. Over the previous eighteen months as Labor's candidate for Reid, my days had been consumed by old-fashioned doorknocking, phone calling, volunteer barbecues, and community surveys. I was balancing a newborn son and fulltime work. I was exhausted.

My last three weeks had been spent on a prepoll booth talking daily to a huge cross section of the population as they voted. Through this I developed an intuitive feel for the electorate's intent. And I knew in my bones I was going to lose. I maintained a brave face. We had hundreds of volunteers who looked to me –we and they were physically and emotionally invested in the campaign. But I knew I was done.

As the dark realisation set in, I asked my local priest to leave a side door open to our church after everyone had left for the day. St Mary's Concord is cavernous and old, designed for over a thousand parishioners, with enormous domed ceilings. There I sat in the dark on a pew to one side, in the vast emptiness of the old church. I was seeking comfort and solace and help. And in humbling myself before God by doing so, I could connect honestly with what I was feeling. I broke down and cried.

Smorgasbord Catholic

I'd grown up listening to Father Ted Kennedy in Redfern, or 'Big Ted' as my family called him (my brother being named in part after him, was known as plain Ted). Big Ted was a radical within the Catholic church and beloved by the community. 'Mum Shirl' (Shirly Smith) once described him next to Jesus Christ as "the greatest man to walk the earth." He truly loved his neighbour, no matter how poor or destitute or broken they were. He was my introduction to the Catholic Church and remains my guiding star of what a good Christian is, or should aspire to be. Since Big Ted, I have always seen the Church (rightly or wrongly) as an institute of love, comfort and meaning. It was natural for me to turn to the church when I was at my lowest.

Yet thinking about the role of faith and politics, I still consider myself an unlikely author on the subject. I am what Cardinal Pell once described as a smorgasbord Catholic. I take what I like from Catholic theology – "love thy neighbour" – and leave the less palatable bits – no sex before marriage, for instance. Despite my undisciplined adherence to its teachings, when I am at my lowest, it is to the church that I turn. Similarly, when my children were born healthy and happy, when my wife and new bubs fell asleep – I dropped to my knees and thanked the Lord Jesus.

Despite my differences and disappointments with the church from time to time, being a Catholic is part of my identity – not the overwhelming part, but an important element, nonetheless. And this is why, during the election, I felt a profound sense of unease when the Prime Minister, having invited a camera crew to take a photo of him praying in his church, was pilloried by many so-called Labor supporters.

Hell on the campaign

Social media viciously attacked him for his overt religiosity and evangelical faith. Putting aside the electoral implications of attacking the religion of 260,000 self-identified Pentecostals spread across marginal seats in Queensland and NSW, the reason I felt so uneasy was these attacks felt like attacks I'd seen on people of other religions – Muslims, Jews or Sikhs – for their visible "otherness". And although I am too young to have personally known a time when being a Catholic placed you on the fringe of society, my parents are not. They reminded me of times they saw signs instructing Catholics not to apply for jobs; how it felt knowing the signs were aimed at them and their parents. I saw the criticism of Morrison in this light and cringed.

Similarly, in the campaign's final days, a journalist questioned Morrison about whether he believed gay people would go to hell. He dismissed the question, but I felt for the PM. Under this line of questioning, was I, as a practicing Catholic, responsible for every distasteful thing the Church or other Catholics said or did? My disappointment was compounded when our campaign weighed in on Morrison's response – it felt as if the PM was being attacked as a representative of his faith.

I can intellectualise why I felt uncomfortable about the attacks on Morrison, but in truth my reaction was instant and visceral. Despite not being of the same type of Christian faith, Morrison and I are still members of the same basic religious group – the same tribe. This is important, because decades of political analysis have shown that voters rarely respond to appeals to their own self-interest. They rarely ask, 'what's in it for me?' what they do ask is 'what's in it for my group?' People are not selfish per se – they are 'groupish'. I clearly wasn't the only one who felt this.

Losing the faith

Labor's Federal Electoral Review pointed to Christians as one of the four key groups who swung away from us that election. It found that "the most pronounced swings were among devout, first-generation migrant Christians… Between them, up to 400,000 voters in these two groups changed their votes at the 2019 election".

This link between first generation migrants and Christians is one Labor MP Stephen Jones grasps. Jones went public after the election with his concerns over the Israel Folau saga. While criticising Folau's views on homosexuality – Jones was a long-time proponent of marriage equality – he said the Australian Rugby Union should not have handled the case as they did. "This is what multiculturalism looks like. It is not just about having a wide variety of interesting food and interesting dances and costumes, actually it is more than that. It is about people's cultures and faiths and all of that interacting with ours," he said. "We can't say on the one hand, 'We support multiculturalism and all that comes with it', and then be offended when the expression of that multiculturalism disagrees with some of our deeply held views."

This interplay between religion and multiculturalism is all the more important when you consider that the best indicator of a person's willingness to vote Labor is how recently they migrated to Australia – and as leading commentators have noted it's also the best indicator in determining how religiously observant a person is.

To be fair, I never fully understood this link until as a candidate I was taken along to the numerous Korean evangelical megachurches frequented by a large portion of my electorate. There I appreciated both the depth and breadth of that particular community's feelings as I saw row upon row of devout believers clap and sing with an intensity far removed from the sedate Catholic services I'd grown up with.

Like reflecting on the frog that was slowly boiled, we can now look back at a series of issues that put Labor and people of faith on different sides in 2019. As Andrew West so eloquently wrote in his election wrap-up: "[we had been asking] faith communities [to] choose between Labor and the God they worship." Debates surrounding marriage equality, abortion, anti-discrimination exemptions, religious freedom – at every possible point we had been framed, and allowed ourselves to be framed, as anti-religion. Some occurred spontaneously. Some were driven by the Liberal Party.

I believe this occurred for two reasons. The first is that we didn't talk about god, faith, religion or any of these issues in a positive context and haven't done so for years. There are those in the party for whom religion is a deep driver of who they are and why they have chosen a life of public service. We need to hear from them and soon. Where they disagree with the party line on issues, they should be given room to voice their concerns. This is difficult, and more easily said than done, but it's necessary if we accept the premise that Labor needs to be a big pluralistic tent.

The second is to understand that conservatives think about issues slightly differently to progressives. As Jonathan Haidt points out in his book *The Righteous Mind*, whereas progressives build our moral frameworks on values such as 'care' and 'fairness', conservatives build theirs on 'sanctity', 'tradition' and 'authority'. Take for instance the question about Catholic schools' antidiscrimination exemptions in 2018. Progressives approached the issue through their fairness framework, which led them to an intractable position. They felt it was unfair to sack a teacher for being who they were (homosexual). To do otherwise was, by definition, "unfair". Conservatives approached the issue with equal intensity through their frameworks of tradition and authority. Any change they reasoned would be a gross incursion by the state into matters of their faith and how they had conducted their affairs for generations.

Keeping the faithful

When progressives talk about religion, we tend to do it from the "care and fairness" frame. For me, these values are why I am a Catholic. It's what I believe the overwhelming messages are of the gospels. But we need to acknowledge that others take different ideas from the same texts. It will, however, take more than a messaging change to reach these small 'c' conservative voters. It will take a change in the way we think about issues and the credence we give to them. If we factor in such perspectives, we might see that much of what motivates these communities is not bigotry and hate, but tradition and culture they see as under attack.

Kevin Rudd was skilled at this. It wasn't just defining himself as an 'Old-Fashioned Christian Socialist' or appearing at a press conference on his way into Sunday Mass, it was that he regularly and thoughtfully related his decision-making to his faith. It was how he talked with sincerity providing a place for Christian voters in his vison. At no time did he ask Christians to choose between their faith and Labor values.

Labor in NSW was founded on working-class Catholics. For me

this is best exemplified by stalwarts like Johno Johnson. If we ever strayed too far from our roots you could expect an earful from Johno, or as I and others experienced from time to time – a walking stick to the back of the head. Faith is quite literally in our DNA we just need to remember it's there.

It's important to acknowledge that no matter what Labor does, there are groups of Catholics for whom big 'C' conservatism will be the driving force of their faith. These voters will never feel comfortable voting for Labor. But it's important to remember that these voters – and even the 'single issue voters' who are doing so much harm in the United States at the moment – do not speak for *all* Catholics or Christians. In fact, they aren't even the majority. Only 41 per cent of regular worshippers vote for the Coalition. 26 per cent vote Labor. Just like the rest of society, this still leaves a large portion of undecided voters eager to be included in the conversation.

We shouldn't forget about the 41 per cent. All too often in modern Labor politics we automatically dismiss those who are rusted on Liberals focus our attention on the swing voter. It's a big part of what is polarising our modern politics. And while it's strategically understandable, it's also what leads voters to distrust politicians assess that they only want to engage for votes. For most Labor MPs I know, this isn't the case. They are motivated by deep rooted values either explicitly based in faith or align with faith substantially. We must do a must better job of keeping the faithful.

* * *

Sam Crosby was Labor's candidate for Reid at the 2019 election. He has been the CEO of a progressive thinktank, The McKell Institute, for the past seven years and has recently moved to the St Vincent De Paul Society as an Executive Director. He has worked in senior roles in State and Federal Government and was an executive at Johnson and Johnson. He holds an MBA from the AGSM and a first-class honours degree in Economics and Social Sciences from USYD. In 2016 he wrote The Trust Deficit (MUP) and he lives in the suburbs of Sydney with his wife and two children.

28. Australia in an Authoritarian World

Kimberley Kitching

There was a time when the benefits of a stable and prosperous liberal democracy, and its superiority over any other model of political and economic organisation seemed self-evident. But it's clear that it's not so obvious in many parts of the world, and indeed in certain age groups in Australia according to the Lowy Institute surveys, and in other democracies, according to Pew Research data. We need to ask why authoritarianism has retained its appeal, even after its proven record of failure over many decades, and even in affluent countries with long histories of democratic government.

I can offer some suggestions. Forty years of largely unrestrained neoliberal economic orthodoxy without balancing this against the rights and needs of wage earners across much of the West has widened the gap between a wealthy, greedy and, in some circumstances, scandalously corrupt elite, and the rest of the population. This has caused an alienation from democratic politics and pushed many towards the false appeal of the fringe, leading to a resurgence of extremist politics. This has been particularly true in the USA and the UK, where the moderate reformers Bill Clinton and Tony Blair have been succeeded by populists in Donald Trump and Boris Johnson. Countries which rejected this model, like Germany and France, have been much less affected, though far from immune. The lesson is that policies which foster economic solidarity are a precondition of stable democracy.

Twenty years into the twenty-first century, we can now look back at the history of the twentieth with some perspective. What some historians call 'the short 20th century' – the period from 1914 to 1991 can be seen as a prolonged struggle of the liberal democratic world against the forces of state oppression. Led first by Britain and France, and then after 1945 by the USA, the democratic world stood against a succession of authoritarian regimes – Imperial Germany, Bolshevik Russia, Fascist Italy, Nazi Germany, Imperial Japan, the Stalinist Soviet Union and Maoist China.

The liberal democratic world won the set-piece engagements of this period – the two World Wars and the Cold War – and it was social democrats who played a critical role. But the period also saw constant relapses into authoritarianism. In Europe after 1918, the twin delusions of nationalist fascism and internationalist bolshevism were too strong to resist. In Latin America, in the Arab World, in post-colonial Africa and Asia, authoritarianism of various kinds usually triumphed. Often it came wrapped in the flag of national liberation. A succession of charismatic authoritarian strongmen (and they were all men, although a contemporary case could be made for the Chief Executive of Hong Kong, Carrie Lam) came and went. We saw Juan Peron in Argentina, Kemal Ataturk in Turkey, Gamal Abdel Nasser in Egypt, Suharto in Indonesia, Saddam Hussein in Iraq – all typical examples, and we could name many more.

After 1945, the liberal democratic idea, inspired by the great victory of the democracies over Nazi Germany and Imperial Japan, made unprecedented progress. A new international architecture was built by the post-war generation of Western leaders – the UN, NATO, ANZUS, the World Bank, the IMF and more recently, the WTO. Germany, Italy, and Japan, humbled by defeat, were successfully remodelled as democratic states and successful economies. India became the world's largest democracy. Fascism was driven from the political mainstream, although communism remained powerful in significant nation states.

Through the Cold War period, from 1945 to 1990, the polar opposite to the Western democracies was the Soviet Union and its satellites, later joined (and then rivalled) by Communist China. As the colonial empires dissolved, many emerging states, particularly in Africa and the Arab world, chose to copy the Soviet model of authoritarian development – the one-party state, the state-controlled economy, the prestige industrial projects, and the five-year plans, all enforced by local versions of the KGB. In the long run this model was a spectacular failure, as these countries became mired in corruption, inefficiency and poverty. Rule by demagogic strongmen was punctuated by military coups. Countries as diverse as Egypt, Myanmar, Tanzania and Venezuela were left bankrupt, their societies permanently damaged. In the long run, authoritarian regimes, whether notionally of the left or the right, always breed corruption, and corruption is always harmful both to economic growth and to political development.

The End of the Beginning of the End

In 1990, history's wheel turned again when the Soviet Union collapsed. Germany was reunited, Ukraine and the Baltic states recovered their independence and fate caught up with Nicolai Ceausescu. At the other end of the political spectrum, the apartheid system in South Africa was dismantled. In the West, some writers hailed these years as the 'The End of History' or the 'The Unipolar Moment.' This, commentators said, was the final triumph of the liberal democratic ideal. The number of functioning democracies rose rapidly, particularly in Latin America and East Asia, but also in Africa. Only the Arab world remained wedded to authoritarianism.

Sadly, the End of History proved to be only one more turn in a long and complex process of historical evolution. Most post-Soviet states, led by Vladimir Putin's regime in Russia, quickly relapsed into authoritarianism. Right-wing extremism re-emerged in Europe and grew powerfully in the USA and Leftist populism, typified by Hugo Chavez's ruinous regime in Venezuela, regained ground in Latin America. China moved from Maoism to unrestrained capitalism without entertaining liberal democratic ideas and the Arab Spring failed to bring democracy to the Arab World. Islamist extremism posed a new threat to liberal values everywhere and the Unipolar Moment ended abruptly with the September 11 attacks on the United States.

Nevertheless, there are stories of democratic transitions which have proven to be stable and, it seems, permanent. This has been particularly true in our own region. Since the 1990s South Korea, Taiwan and Indonesia have established and successfully maintained stable and increasingly prosperous democracies. It would have been a bold prophet who predicted in 1990 that Indonesia would become the most successful democracy in the ASEAN grouping, but that is now the fact. Even Myanmar, after decades of enforced isolation under the 'Burmese Way to Socialism', holds successful democratic elections, although the army retains effective control. The experiences of these countries shows entrenched authoritarian systems can evolve – without revolution or civil war – into stable, prosperous liberal democracies.

Though, when we look across ASEAN, a different tale also presents itself. Thailand remains under de facto military control, despite a new, student-led movement calling for democratic reforms to the country's constitutional monarchy. In the Philippines, President Duterte has continued his use of extrajudicial killings to supress any opposition to his strong-man rule. Brunei is an authoritarian absolute monarchy which recently adopted *Hudud* – a severe form of punishment for criminal breaches of Sharia Law. Cambodia continues to be one of the most corrupt kleptocracies in the world, and Laos and Vietnam effectively remain one-party socialist republics.

Australian exceptionalism

Throughout this century of turmoil, Australia was one of a handful of nations to retain liberal democratic institutions without serious challenges from the right or left. Although we tend to think of Australia as a new country, it is in fact one of the oldest democracies in the world – a tradition of democratic government stretching back to the 1850s with state (or then colonial level) governments. We should be proud of our inheritance of Westminster institutions and traditions, not apologetic about them. This is a point on which I sometimes find myself in disagreement with some of my 'progressive' friends. Indeed, even some of my own colleagues.

Yes, Australian democracy was founded in the wake of a brutal dispossession of indigenous Australians. Indeed, even today, indigenous Australians die younger than other Australians. For many decades it was the exclusive property of white English-speaking men and not women. We have many disgraceful episodes in our past – notably the White Australia Policy, the Stolen Generation and decades of institutional abuse of many kinds. Yet, our Westminster institutions and the constitution that today's Australia has inherited, have adapted with remarkable success to changing ideas about democracy, society, and morality.

An ever-expanding franchise of democracy and democratic institutions is inherently a good thing, and it is the only proven way to build a lasting, fair society and nation-state. 'Australia for the White Man' is as dead as *The Bulletin*, on whose masthead that slogan appeared until 1961. Women and Indigenous Australians gained the right to vote. We expanded the rights of labour through the efforts of free trade unions. We established and sustained a free and boisterous media, notably by the inclusion of a highly respected state broadcaster. We absorbed millions of migrants from every cultural background so they too could become democrats. In the 1990s we had a mature debate about the constitutional monarchy and its place in modern Australia – a debate we expect to resume at some point. And most recently, we changed the definition of marriage by a democratic process. Despite often fierce controversies, we did all this, almost always without violence.

Western horizons

Despite our geographic location off the coast of South-East Asia, and our increasingly non-Western population mix, in a cultural and institutional sense Australia remains very much a Western country. Much as we may like to decry our British colonial history, Australia has benefitted from that heritage. Liberal democracy had its origins in Europe and North America, but we must not give any credence to the notion that it is in its essence a 'Western idea', and therefore by extension, to be disregarded or not applicable elsewhere. The idea of human freedom, and its practical application through political democracy, is a universal idea central to the rights and soul of humanity. And of course, democracy is quite fragile. And radical. Throughout history, it has usually been might that is right. So the idea that every person is franchised, and has an equal say, is quite a radical concept.

People in Latin America, Africa, the subcontinent, and East Asia have repeatedly shown that given the chance they prefer freedom to despotism. Countries as diverse as Chile, South Korea and Ghana, as populous as India and Indonesia, and as historically conflicted as South Africa, have all become successful democracies. As I write this, people in Russia and China, Egypt and Syria, Cuba and Venezuela, Vietnam and Cambodia, and particularly at the moment in Hong Kong, are risking their freedom and their lives in the name of these ideals – in a word, to be free.

There are many valid criticisms to be made of the Western democracies and their role in the world, particularly in the present moment. The unrestrained free-market capitalism of the 1980s was dominant in the English-speaking world and increased economic inequality and social dysfunction – thereby unstitching the very social capital that gave everybody a stake and agency so critical to a functioning democracy. We saw the political consequences of that era in the Trump presidency, the ill-considered consequences of Brexit, and similar upheavals in other countries across Europe. I am far from content with things the way they are, and I believe democracy is an ideal that needs to be actively defended – recent history shows us why.

But I also become annoyed when I hear Western academics and intellectuals, secure in their taxpayer-funded jobs, telling us that this or that model of anti-Western authoritarianism is superior to liberal democracy and market economies. I recall that it wasn't long ago that many of these people were telling us about the superior efficiency of Mussolini's Italy (*he made the trains run on time!*), or Stalin's Soviet Union, or Chairman Mao's China. They were wrong then and they are wrong now. I will strongly oppose any such notions gaining ground in the Australian Labor Party and the wider labour movement. I think most Labor voters will agree with me. Having said that, I fully accept that liberal democracy is not something the West can impose on the rest of the world – although the US successfully did so in post-war Japan. Most of the democratic governments the colonial powers left behind by them in Africa and Asia had shallow roots and soon succumbed to authoritarianism of the right or left or to military rule. It took many years for democratic sentiment to develop organically in these countries.

Obviously, there is a link between economic progress and democratic political progress. It's not an accident that South Korea and Taiwan become more democratic as they grew more affluent. That has also been true in Mexico and other Latin American countries. But it's not a universal rule. Thailand's per capita GDP has doubled in fifteen years, but it is still suffers regular military coups. Cambodia has politically gone backwards even as it has advanced economically. China's 'market Stalinism' offers an alternative route to aspiring dictators everywhere. I would argue, however, that an economic system that fosters economic growth, even at the price of some inequality, is more likely to see the success of democratic institutions than a system which imposes an equality of poverty in the name of 'social justice'. I have visited Cuba, and was quite stunned when our guide (and watcher) Julio said in a response to my question about computers for school children that 'all school children would have to wait until all could have the same resources'. Even when I pointed out that if one family wanted to save for a computer for their children, or work another job, they should be able to do so and buy one, he insisted that it was right that everyone wait until they could all have one. And of course, there is inequality and a lack of social justice, but hypocrisy aplenty, in an authoritarian country.

Stable democracies like Australia can continue to serve as models of liberal democratic government. It's not very fashionable to quote Hillary Clinton these days, but she was right when she said (of the United States) that "the power of our example is more important than the example of our power." The same is true, on a smaller scale, of Australia. We can and do offer practical help to our regional neighbours. We can point to the good work Australia has done in East Timor, Papua New Guinea and the Solomon Islands. We can do more to help our Pacific Island neighbours. We can speak up for individuals who fight for democracy in Hong Kong, Myanmar and Vietnam. Most importantly, and at the present juncture, we can help our neighbours resist the economic benefits on offer while Beijing expands its regional economic and strategic hegemony. Resistance to China's attempts to enmesh countries in its web of influence should be encouraged.

Since the end of the Cold War, and at an accelerated pace in the past two decades, globalisation and deindustrialisation have caused the decline of trade unionism and social democratic politics in many countries. This has left the working-class voters in forgotten communities economically exposed and susceptible to the allure of simplistic solutions offered up by populists. This has been coupled with a crisis of self-confidence among the elite. The strange appeal of authoritarian ideologies to the educated cultural elites goes back at least to the 1920s – and may partly be explained by relative deprivation theory – but usually fades during periods of prosperity and stability.

Not surprisingly, these flirtations have recently resurged. Locally, we can see the harmful effects of this in the rise of influential apologists for the Chinese Communist Party in Australian universities, the corporate sector and other institutions. I would add that beyond those on the fringe engaged in esoteric arguments about the intellectual purity of, for example, Communism, a much more insidious force is at play with the continued influence on decision-making from those, who despite having enjoyed long and illustrious careers in the fields of international diplomacy and policy-making, remain actively invested in promoting a world that no longer exists, to the detriment of our nation's peace and security. This is a dangerous trend which needs to be exposed and opposed. These are the types that hedge every criticism of the CCP regime with a qualified, equal and proportionate criticism of the United States. It harks back to a self-loathing form of cultural cringe that we spent decades in Australia trying to escape. While it is true that throughout its history, the United States has faced varying assaults on the vision of its Founding Fathers, its democratic ideals, norms and values, underpinned by an independent judiciary and separation of powers, have held up. Some commentators have been recently pontificating about the demise of American democracy, but I have never had a moment of doubt. And indeed, what we have seen in the recent US election is the largest voter turnout in its history, and democracy supported by its institutions.

More recently, and more broadly in democracies worldwide, the rise of social media and fake news, attacks on the mainstream media, and the tribalisation of politics and the breakdown of democratic consensus, has had a seriously harmful effect on democratic institutions. The institutions have also shown themselves to be far from perfect. The net effect of these has been to take the shine off the system overall and leave a sense that those 'running the game' are in it for themselves, and that the idea of public service has disappeared. Such disillusionment – while understandable – is poison to a democracy internally while providing easy propaganda wins for authoritarians eager to show people that democracy itself is an illusory lie. In recent years, we have also wasted real and tangible opportunities to entrench the ideals of liberalism, the free market and multilateralism. The United States' decision to walk away from the Trans-Pacific Partnership will be viewed in decades to comes as a major strategic own goal – not just because of the message it sends to countries in the Asia-Pacific about its reliability as a regional partner, but also because it has essentially vacated the field to an assertive China that has shown its clear desire to upend the regional economic and security architecture that has been in place since the end of the Second World War.

All these trends are present in Australia, although we have resisted the worst of them. We retain fairly strong unions and a viable centre-left (or moderate!) political party. We have a relatively pluralist broadcast media, and while the alienation of the intellectual elite is present, it is not as strong as in Europe or the USA. In this context we need to do more to empower students and staff to resist authoritarian politics and foreign influence in our universities. Governments must also play their part by actively promoting democratic values. This needs to be done through campaigns across traditional and social media platforms, by implementing compulsory civics classes in schools, instituting ethics and morality standards at universities, and by engaging and talking in an inclusive but honest way with our immigrant communities.

While the world will continue to grapple with the dichotomy of democratic ideals and those of authoritarianism, Australia should continue to play its part as a good global citizen and role model in our region. To do this we need strong unions and a strong Labor Party to lead the fight against harmful trends and to maintain the strength and vitality of our democracy. These are the reasons I entered politics and became a Labor Senator. I am proud of Labor's internationalist history and struggle to defend and strengthen Australian democracy over more than a century. But that struggle never ends. I look forward to the next chapter in this long story. I belong to the Australian Labor Party because I want to see political democracy and the free market system made to work for the benefit of all Australians, not just those who are entrenched at the top in our economic or cultural elite.

* * *

Kimberley Kitching is a Labor Senator for Victoria. She serves as the Deputy Manager of Opposition Business in the Senate and Shadow Assistant Minister for Government Accountability. She is also the Chair of the Senate on Foreign Affairs, Defence and Trade References Committee. Prior to joining the federal Labor team in the Australian Parliament in 2016, Kimberley practised as a lawyer, worked in several private companies in leadership positions, was a senior adviser to the Treasurer of Victoria and the Victorian Minister for Industry, Trade, Major Projects and Information Technology, was a Melbourne City Councillor and the General Manager of the Health Workers Union in Victoria where she helped restore good governance and financial strength. Kimberley's most important job as a Labor Senator is to advocate for Australian families and workers so that they can continue to enjoy the prosperity and security that makes Australia such a great country.

29. Securing Australia

Daniel Mulino

'We don't make things in Australia anymore'. This decades-old lament has been given new meaning in 2020. The coronavirus pandemic and its impact upon national economies and the supply chains which connect them has stimulated renewed interest in industrial policy globally. Countries that became reliant on overseas manufacturing and globalised supply chains for strategically important products have become acutely aware of the downsides to offshoring production. Around the world, governments are rediscovering the significance of domestic production and secure supply chains in terms of building economic and industrial resilience.

The rediscovery of the relationship between domestic production and national economic security raises two questions that are worth disentangling. First, what should we make in Australia? Second, if we make something in Australia: does it matter if we assemble prefabricated parts here – or should we aim to make some things from scratch, with local sourced components and raw materials?

The first question goes to the issue of what Australia should specialise in. Given the size of our economy, we can't build everything (certainly not well or efficiently). Autarky would dramatically lower our standard of living. Forget iPhones, laptops that halve in price every year while doubling in processing speed, or even Nutella on your morning toast (Nutella being the product of a well-documented and highly sophisticated global supply chain). Economists dating back to David Ricardo in the eighteenth century have suggested the principle of "comparative advantage" as the best guide for what each country should specialise in. To some extent, market forces will guide the economy towards appropriate areas of specialisation, often through trial and error at the firm level. However, most trading nations don't leave such matters entirely to the market: consider the MITI in Japan, the Springboard Innovation Promotion Agency in Germany and multiple state agencies in China. This isn't to support wanton bureaucratic interference, but laissez faire shouldn't be the benchmark simply because the market works well in many contexts. Industry policy needs to take into account of risk, externalities and coordination issues.

This chapter will focus on the second question, which is far more prominent after the COVID-19 pandemic and the exposure that many countries felt in accessing essential goods such as PPE, medical equipment and medicine. This exposure raised the spectre of global supply chain risks for strategically important products. Even in a world that remains highly specialised, countries will need to consider supply chain risk and not just price when considering *how* to participate in the production of goods and services and, where not producing essential goods locally, how to ensure access to essential goods and services.

Risky business

During the height of the COVID-19 crisis, many countries engaged in a frantic, zero sum battle for finite stocks of PPE, medical equipment and medicine. Prices went up and many were left without access. In a world of global supply chains, this could just as easily have been defence equipment or key industrial inputs such as fuel. Australia, as a medium size economy whose trade relationships are highly specialised both in terms of industry and country of destination, is particularly exposed.

As the dust settles, many have started to ask how best to manage the risks associated with complex, vulnerable supply chains. What is the best way to manage these risks? Not autarky. Instead, the best response will involve a set of policies to build resilience while maintaining as many of the benefits of global engagement as possible.

There are three key aspects to Australia's growing exposure to disruption in access to strategically important goods, risks we share with other developed countries.

First, while specialisation has boosted productivity growth, it has led to small and medium sized economies becoming totally reliant on imports of many goods, including items that could be considered strategically important. At its heart, specialisation can involve a trade-off between productivity and risk.

Second, supply chains have become increasingly global, which has resulted in some supply chains becoming enmeshed in strategic relations with other countries. The more complex are supply chains, the more likely they are enmeshed with foreign policy tensions.

Finally, supply chains have become susceptible to concentration and bottlenecks. This can take the form of either the availability of raw materials or intermediate goods or the capacity to produce final goods. Some inputs are highly concentrated, including endowments of natural resources such as rare earths and the production of some of the key inputs used in the production of medicines. This leaves many upstream producers exposed to market power. In addition, the production of some final goods has become highly concentrated. Magnets and lithium batteries, both of which have highly concentrated production footprints, are both critical components of many renewable energy mechanisms.

Each of these factors has arisen for good reason, most particularly the productivity gains arising from specialisation and the benefits these have created for consumers. However, while beneficial in many respects, recent trends in the global economy have also increased the risks associated with accessing goods in moments of global tension or unexpected disruptions such as pandemics. This creates a trade-off between price and access that needs to be re-examined in a post-COVID world.

Classifying goods and services as "strategically important" (or not) is more than binary exercise. Rather, a number of criteria must be taken into account in relation to each good to determine the premium placed on it by governments: how directly it relates to core functions of government such as the defence of the nation or the provision of health services in a pandemic; how integral it is to overall business competitiveness; how substitutable the good is; and how multi-purpose the good is (e.g. does it have uses in times of non-emergency?). Strategically important goods include a wide range of products, from the relatively simple, such as fuel and PPE, through to highly sophisticated goods we would struggle to manufacture in isolation, such as military aircraft and advanced 3D printers.

National levers

To increase Australia's resilience, there are four main levers available to government. First, for some goods that we can't produce here, storage is an option. Think fuel, particularly with refining all but having been wound down in Australia – and the recent decision of BP to end refining at its Kwinana plant a further blow to local self-sufficiency. Second, we can improve international access through agreements, although when push comes to shove during a crisis, many agreements can be worth little more than the paper that they're written on. The third lever is the diversification of supply chains. Globalisation can result in a "price first" determination of supply. It is entirely appropriate to leave the risk vs price trade-off for imports and exports in the hands of each individual company in the economy. However, for some strategically important products, government has a role to play in actively diversifying access points. Where multiple production points exist, government should consider the merits of diversifying relationships, even if this comes at a cost premium.

For example, Australia has significant market share in many rare earth elements (REEs). We could use this leverage to engage in partnerships with our trading partners and allies to develop more diversified manufacturing options, where production is currently highly concentrated. Given the important role of REEs in the production of strategically important goods such as magnets, batteries and renewable generation components – such diversification could be of vital importance both economically and for national security.

Labor's national mission

The final lever is closely intertwined with the mission and philosophy of the Australian Labor Party – the recognition that domestic production capability is a vital dimension of national economic strength and that the Australian Government has an important role to play in establishing firm foundations for sustainable Australian manufacturing. Self-reliance across the entire supply chain is the ultimate form of security and cannot be achieved without broad and deep manufacturing expertise and capability.

It is worth examining the health and medical equipment sector as a case study, both due to the issues raised by the COVID-19 pandemic – but also as this is an area where Australia is already internationally competitive. This is success that we could build on with appropriately targeted government intervention.

For some products, such as ventilators, PPE and hand sanitiser, onshore supply chain security has proved possible at short notice, often as a result of repurposing and retooling existing manufacturing plant to deliver goods deemed essential to the health battle against COVID-19. Some of this can be achieved by repurposing existing manufacturing capacity. For example, Australian distillers shifted to hand sanitiser production at short notice at the outset of the pandemic while textile, clothing and footwear (TCF) production facilities were quickly repurposed to manufacture a range of PPE. Similarly, several medical equipment manufacturers such as ResMed were able to produce ventilators at short notice.

Australia also has the building blocks of capability that could be developed in the production of drugs and vaccines. This includes one of the strongest medical research ecosystems in the world and the industrial might of companies such as CSL, Cochlear and ResMed. During parts of 2020, CSL was the largest company on the ASX by market capitalisation. While repurposing existing production facilities at short notice has provided valuable resources during a crisis, a higher level of permanent local production could be encouraged by government through subsidies to individual firms or through targeted procurement practices. This could take a number of forms, including favouring domestic suppliers when building the national stockpile and also for ongoing purchases by large public entities such as hospitals. This would not invalidate a broader commitment to free trade and international integration but, rather, would recognise that non-price factors (such as reliability and resilience to international supply chain disruptions) are valid considerations in a holistic assessment of value for money. Governments could also favour industries or firms where there is a realistic potential for creating a sustainable export market.

Governments *could* do all of these things. But the Morrison Government has not. The 2020-21 Commonwealth budget included a $1.5 billion measure to support Australian manufacturers scale-up, improve their competitiveness and build more resilient supply chains. Yet despite the Morrison Government's vague platitudes about the importance of domestic manufacturing to supply chains and economic resilience, the sad reality is that this Government has allowed Australia's industrial base to atrophy even further during the COVID crisis, especially in strategically sensitive sectors.

In the last month alone, American pharmaceutical giant Pfizer announced that it will be pulling the shutters down on its Perth factory, with hundreds of advanced manufacturing jobs, invaluable skills and the capacity to produce essential oncological medicines set to be lost. More extraordinary still, given the nature of the pandemic that's wrought havoc on the world in 2020, is the decision of British manufacturer GlaxoSmithKline to close its plant in Melbourne that manufactures respiratory products. It's not the role of government to take on a corporatist economic planning role. But it is the obligation of a responsible government to use the levers it does possess as the nation's largest purchaser and R&D investor to ensure Australia has a critical mass of manufacturing expertise in strategically sensitive sectors.

Governments can also use market mechanisms to provide incentives for private firms to develop manufacturing capacity that is deemed essential to national economic security. One option of enabling private firms to compete for opportunities to partner with government and to co-invest in new manufacturing plant was illustrated by an innovative approach to urban renewal in the US. In 2011, New York City conducted an auction among universities and tech companies to build a new applied science and technology precinct with a grant of donated publicly owned brownfield land and a US$100M grant.

Cornell University was ultimately successful in beating off competition from a range of other world-leading institutions. Its winning bid secured a new campus occupying 2.1 million square feet, accommodating 2,500 students and costing more than USD$2 billion to build. The auction enabled the City of New York to avoid 'picking winners' while extracting the most competitive and value-creating bids, as part of the City's plan to attract technology-oriented educational institutions and firms to compete against Silicon Valley and Boston's high-tech knowledge economy.

Another option is for government to partner with private enterprise to scale-up manufacturing capability. Areas like Sunshine North, Brooklyn and Braybrook in my electorate of Fraser are already home to some of Australia's most innovative and efficient manufacturing firms – many of which have ramped up or pivoted their production to deliver essential goods during COVID-19. This capability is replicated across the country and forms the skilled manufacturing base upon which Australia can build a more resilient and secure economic future.

Australian manufacturing can deliver a safer Australia and more quality jobs, but it needs the ability to fund the delivery of world-class outcomes. Advanced manufacturing firms in my electorate have reported that Australian capital markets are often reluctant to fund nascent innovation or to help emerging products and ideas scale-up to a level where they can provide sovereign industrial capacity or exports.

Role for government

Government has a role to play in addressing this market failure and enabling innovative Australian firms to increase local production and jobs. This could involve providing a form of investment guarantee, partnering with superannuation firms to provide venture capital or enabling manufacturing firms to invest in new fixed capital by borrowing with the security of the Government's balance sheet behind them.

Even if it isn't possible to achieve self-reliance across an entire supply chain, increasing the footprint of domestic manufacturing should be examined for each key strategic product. For some products, there may be too many elements to the supply chain to produce all domestically. For example, the production of a vaccine will include: the mass production of antigens and recombinant proteins; the production and processing of excipients (the formulation production referred to above); possibly, the production and processing of preservatives; the production and maintenance of chemical processing equipment; glass vials; packaging; storage; and the medical R&D underpinning the development of new medicines and vaccines. Australia is already at the forefront of many aspects of this supply chain and it is worth exploring whether government should partner with stakeholders in filling any gaps. This could include large firms (such as CSL); universities; manufacturers; and logistics firms. Even if it isn't possible to become fully self-sufficient, a greater degree of resilience will both reduce risk and also increase the value-add in a sector which already contributes so strongly to local employment and economic output.

One of the key considerations in determining how much Australia should focus on a particular supply chain will be how a product or service can be repurposed. For example, a sophisticated 3D printer that could be used at short notice to help manufacture a ventilator, will be useful for many purposes and will benefit the broader economy other than at times of emergency.

The Australian Government should undertake a detailed audit of what manufacturing, logistics, chemical processing, energy and IP capacity would be required in order to achieve more self-reliance in relation to key strategic goods and services. To the extent that this requires greater onshore capacities in any of these areas, government should explore which policy tools are most appropriate. This should then be activated through a whole-of-government process with clearly defined KPIs.

The COVID-19 pandemic has highlighted some risks arising from globalisation, economic integration and specialisation. These broader global trends have produced massive benefits – but there is often a trade-off whereby the gains from specialisation and integration can also increase reliance and risk, particularly for small and medium-sized economies. Australian firms are already world leaders in many areas of industrial production, with the health sector a standout example. Government can build on this success to date by using the power of its procurement, by managing competitively tendered processes to allocate development zones and by subsidising investment in firm-specific and sector-specific human capital. Building innovative ecosystems will create high wage employment, more diversified exports and economy-wide spill-overs that will boost productivity.

The economy is already moving us towards a future in which we are more resilient in strategic sectors, with CSL's world-beating performance a good example. The innovative potential of CSL is replicated on a smaller scale in firms scattered throughout the Australian economy. National leadership by the Australian government could allow that potential to thrive, building on our success to date and create a more resilient and prosperous future.

* * *

Representing the Australian Labor Party, Dr Daniel Mulino was elected to the Australian Parliament at the 2019 Federal Election as the first Member for Fraser, a new electorate in Melbourne's western suburbs. Daniel is an economist by profession, with bachelor and master's degrees from the ANU and University of Sydney, and a doctorate from Yale University. He has lectured at Monash University and was economic adviser to the previous Minister for Financial Services. Before entering the Australian Parliament, Daniel served the Victorian community as a member of the Victorian Parliament. He was Parliamentary Secretary to the Treasurer between 2014 and 2018. Working closely with the Treasurer, Daniel helped deliver major new infrastructure projects across Victoria and developed innovative new financing structures for community projects. He is a member of the House of Representatives Economics Committee and the Joint Standing Committee on Trade and Investment Growth.

30. Trials, Tribulations and Triumphs in the Northern Territory

Selena Uibo

My Territory

The Northern Territory is a place of wonder. More than 65,000 years of Aboriginal culture, heritage, and tradition. Our lands and waters hold generations of stories and teachings – and are home to some of the most beautiful places on the planet. We are also a Territory of complex challenges, disadvantage, and inequality, and one of the highest Aboriginal incarceration rates in the world. It's a tragic reality, but what drives me is the prospect of positive generational change through bold legislative and policy reform.

I am a proud Aboriginal woman. My mother is a Nunggubuyu woman from Numbulwar and Wanindilyakwa from Groote Eylandt, and my father is a second generation Australian from Sydney with Estonian, Irish and South African heritage. I have fond memories of growing up as a Territory kid. For the first ten years in the town of Batchelor located approximately 100km south of Darwin. I remember running and riding around the small community with my friends and always feeling safe. Our home was one of the usual hangout spots for my older sister's friends and mine. We had chooks, ducks, cats, rabbits, mice, fish, and a tortoise! Our community was one where kids played in the street until dark and then went home for dinner. If a family went away for holidays, another family would help out feeding animals, watering the garden and checking on the house. A place of family, friends and connected community.

On our family holidays we either went to Sydney to visit my father's family or to Numbulwar to visit my mother's family. I loved visiting both families for different reasons: Sydney with its big, bustling, exciting city and trains. Numbulwar for the sand, fishing, campfires and hunting bush trips. When I was 10 years old our family moved to Darwin where I finished all my schooling in public education.

Whilst my memories and love for the Territory are positive, I also grew up watching the challenges plaguing the Territory unfold. I've seen and felt the racism, I've watched families be torn apart by addiction, and I've experienced the effects of generational trauma, and violence in our communities. I've watched immense potential go to waste because of circumstance and a lack of opportunity.

Being the youngest Aboriginal Affairs Minister in the Northern Territory is a privilege, and one I have never taken for granted – and I hope young people look at our progressive and diverse Labor Government and realise that they truly are the future of this great place. Being a Minister gives me a platform and the power to implement bold reforms that will ensure generational change – and I will do everything I can to make sure that becomes a reality.

As the second and the longest-serving Aboriginal Attorney-General, I know the expectations are high, I know there are critics, and I know all eyes are on what we do next to ensure justice in the Territory, and justice for Aboriginal Territorians. Some see the fact that I'm not a lawyer as something that is detrimental to my ability to be an effective Attorney-General. As an Aboriginal woman and teacher, I see myself as having an advantage. The Territory is my home. The challenges we face are ones I have experienced. I have taught students in some of the most remote parts of our country. I have seen years later, some of the same students caught up in the justice system. I understand the justice system as it stands is letting down Aboriginal Territorians and victims of crime alike. And I am not afraid to implement the bold reforms necessary to ensure both safer communities, and better futures for our people.

Achieving justice through the Aboriginal Justice Agreement

Aboriginal Territorians are incarcerated at one of the highest rates in the world. Achieving justice in the Northern Territory means understanding the importance of innovative community-led, place-based initiatives that address our shameful incarceration rates, reoffending, and the drivers of crime. We are simply not going to get different results if we keep doing things the same way. It means recognising the older models that continue to fail victims, offenders, and communities, and acknowledging the merit and opportunities that lie in preventive justice, and Alternatives to Prison models. It's why I'm proud of our Government's commitment to an Aboriginal Justice Agreement.

The Aboriginal Justice Agreement will ensure we reduce reoffending and imprisonment rates of Aboriginal Territorians. It means engaging and supporting Aboriginal leadership and improving justice responses and services for Aboriginal Territorians. Our Youth Justice System in the Territory alone costs us $40 million a year. One thing that continues to be overlooked, is that justice reform is not a battle between left and right values. The economic implications of a justice system that does not work are blatant. The cost to taxpayers, the cost to businesses, the cost to the community. It's time to get serious about looking at doing things differently. A way that incorporates the social, cultural, and economic factors that can impact justice in the Northern Territory, and a way that focusses on how we can be successful in locally driven justice agreements.

We've already taken integral steps in preparation for our bold reforms. We are the first Territory Government to implement a specialist approach to addressing domestic and family violence, with a specific Domestic and Family Violence Court approach. We established a 'Back on Track' program that provides youth offenders with opportunities to reconnect with country and culture, and participate in learning camps as alternatives to youth detention, and our Government opened the Alice Springs Alternative to Custody Life Skills Camp for Aboriginal female prisoners. Over the next four years, we'll be looking at implementing the Aboriginal Justice Agreement, looking at the Law Reform Committee's recommendations in relation to mandatory sentencing, strengthening the *Anti-Discrimination Act* and raising the age of criminal responsibility. They are all integral reforms that will change the legal landscape of the Territory for generations to come.

Local decision making

If we want to look to progress as a whole – we need to look at tackling the issue of disadvantage holistically. I'm committed to making positive generational change a reality and local decision-making underpins that change. Supporting and investing in strong Aboriginal governance is necessary to ensure local people drive local solutions, and that Aboriginal organisations are supported in managing local decision making. It is not a transition that will happen overnight, but the impacts of handing back control will enable stronger futures for generations to come. We have a 10 year plan that will provide a pathway so that communities can have more control over their own affairs. It's about recognising that communities understand what they need and what will and will not work more than anyone else. It's about empowerment. It's about the futures for their families.

Local decision-making and extensive and honest consultation is at the heart of creating real and effective change – and we're going to give our reforms enough time to work. Local decisions are the best decisions, and I'm proud of our Territory Labor Government's progress in handing back power and ensuring community control. We have already signed the Groote Archipelago Local Decision-Making Agreement with the Anindilyakwa Land Council in Groote Eylandt, handing back control of education, justice, health and governance to the local community.

The tangible benefits of local decision-making are already coming to fruition with more local jobs, an empowered community that takes pride in their achievements, and more opportunities than ever before.

Treaty, truth-telling and reflection

The history of Aboriginal Australia is devastating and traumatic, but it's one that needs to be acknowledged and addressed. Centuries on from colonisation, Aboriginal Territorians are still suffering at the hands of structures we had no say in, and battling demons faced as a result of intergenerational trauma and a lack of opportunity. Treaty Commissioner Professor Mick Dodson AM, alongside Deputy Commissioner Ursula Raymond have embarked upon the challenging role of listening to Aboriginal voices across the Territory in order to begin the vital process of creating a Treaty in the Territory. Part of that process is understanding the importance of truth-telling and reflection – and the role they play in healing generations of hurt. It is fundamental to progress to ensure we recognise what has happened in the Territory. The difference of place, the difference of families, the difference of success for families. A Treaty will set the necessary foundation for future agreements between Aboriginal Territorians and any Northern Territory Government that is in power. It is about safeguarding truth and control – and making sure progress that is made cannot be easily undone.

Looking to the future

My journey into politics was a learning curve. I was lucky enough to have Labor Party mentors such as Warren Snowden, Malarndirri McCarthy, Lynne Walker, Marion Scrymgour, Paul Henderson and Peter Wellings, and support from a Labor family founded on values that drive what I do. Having just come out of the 2020 NT election campaign, I experienced misogyny, being not just a woman, but an Aboriginal woman, and the lateral violence that happens in different contexts. It's something I will make my mission to call out.

My experience taught me that accepting that kind of behaviour and attempts to pull down female leaders is not good enough – it cannot always be someone else's job to fight the unacceptable. I will always be someone who does everything in my power to build up the people around me. That's how we create future leaders who will go on to change the world for the better. The future of progressive politics depends on it.

Achieving generational change takes courage, commitment and

perseverance. It takes having a vision of better futures for our kids, better opportunities, and a strong focus on economic drivers that will empower our communities. In many ways, our lives and the paths we end up taking start at the very beginning. Where we are born, what we see and feel, what we are taught, what we believe is possible. Our commitment to the Families as First Teachers program acknowledges this – and is a cornerstone of our commitment to positive generational change in the Northern Territory. I see Territory children being raised by families who have the skills and support necessary to love them and guide them towards a life of fulfilling their true potential. Living within structures and amongst services that were designed by their communities – to ensure they get the support they need to flourish.

An important foundation of our great Labor movement is having a vision of what needs to change – and being pragmatic about making it a reality. We are a party of bold reform and change. We are a party that leaves no one behind. In the Northern Territory, we have a long way to go, but under our Territory Labor Government, positive generational change will be a reality. We are planting the seeds to grow the trees to provide the shade for the future generations to enjoy. When I look at my daughter Radiance, I see so much love, hope and opportunity. I think about the ways in which the Territory shaped me. I reflect on all of the ways it will change in the coming years. And I am proud of the place she will grow up to call home – just as I did.

* * *

Selena Uibo was born and bred in the Northern Territory. Her mother is a Nunggubuyu lady from Numbulwar and Wanindilyakwa from Groote Eylandt and her father is a second-generation Australian who was born in Sydney. Selena speaks English, Kriol and some of the Wubuy language of Numbulwar. Selena studied a Bachelor of Arts/ Bachelor of Education at the University of Queensland in Brisbane, where she graduated as Valedictorian before commencing her teaching profession in the NT. Selena received the NT Award for Excellence in Teaching, and was awarded a Commonwealth Bank Foundation Award for teaching financial literacy to her secondary students in Numbulwar. In 2016, Selena successfully contested the seat of Arnhem as a Territory Labor candidate. In June 2018, Selena was promoted to Cabinet as the ninth Cabinet Minister, as Minister for Education and Workforce Training, and in January 2019, she became the Minister for Aboriginal Affairs. At the 2020 NT Election, Selena retained the seat of Arnhem and became the Attorney-General, Minister for Justice, Minister for Aboriginal Affairs, Minister for Treaty and Local Decision Making, and Minister for Parks and Rangers.

www.ingramcontent.com/pod-product-compliance
Lightning Source LLC
Chambersburg PA
CBHW050337270326
41926CB00016B/3496